Puppies

maranGraphics™

&

THOMSON

COURSE TECHNOLOGY

Professional ■ Technical ■ Reference

MARAN ILLUSTRATED™ Puppies

Distributed in the U.S. and Canada by Thomson Course Technology PTR. For enquiries about Maran Illustrated™ books outside the U.S. and Canada, please contact maranGraphics at international@maran.com

For U.S. orders and customer service, please contact Thomson Course Technology at 1-800-354-9706. For Canadian orders, please contact Thomson Course Technology at 1-800-268-2222 or 416-752-9448.

ISBN-13: 978-1-59863-283-5
ISBN-10: 1-59863-283-3

Library of Congress Catalog Card Number: 2006927122

Printed in the United States of America

06 07 08 09 10 BU 10 9 8 7 6 5 4 3 2

Trademarks

Important

Copies

Educational facilities, companies, and organizations located in the U.S. and Canada that are interested in multiple copies of this book should contact Thomson Course Technology PTR for quantity discount information. Training manuals, CD-ROMs, and portions of this book are also available individually or can be tailored for specific needs.

maranGraphics™

maranGraphics Inc.
5755 Coopers Avenue
Mississauga, Ontario
L4Z 1R9
www.maran.com

THOMSON
COURSE TECHNOLOGY
Professional ■ Technical ■ Reference

Thomson Course Technology PTR, a division of Thomson Course Technology
25 Thomson Place ■ Boston, MA 02210 ■ http://www.courseptr.com

maranGraphics is a family-run business

At **maranGraphics**, we believe in producing great books—one book at a time.

Each maranGraphics book uses the award-winning communication process that we have been developing over the last 30 years. Using this process, we organize photographs and text in a way that makes it easy for you to learn new concepts and tasks.

We spend hours deciding the best way to perform each task, so you don't have to! Our clear, easy-to-follow photographs and instructions walk you through each task from beginning to end.

We want to thank you for purchasing what we feel are the best books money can buy. We hope you enjoy using this book as much as we enjoyed creating it!

Sincerely,

The Maran Family

We would love to hear from you! Send your comments and feedback about our books to family@maran.com

To sign up for sneak peeks and news about our upcoming books, send an e-mail to newbooks@maran.com

Please visit us on the Web at: .
www.maran.com

CREDITS

Author:
maranGraphics
Development Group

Content Architects:
Kelleigh Johnson
Andrew Wheeler

Technical Consultant:
Allison Litfin

Project Manager & Editor:
Judy Maran-Tarnowski

Copy Developers:
Dana Grimaldi
Andrew Wheeler

Editor:
Jill Maran Dutfield

**Photographer, Layout Designer
& Photographic Retouching:**
Sarah Kim

**Layout Designer &
Photographic Retouching:**
Mark Porter

Indexer:
Kelleigh Johnson

Post Production:
Robert Maran

**Publisher and General Manager,
Thomson Course Technology PTR:**
Stacy L. Hiquet

**Associate Director of Marketing,
Thomson Course Technology PTR:**
Sarah O'Donnell

**Manager of Editorial Services,
Thomson Course Technology PTR:**
Heather Talbot

ACKNOWLEDGMENTS

Thanks to the dedicated staff of maranGraphics, including Dana Grimaldi, Kelleigh Johnson, Sarah Kim, Jill Maran Dutfield, Judy Maran-Tarnowski, Robert Maran, Ruth Maran, Mark Porter and Andrew Wheeler.

Finally, to Richard Maran who originated the easy-to-use graphic format of this guide. Thank you for your inspiration and guidance.

M. Allison Litfin B.A., C.P.D.T. is the owner of Lifetime Dog Training and has been a trainer since 1990, working both as an obedience instructor in a class setting and as a private consultant in owners' homes. She specializes in helping young puppies get started on their lives with their new families.

Although she is primarily dedicated to family dog obedience training, Allison regularly competes with her own dogs in various dog sports and is a Rally Obedience judge.

Independently certified by the Certification Council for Pet Dog Trainers through the Professional Testing Corporation of New York, Allison regularly attends accredited seminars and workshops as part of her professional development. She is a member in good standing of the Association of Pet Dog Trainers (US), the Canadian Kennel Club, the Canadian Association of Professional Pet Dog Trainers and the Canadian Association of Rally Obedience.

Allison shares her life with three wonderful dogs and a very patient family; her son's first word was "dog!"

A few words from Allison:

My philosophy of dog training can be summed up as: "The earlier, the better." It's my hope that this book, filled with information about the development, raising and training of puppies, can answer some of the numerous questions new puppy owners have and help people get off to a good start on many happy years with their family dog. I would like to thank the dedicated staff of maranGraphics for their patience and expertise in producing Maran Illustrated Puppies—it's truly a labor of love.

I have been fortunate over the years to have had the opportunity to learn from and train with the very best—thank you! And thanks also to my patient teachers and best friends, past and present: Susie, Luke, Luka, Bean, Diva, Grace and Joy... I love you all.

This book is dedicated to puppies everywhere. May you all live happily ever after!

maranGraphics would like to thank all of our friends who participated in this book.

Ace
Norwegian Buhund
Georgina Cornell

Barrett
Labrador Retriever
Marianne Voogt

Bazil
Irish Red and White Setter
Anita Geier-Champ

Bobby
Golden Retriever
Rob Paterson

Breeze
Australian Shepherd
Linda Barton

Brown Boy
Golden Retriever
Rob Paterson

Cuddles
Golden Retriever
Rob Paterson

Daisy
German Shepherd
Natasha Buckham, Tanis
Buckham and Carol Armit

Fosse
Golden Retriever
Cassandra Hartman

Georgie
Pug
Peggy Doyle

Herbie
Pug/Boston Terrier Mix
Kelleigh and Mark
Johnson

Jazz
Golden Retriever
Dan and Nicole Kuntz

Joplin
Golden Retriever
Rob Paterson

Joy
Labrador Retriever
Allison Litfin

Lucy
Poodle/Miniature Schnauzer Mix
Andrea and Steve Eljuga

Peachie
Labrador Retriever
Don Willoughby

Raine
Shetland Sheepdog
Kelly Morrow

Reese
Nova Scotia Duck Tolling Retriever
Laurie Gleiser

Rowan
Golden Retriever
Mary Barrett

Skye
Scottish Terrier
Anne Campbell and Janet Lenover

Sunny
Yorkshire Terrier
Effie Leduc

Timber
German Shepherd
Natasha Buckham, Tanis Buckham and Carol Armit

Labrador Retrievers featured on the cover
Liz Gingell and Phyllis Anderson
Ginander Labradors

Table of Contents

Table of Contents

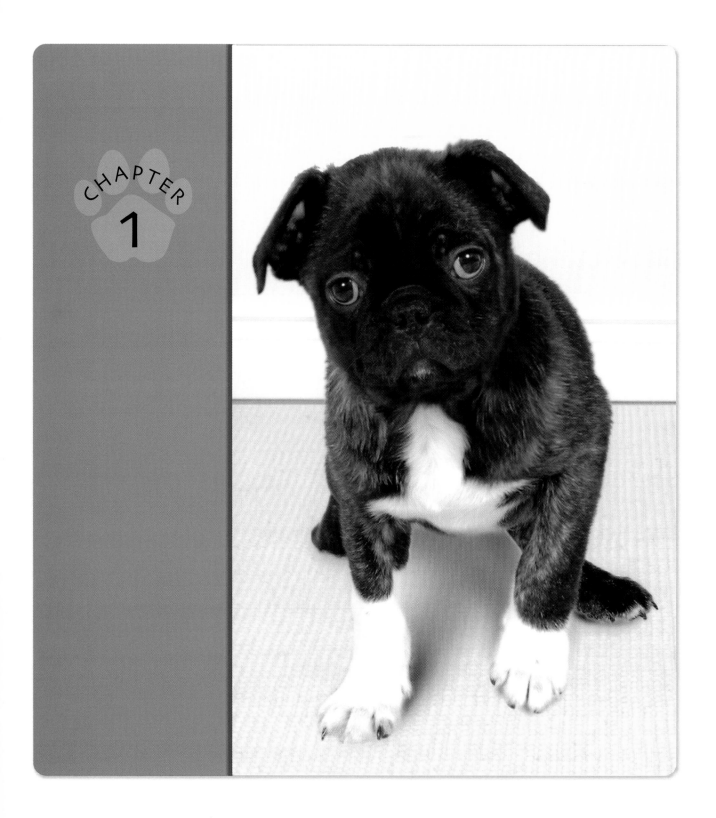

CHAPTER
1

Picking a Puppy

Are You Ready for a Puppy?

Having a puppy can be like living with a toddler—rewarding and challenging at the same time. It's a good idea to think about whether your lifestyle can accommodate caring for a puppy before you bring one home.

Puppies are social animals, so they need to be with people. If you want to include a puppy as part of your family, you may have to change your daily routine to accommodate his social needs and properly train him. For example, young puppies must be fed and taken for bathroom breaks several times a day.

If you're not up for the challenge of raising a young puppy, you may want to consider getting an older one. Puppies over six months old are often housetrained, but they may need additional training to discourage undesirable behaviors that a previous owner may have allowed.

Time Commitment

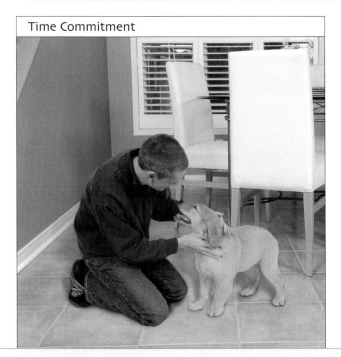

- A puppy is a long-term commitment. Most dogs live for 8 to 15 years, so you must be prepared to care for your puppy for many years after puppyhood.
- Puppies require a lot of interaction with their owners to be properly trained and socialized.

- All puppies need to be fed and taken outside for housetraining and exercise several times every day, without exception.
- If you spend a lot of time away from home, you should reconsider your decision to get a puppy.

Lifestyle Considerations

- Before you get your puppy, you must evaluate how a puppy will fit into your life.
- Consider how other family members and pets will adjust to having a puppy in the home.

- Make sure you understand how big your puppy will grow. Research and try to spend time with adult dogs of the breeds you are considering.
- If you live in a small apartment or house without a fenced yard, you should consider a smaller or less-energetic breed.

I have young children. What type of puppy should I get?

Tip If your children are very young, it may be a good idea to wait to get a puppy until they are older. Puppies require a lot of attention—they need to be housetrained, socialized and exercised regularly. If you try to care for young children and train a puppy at the same time, you may find yourself taking on too much at once. The best time to get a puppy is once your children have started school and are over 6 years of age.

 I sometimes work long hours, but would still like to get a puppy. What can I do?

Tip You can hire a dog walker to exercise your puppy during the day. Even if your puppy cannot go for walks because he's not yet fully vaccinated, a dog walker can play with your puppy in your house or the backyard. Another option is for you and your family to stagger your schedules to decrease the time your puppy is alone. If you travel extensively or regularly work long hours, you should postpone getting a puppy until your schedule is more flexible.

Financial Commitment

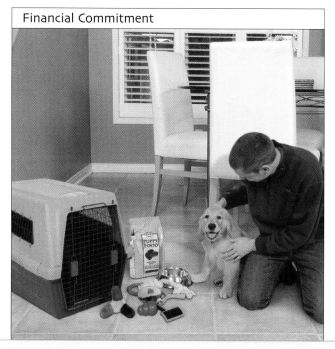

The Need for Patience

- Getting a puppy is a serious financial commitment.

- Aside from the initial purchase price of your puppy, you must consider the cost of food, toys, training classes and supplies, grooming equipment, visits to the veterinarian and medication.

- Some breeds require a greater financial commitment because they are more prone to health problems or have special grooming needs.

- Puppies require generous amounts of patience.

- While proper puppy-proofing (see page 56) and supervision are essential, you should be prepared to lose a few items as your puppy goes through his chewing stage.

- When housetraining your puppy to eliminate outside, you need to be ready for the occasional accident in the house.

- If the chewing stage and housetraining seem like too much trouble, consider an older puppy that has gone through the chewing stage and has already been housetrained.

Guide to Popular Breeds

Purebred Dogs

A purebred dog is a dog whose mother, father and ancestors are all the same breed.

There is an abundance of information available in books and on the Internet about each dog breed. By researching a breed of interest, you can find out about the adult appearance, size, personality and behavior of dogs of that breed. This information can help you make an informed choice about what kind of dog may be right for you.

Choosing a purebred puppy gives you an idea of what your dog may be like, but it is important to remember that each dog is an individual and may display characteristics outside of his breed.

Mixed Breed Dogs

A mixed breed dog is a dog whose parents are different breeds. For example, a Cockapoo has a Cocker Spaniel parent and a Poodle parent. Mixed breed dogs, just like purebred dogs, can make loyal and affectionate pets.

It can be difficult to determine what the adult appearance, size, personality and behavior of a mixed breed dog will be, but his dominant physical features may provide some clues. For example, if he looks a lot like a Poodle, he may grow up with Poodle-like characteristics and personality.

AMERICAN KENNEL CLUB ℠

The American Kennel Club

The American Kennel Club (AKC) is a not-for-profit organization that maintains the world's largest registry, or list, of purebred dogs and currently recognizes 153 different breeds. A dog that is registered with the AKC is a purebred dog whose lineage has been recorded for multiple generations. The AKC does not guarantee the health or temperament of the dogs it registers. To find out more about the AKC, you can visit them on the Web at www.akc.org.

The AKC uses seven groups to categorize dog breeds—Sporting, Toy, Terrier, Hound, Working, Herding and Non-Sporting. The groups are based on the jobs the dogs were originally bred to do.

Guide to Popular Breeds:

The Sporting Group

The Sporting group includes dogs originally bred to work with hunters. This group includes retrievers, spaniels, pointers and setters.

Sporting dogs are generally intelligent and friendly and require regular, vigorous exercise.

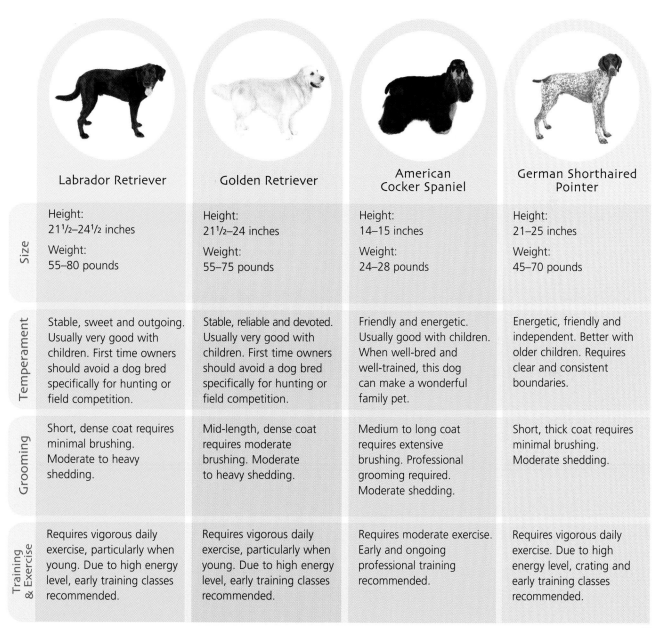

	Labrador Retriever	Golden Retriever	American Cocker Spaniel	German Shorthaired Pointer
Size	Height: 21½–24½ inches Weight: 55–80 pounds	Height: 21½–24 inches Weight: 55–75 pounds	Height: 14–15 inches Weight: 24–28 pounds	Height: 21–25 inches Weight: 45–70 pounds
Temperament	Stable, sweet and outgoing. Usually very good with children. First time owners should avoid a dog bred specifically for hunting or field competition.	Stable, reliable and devoted. Usually very good with children. First time owners should avoid a dog bred specifically for hunting or field competition.	Friendly and energetic. Usually good with children. When well-bred and well-trained, this dog can make a wonderful family pet.	Energetic, friendly and independent. Better with older children. Requires clear and consistent boundaries.
Grooming	Short, dense coat requires minimal brushing. Moderate to heavy shedding.	Mid-length, dense coat requires moderate brushing. Moderate to heavy shedding.	Medium to long coat requires extensive brushing. Professional grooming required. Moderate shedding.	Short, thick coat requires minimal brushing. Moderate shedding.
Training & Exercise	Requires vigorous daily exercise, particularly when young. Due to high energy level, early training classes recommended.	Requires vigorous daily exercise, particularly when young. Due to high energy level, early training classes recommended.	Requires moderate exercise. Early and ongoing professional training recommended.	Requires vigorous daily exercise. Due to high energy level, crating and early training classes recommended.

The Toy Group

The Toy group includes small, long-lived dogs that were originally bred to be companions for people. Many dogs in the Toy group require only minimal exercise and are ideal for people with limited living space.

	Chihuahua	Pug	Shih Tzu	Yorkshire Terrier
Size	Height: Approximately 5 inches Weight: Up to 6 pounds	Height: 10–11 inches Weight: 14–18 pounds	Height: 8–11 inches Weight: 9–16 pounds	Height: 7–9 inches Weight: 3–7 pounds
Temperament	Intelligent, feisty and devoted to owner. Can be barky, snappish and territorial, if not properly socialized. Not suitable for children.	Easygoing, playful, charming and even-tempered. Good family pet. Good for first time owners.	Outgoing, friendly and fun-loving. True companions. Good for first time owners.	Clever and devoted to owner. Can be barky and snappish if spoiled. Better with older children.
Grooming	Smooth-coated variety requires minimal brushing. Long-coated variety requires moderate brushing. Minimal shedding.	Short, smooth coat requires minimal brushing. Heavy shedding.	Long, dense coat requires daily brushing. Professional grooming required. Minimal shedding.	Long, fine coat requires daily brushing. Professional grooming required. Minimal shedding.
Training & Exercise	Requires minimal exercise. Early and ongoing socialization is important to avoid behavior problems.	Requires minimal exercise. Ongoing training provides mental stimulation for this clever dog.	Requires minimal exercise. Ongoing training provides mental stimulation for this intelligent dog.	Requires moderate exercise. Early and ongoing professional training recommended.

Guide to Popular Breeds:

The Terrier Group

Terriers were originally bred to hunt small animals. Their lively, self-confident personalities make Terriers good watchdogs, but chasing, barking and digging can be a problem for these dogs.

	Airedale Terrier	Miniature Schnauzer	Scottish Terrier	West Highland White Terrier
Size	Height: Approximately 23 inches Weight: 45–50 pounds	Height: 12–14 inches Weight: 13–15 pounds	Height: Approximately 10 inches Weight: 18–22 pounds	Height: 10–11 inches Weight: 15–19 pounds
Temperament	Playful, fun-loving, active and protective of owner. A hardy, adaptable dog.	Active, spirited, self-assured and sensitive. Prone to barking.	Feisty, independent and devoted to owner. Better with older children.	Friendly, lively and playful. Better with older children.
Grooming	Wiry coat requires weekly brushing. Professional grooming required. Minimal shedding.	Wiry coat requires regular brushing. Professional grooming required. Minimal shedding.	Wiry, dense coat requires regular brushing. Professional grooming required. Minimal shedding.	Straight, stiff coat requires brushing several times a week. Professional grooming required. Minimal shedding.
Training & Exercise	Requires plenty of exercise. Early and ongoing socialization and professional training recommended.	Requires moderate exercise. Training classes recommended.	Requires moderate exercise. Early and ongoing socialization and training classes recommended.	Requires moderate exercise. Training classes recommended.

The Hound Group

Hounds were originally bred to hunt by scent or sight. Scenthounds, including the Beagle, Dachshund and Basset Hound, enjoy following their noses. Sighthounds, including the Greyhound and Whippet, enjoy a good run.

	Beagle	Basset Hound	Dachshund	Greyhound
Size	Height: 10–15 inches Weight: 18–30 pounds	Height: 14–15 inches Weight: 40–55 pounds	Height: 5–9 inches Weight: 10–32 pounds	Height: 26–30 inches Weight: 60–70 pounds
Temperament	Cheerful and curious. Good with children. Howling, barking and following his nose into trouble can be problems.	Good-natured, pleasant and sociable. Howling and begging can be problems. Usually good with children.	Clever, persistent and playful. Digging and barking can be problems. Better with older children.	Gentle, quiet and affectionate. Good family pet. Destructive chewing may be a problem.
Grooming	Short coat requires minimal brushing. Regular ear care required. Moderate shedding.	Short, smooth coat requires minimal brushing. Regular ear care required. Minimal to moderate shedding.	Long and wire-haired coats require moderate brushing. Smooth coat requires minimal brushing. Minimal to moderate shedding.	Short, smooth coat requires minimal brushing. Minimal shedding.
Training & Exercise	Requires plenty of exercise. Early and ongoing training classes recommended.	Requires moderate exercise. Food rewards are an especially good training tool for this dog. Challenge to housetrain.	Requires minimal to moderate exercise. Early socialization and training classes recommended. Challenge to housetrain.	Requires moderate exercise in a fenced area. This dog requires positive, sensitive training.

Guide to Popular Breeds:
The Working Group

Working dogs are powerful, intelligent dogs who were originally bred to perform a variety of tasks. Working dogs can be great companions for experienced owners who make training and socialization a priority.

	Boxer	Doberman Pinscher	Rottweiler	Siberian Husky
Size	Height: 21–25 inches Weight: 60–75 pounds	Height: 24–28 inches Weight: 60–85 pounds	Height: 22–27 inches Weight: 85–115 pounds	Height: 20–23½ inches Weight: 35–60 pounds
Temperament	Fun-loving, athletic and courageous. Patient with children. Can be overly exuberant.	Loyal, energetic and athletic. A sensitive dog that must be treated in a positive manner. Suitable for experienced owners.	Confident, courageous, powerful and protective. May be assertive. When well-bred and well-trained, this dog can be suitable for experienced owners.	Good-humored, friendly and outgoing. Destructive digging or chewing a problem if not adequately stimulated.
Grooming	Short, smooth coat requires minimal brushing. Minimal to moderate shedding.	Short, smooth, shiny coat requires minimal brushing. Minimal shedding.	Short, dense coat requires regular brushing. Moderate shedding.	Mid-length, thick coat requires weekly brushing. Heavy shedding in spring and fall.
Training & Exercise	Requires plenty of exercise. Early training classes and socialization recommended.	Requires vigorous daily exercise, especially when young. Early and ongoing professional, positive training recommended.	Requires plenty of exercise. Early and ongoing socialization and professional training recommended.	Requires vigorous daily exercise in a securely fenced area. Early professional training recommended

The Herding Group

Dogs in the Herding group were originally bred to herd livestock. Herding dogs are intelligent, energetic and often independent. They can be prone to barking.

	Collie	German Shepherd	Pembroke Welsh Corgi	Shetland Sheepdog
Size	Height: 22–26 inches Weight: 50–75 pounds	Height: 22–26 inches Weight: 60–100 pounds	Height: 10–12 inches Weight: 25–30 pounds	Height: 13–16 inches Weight: 15–20 pounds
Temperament	Loyal, alert and sensitive. Can be nervous and barky.	Intelligent, versatile and independent. Thrives when given a job to do. Better suited to an experienced owner.	Intelligent, friendly and active. Big dog attitude in a small body. Good with children.	Intelligent, playful and devoted to owner. Can be nervous and barky. Better with older children.
Grooming	Mid-length to long, dense coat requires weekly brushing. Moderate to heavy shedding.	Mid-length, dense coat requires regular brushing. Heavy shedding in spring and fall.	Mid-length, thick coat requires brushing several times a week. Sheds heavily.	Long, dense coat requires regular brushing. Moderate shedding, with heavy shedding in spring and fall.
Training & Exercise	Requires plenty of exercise, especially when young. Early and ongoing training and socialization recommended.	Requires vigorous daily exercise. Early and ongoing socialization and professional training is required.	Requires plenty of exercise. Early training and socialization recommended.	Requires plenty of exercise. This dog generally excels at obedience and agility training.

Guide to Popular Breeds:

The Non-Sporting Group

The Non-Sporting group is made up of dogs that do not fit into any other group. This group contains a wide variety of dogs that differ greatly in appearance and personality.

	Bichon Frise	Boston Terrier	Bulldog	Poodle
Size	Height: 9–12 inches Weight: 7–12 pounds	Height: 12–14 inches Weight: 15–25 pounds	Height: 14–16 inches Weight: 40–50 pounds	Height: Under 10 (Toy), 10–15 (Miniature), Over 15 (Standard) Weight: 5–7 (Toy), 14–17 (Miniature), 45–75 (Standard)
Temperament	Stable, social and playful. Good for first time owner. Good with children.	Lively, friendly and affectionate. Good family pet.	Easygoing, charming and loyal. Prone to a number of health problems.	Intelligent, dignified and active. Toys and Miniatures are prone to barking. Standards are energetic and make good family pets.
Grooming	Curly, fine coat requires daily brushing. Professional grooming required. Minimal shedding.	Short, shiny coat requires minimal brushing. Skin folds on face require regular cleaning. Minimal shedding.	Short, smooth coat requires minimal brushing. Skin folds on face require daily cleaning. Minimal shedding.	Curly, dense coat requires regular brushing. Professional grooming required. Does not shed.
Training & Exercise	Requires moderate exercise. Early socialization and training classes recommended.	Requires moderate exercise. Early socialization and training classes recommended.	Requires minimal exercise. Training classes recommended.	Toys and Miniatures require moderate exercise. Standards require plenty of exercise. Training classes recommended.

Buying From a Breeder

You can find a puppy for sale just about anywhere, but that doesn't mean you should buy from the first place you visit. If you would like to make a purebred puppy a part of your family, you should thoroughly research your chosen breed and purchase your new companion from a reputable breeder. Buying a puppy from a reputable breeder will give you the best chance of raising a dog that is healthy, even-tempered and free of behavioral problems.

ABOUT REPUTABLE BREEDERS

Passionate About Their Breed

Reputable breeders are passionate about improving the breed that they raise. They have a breeding plan which outlines the physical attributes and characteristics they wish to produce in their puppies. Many good breeders also show their dogs in competition and are involved in breed clubs.

Knowledge and Support

Reputable breeders are very knowledgeable about the history of their breed and any related health issues or specific needs. Good breeders should be happy to answer all of the questions you have about a puppy. Expect breeders who really care about their puppies to ask you a lot of questions about your family and lifestyle. Good breeders will also be available to give you advice after you have taken your puppy home.

Health Certificates and Guarantees

To minimize health problems in their puppies, reputable breeders do not breed dogs with known health problems. The dogs they do use for breeding are tested for any hereditary ailments that are common to their breed, such as hip dysplasia and eye problems. You should ask to see the health certificates of the parents of any puppy you are considering. As well, reputable breeders will give you a written guarantee of the health of any puppy you bring home.

ABOUT REPUTABLE BREEDERS continued

Home-Raised Puppies

Reputable breeders often raise their puppies in their own homes. When raised in a home environment, puppies become used to living with humans and are generally more accepting of new sights and sounds. Breeders can closely observe puppies raised in their homes and should have a good idea of which puppy will best fit in with your family.

Mother On-Site

Reputable breeders will have the mother of their puppies on-site and should be happy to let you meet her. If the mother seems to be a relaxed, confident dog, there is a good chance her puppies will develop a similar disposition. Breeders may also have the father on-site.

Puppy Development

The breeder plays an important role in a puppy's social, mental and behavioral development. Good breeders will spend time with each of their puppies, handle them frequently and begin the puppies' socialization. By providing an interesting environment and exposing their puppies to a variety of objects, people and different experiences, good breeders work to stimulate all aspects of their puppies' development.

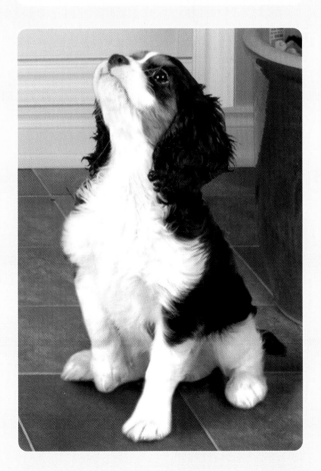

Contracts

A reputable breeder will ask you to sign a contract that outlines both their responsibilities and your responsibilities. Good breeders are normally willing to take the puppy back if the puppy does not work out with your family.

CONTINUED >

ABOUT REPUTABLE BREEDERS continued

Pedigree

A pedigree outlines a puppy's family history. Ask your breeder if they can provide you with a pedigree for your puppy. Your puppy's pedigree should show family history going back at least three generations.

AKC Registration

A reputable breeder of a dog breed recognized by the American Kennel Club (AKC) will provide you with an application to register your puppy with the AKC. Keep in mind, however, that AKC registration does not guarantee the puppy's health or temperament.

FINDING A REPUTABLE BREEDER

To find a reputable breeder, you can talk to dog owners, veterinarians and professional dog trainers. You can also check with the American Kennel Club (AKC) and various breed clubs.

If you have an uneasy feeling about a breeder, you should find another breeder who you feel more comfortable with. It is well worth your time to look for the best breeder you can find. The care with which a dedicated breeder produces and raises their puppies gives the puppies the best start in becoming healthy, stable family dogs.

Questions to Ask a Breeder

To help determine whether you are dealing with a reputable breeder, you can ask the following questions.

- Do you have any references that I can contact?

- Have your puppies been vaccinated? If so, which vaccinations were given and when were they administered?

- Are your puppies tattooed or microchipped for identification?

- Do you temperament-test your litters? Can you help me choose the right puppy for my family?

- Which characteristics do you strive to produce in your dogs?

- Have your dogs earned any competition titles?

DISREPUTABLE BREEDERS

Unfortunately, there are people who produce puppies purely for money, without regard for their puppies' well being. Buying a puppy from someone other than a reputable breeder can lead to major health and behavioral issues that can result in expensive veterinary and training bills.

Signs that you may be dealing with a less-than-acceptable breeder include:

- There is a huge number of dogs on-site.
- The breeder does not ask any questions about you and your family.
- The breeder claims that their puppies are purebred but does not offer any papers.
- The breeder wants you to take a puppy home before 7 weeks of age.

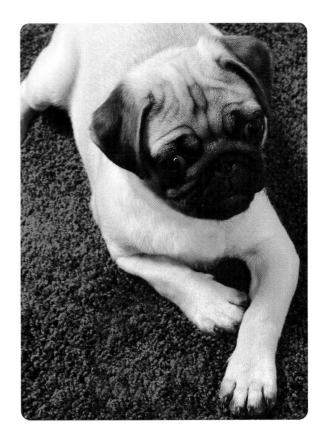

OTHER PUPPY SOURCES

Shelters and Rescue Groups

It can be difficult to find puppies at an organization that cares for unwanted dogs, as they most often offer only adult dogs for adoption. Occasionally, however, they do have puppies available for adoption. These organizations will sometimes have helpful information on the puppies' background. You can be successful in raising a puppy from a shelter or rescue group, but be aware that you may have to help build the puppy's confidence or deal with a few behavioral issues.

Newspaper Ads and the Internet

Newspapers and the Internet can be useful resources for locating reputable breeders. However, you should be wary of buying a puppy from any source that will not allow you to meet the breeder and the puppy's mother. Buying from these sources means that the background of the puppy, which can have a huge effect on a puppy's temperament and health, will be a complete mystery.

Uncovering a Puppy's Personality

Each puppy has a unique personality for you to discover. To find the puppy that is the best match for you and your family, look beyond the puppy's appearance to determine if his temperament and personality will complement you and your family. For example, a timid puppy may not do well in a family with lots of children and activity and an energetic puppy may be more than a retiree bargains for.

To determine a puppy's personality, watch how he interacts with his littermates and with people, as well as how he plays with you on his own. After you bring your puppy home, accept him for whatever personality he has and make it your goal to train and raise him to be a happy, stable dog.

Energetic Puppies

- Energetic puppies love to play and wrestle with their littermates and will jump up with their tails wagging when you appear. They are usually confident, clever and bossy.

- A puppy with this spirited type of personality will be a lot of work, but will also be a lot of fun.

- With an energetic puppy you have to establish your leadership and make the time to train him well to avoid having him become a bossy, difficult pet.

Relaxed Puppies

- Relaxed puppies will defend themselves in games with their littermates, but have a lower energy level than other puppies and spend more time quietly exploring.

- A puppy with this laid-back type of personality is undemanding and has a good tolerance for noise and confusion.

- A relaxed puppy is ideal for families with children.

Are there any other ways to determine a puppy's personality?

When observing a puppy, observe the puppy's parents as well. Puppies inherit their temperament from their parents just as they inherit their appearance or the length of their coat. If you do not want an aggressive or shy puppy, avoid puppies whose parents display these traits. If a puppy has a pleasant, relaxed parent, the puppy has a good chance of ending up with the same qualities. You can also try a few simple personality tests to help determine a puppy's personality type. For more information, see page 32.

Can the breeder help me in choosing a puppy that is right for me?

Yes. It's the breeders' responsibility to match puppies with the best potential owners, so they will make an honest effort to steer you in the right direction. Breeders have had more time to observe each puppy's personality traits and can judge how a puppy's personality complements you and your family.

Passive Puppies

- Passive puppies are shy and submissive with their littermates.
- While the other puppies may run to greet you when you enter, a puppy with a passive personality may just sit quietly watching you.
- A passive puppy needs calm, sensitive handling and a training program that focuses on patience and positive reinforcement.

Timid Puppies

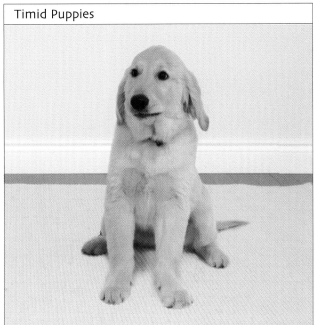

- Timid puppies show fear with their more dominant littermates. While the other puppies play and wrestle, the timid puppy may simply chew on a toy in a corner by himself.
- A puppy with this sensitive type of personality may startle at a loud noise or sudden movements by people in a room.
- A timid puppy is not the best choice for a family with children. He will need a lot of support and a training program that builds up his confidence.

Picking Your Puppy

Meeting a puppy for the first time is a little like going on a blind date—you're never sure what to expect. Fortunately, it may be easier to find a puppy whose personality will match your lifestyle than it is to find your human soul mate. Once you have decided what personality traits you are looking for in a puppy (see page 30), you can perform some simple tests to help you determine the personality of each puppy you meet.

In addition to testing the puppies in a litter, you should take the time to talk to the breeder. As someone who has watched the puppies since they were born, the breeder will be a valuable source of information.

About Picking Your Puppy

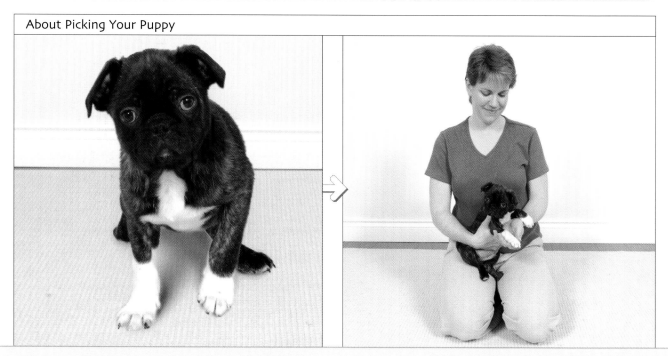

- You can perform a few simple tests with prospective puppies to help you determine the personality of the puppies.

  Note: You should try to perform the following tests when the puppies are at least 7 weeks old.

- You should test each puppy separately, away from his littermates. A puppy's confidence level may change when he is on his own.

- If possible, try to perform the tests in a room the puppy has never been in before. Taking the puppy away from the area he is accustomed to can also affect his confidence level.

- For best results, the person performing the testing should be a person the puppy does not know.

- Before performing the tests, try to make sure the puppy has gone to the bathroom.

- Avoid performing the tests immediately before or after the puppy's usual mealtime.

Is there anything else I should keep in mind when performing these exercises?

Try to remember that when you test a puppy's personality, you are only seeing what the puppy is like on a specific day and time and in a single environment. Before you make a decision, visit and test the puppies that you are interested in more than once. A couple of trips to the breeder can give you a much better idea of what a puppy's personality is like.

 Will a puppy's personality always remain the same?

A puppy's personality can be greatly affected by the environment that he lives in. Once your puppy comes home, you will be able to influence your puppy's developing personality and behavior by spending time with him. If you focus on training and socializing your puppy, you will have an excellent chance of raising the kind of dog you want to share your life with.

Come To Me Test

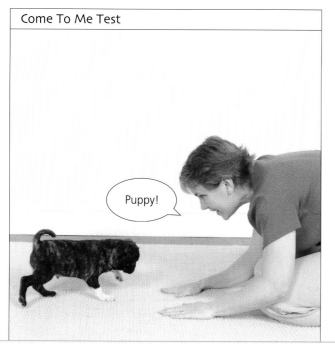

Puppy!

1 Kneel on the floor a short distance from the puppy.

2 Say "Puppy" in a cheerful tone and pat the floor in front of you to get the puppy's attention.

- Look for a puppy that responds quickly and comes to investigate you. This puppy is likely to be people oriented as an adult.

- A puppy that comes very slowly or not at all may be timid or undersocialized and may not be a good choice for a novice puppy owner.

Touch Test

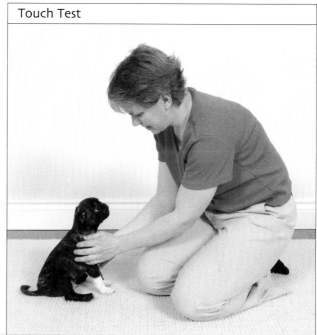

1 Kneel on the floor in front of the puppy.

2 Gently stroke the puppy all over to see his reaction to being touched and handled.

- Look for a puppy that is relaxed and content while being touched and handled.

- A puppy that seems distressed or tries to run away may be very independent or timid and may not be a good choice for a novice puppy owner.

CONTINUED

Picking Your Puppy continued

When you are evaluating a puppy's personality, there are a couple of things to keep in mind. First, puppies should be as relaxed as possible during testing, so avoid doing anything that may potentially frighten them. Second, puppies who have been recently vaccinated may feel under the weather, so ask the breeder to give the puppies at least two days to feel better before you arrive to evaluate them.

If you know someone who has experience with evaluating puppies, ask the breeder if they can come with you. A second opinion can be helpful.

The most important reason to perform these tests is to make you familiar with the personality of your new puppy. Once you know what your puppy is like, you can start to plan his training and socialization to bring out his best qualities.

Cradling Test

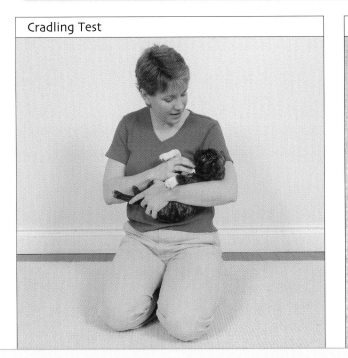

1 Kneeling on the floor, pick up the puppy and cradle him in your arms, with his back towards the floor.

2 Try to keep the puppy in the cradled position for one or two minutes.

- Look for a puppy that is willing to relax in your arms. This puppy will likely be easy-going.

- A puppy that struggles or even tries to bite you may be very independent or may need more socialization to become comfortable with new situations.

Noise Test

1 Kneeling on the floor a short distance from the puppy, make a loud noise, such as dropping your keys on the floor.

- Look for a puppy who startles at the noise but goes to investigate. This puppy has likely been well socialized and is comfortable with new sounds.

- A puppy that runs away and will not return may be timid or undersocialized and may not be a good choice for a novice puppy owner.

Is there another test I can perform to evaluate a puppy?

You can perform a simple test to determine how well a puppy responds to food rewards. Kneel on the floor facing the puppy and hold a treat close to his nose. Move the treat up above the puppy's head, between his eyes and toward the back of his head, always keeping it within sniffing-distance. A puppy that follows the treat with his nose and ends up in a Sit position is likely to respond to food incentives and should be easier to train than a puppy who ignores the treat.

Lift Me Test

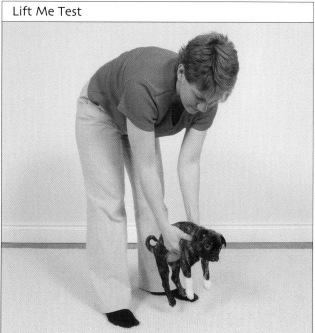

1 Standing near the puppy, interlace your fingers with your palms facing up under the puppy's belly. Gently lift up the puppy so his paws come up a few inches off the floor.

2 Hold the puppy in this position for about 30 seconds.

- Look for a puppy that is relaxed while he is suspended off the floor. This puppy will likely be easy-going.

- A puppy that struggles excessively may need more socialization to become comfortable with new situations.

Come With Me Test

1 Standing near the puppy, turn and slowly walk away from the puppy while encouraging the puppy to follow you.

- Look for a puppy who willingly follows you for at least a short distance. This puppy is likely to be people oriented as an adult.

- A puppy that shows no interest in following you may not be a good choice for a novice puppy owner.

Adopting an Older Puppy

Bringing home an older puppy, generally between the ages of 12 weeks and 1 year, is an option you should consider carefully. Depending on how much care, attention and training the puppy has received from a breeder or previous owner in the past, you may end up inheriting problems someone else created.

While adopting a younger puppy, between 7 to 12 weeks old, allows you to start training and socializing with a blank canvas, you do not necessarily need to rule out an older puppy. Take the time to find out how much socialization the older puppy has had with people as well as with other animals if you have other pets. You should also check to see how far along the puppy is with housetraining.

Benefits of Older Puppies

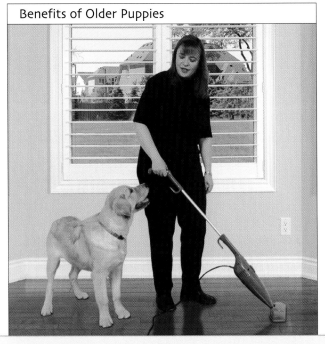

- Many people get their puppies when they are between 7 and 12 weeks old. However, deciding to make an older puppy a part of your family has several benefits.

- A puppy that is 6 months or older may have grown out of many puppy behaviors, such as excessive biting and chewing, and may already be housetrained.

- Older puppies that have been properly socialized—made comfortable with a variety of places, situations, people and sounds—may be calmer and more tolerant of household noise.

Considerations for Older Puppies

Questions to ask current owners:

✓ How old is the puppy?

✓ Why are the owners looking for another home for the puppy?

✓ How many homes has the puppy had?

✓ Has the puppy had any training?

✓ Is the puppy used to being in a crate?

✓ Does the puppy have any bad habits, such as aggression, excessive chewing or house soiling?

- There are several questions you should ask the breeder or current owner of a puppy that is older than 12 weeks before you decide to make the puppy a part of your family.

- If you are thinking of bringing an older puppy into a home with children, you should introduce your children to the puppy before you bring the puppy home. If the puppy displays any undesirable behaviors, you should not bring the puppy home.

What should I do after I adopt an older puppy?

Tip

You should find a dog trainer and get started with training classes right away. A good trainer will introduce you and your puppy to basic obedience practices. The trainer should also help you understand any troubling behaviors your new puppy may have and work with you to help your puppy become a stable, friendly companion.

Should I adopt an older puppy from a shelter?

Tip

If you adopt an older puppy from a shelter, keep in mind there are some additional risks. If the puppy came to the shelter from another home, find out why, especially if you have children. The puppy may need extra work to become accustomed to children. You should also find out what vaccines the puppy has received and if he has been exposed to other dogs who were sick.

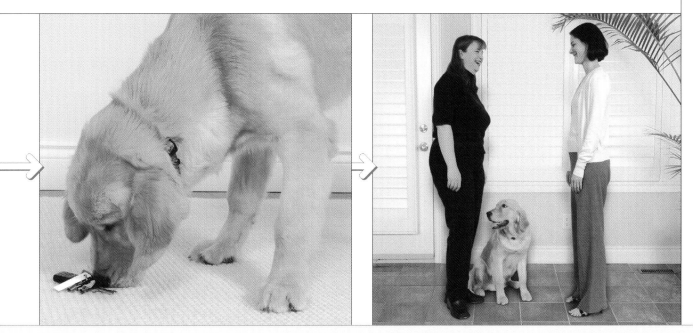

- Older puppies that have been neglected may be unpredictable, fearful or aggressive.

- Try tossing a set of keys on the floor or clapping your hands to determine the puppy's reaction to being startled. If the puppy is very upset by the noise, you may want to reconsider bringing the puppy home with you.

- You should also ask the puppy's current owner to lift the puppy up off the floor for you. If the puppy shows a lot of fear or frustration, this may not be the puppy for you.

- Try to find out how much time the puppy has had getting used to people and experiences in the outside world.

- Older puppies that have not been adequately socialized may require a great deal of training and careful introductions to new situations.

- As a rule of thumb, the more time a puppy spends with his littermates, the less he learns about humans. Under-socialized older puppies may be difficult to communicate with and may be shy.

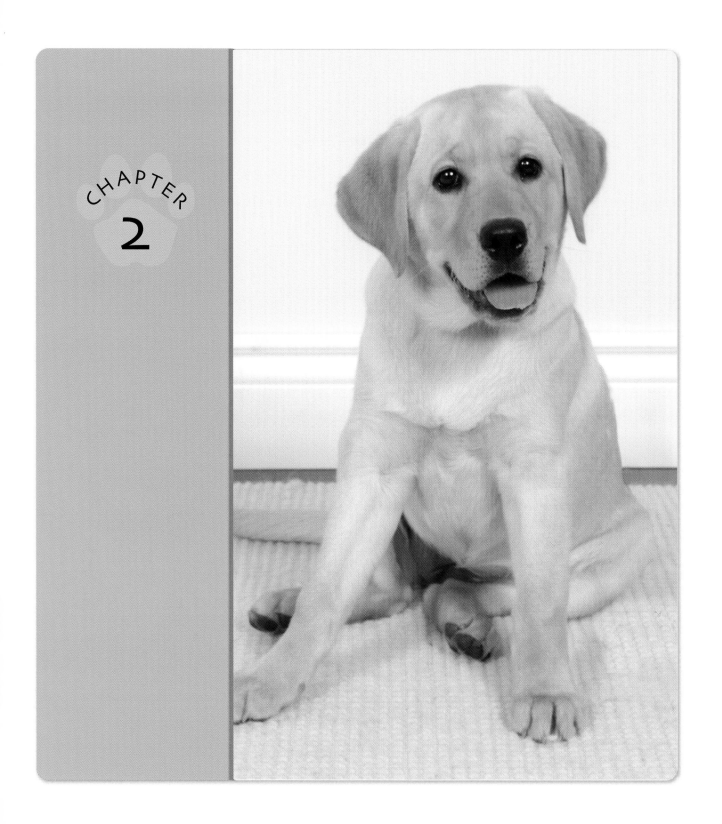

CHAPTER

2

Preparing for Your Puppy

Crates, Gates and Enclosures

There are a variety of enclosures, including crates, gates and outdoor dog runs or exercise pens, to help keep your puppy safe and out of mischief. Do not feel that you are punishing your puppy when you place him in a crate. Dogs naturally like the den-like, protective environment of these types of enclosures. A child-safety gate will also keep your puppy in a limited area of the house, just as outdoor exercise pens will keep him from areas of the yard that you want to protect.

Crates, also called kennels, are also useful tools when training. For more information on using crates in housetraining, see page 78. For information on crate training your puppy, see page 70.

Crates

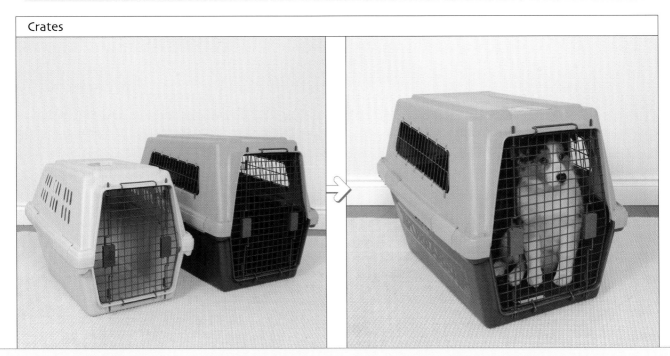

- A crate is a metal or plastic box with a wire-mesh door that can be latched shut.

- You should have a crate to provide a secure spot where your new puppy can go when you are not able to supervise him.

- Enclosed plastic crates provide a safe, den-like environment that most puppies find comforting. This type of crate is also useful for when you need to travel with your puppy.

- Any crate you purchase should be large enough for your puppy to stand up, turn around and lie down in.

- A crate that is too large will allow your puppy to eliminate in one part and sleep in another, which can create problems for housetraining.

- If you purchase a crate that will fit your puppy when he is full-grown, you should also purchase a crate divider with which you can create a smaller space while your puppy is little.

Tip

Should I put towels or blankets into my puppy's crate?

Placing towels or blankets in your puppy's crate can be dangerous. The material is a choking hazard for inquisitive and chewing puppies. Because towels and blankets absorb urine, they also limit the effectiveness of crate training. When your puppy is older, you can introduce, with supervision, a blanket into his crate. Until then, only place a safe chew toy in the crate with your new puppy.

Tip

I want my puppy to be comfortable. Can I buy a dog bed for him?

Dog beds can provide your puppy with a soft, comfortable place to lie down. Until your puppy is housetrained and past the chewing stage, however, you should place the dog bed in a common area of your home where you can supervise. You should not place the bed in the puppy's crate. A dog bed you purchase should have a zippered outer shell that can be removed and washed and an inner pillow that can be wiped clean.

Gates

Outdoor Enclosures

- You can use a child-safety gate to keep your puppy in one room.

- Until your puppy is fully trained, you can keep him confined to a small area of your home until he earns more freedom through good behavior. Gates can be moved to gradually give your puppy access to more of the house.

- Before your puppy is housetrained, it is best to confine him to a room that has tile or vinyl floors so that any accidents can be easily cleaned up.

- If you do not have a fenced yard, a folding exercise pen or fenced dog run is a great alternative for times when you want to let your puppy play outside.

- In warm weather, it is important to set up your exercise pen or dog run in a shaded area.

Note: A puppy should always be supervised while outside to prevent him from troublesome behavior such as digging or chewing on shrubs.

Feeding Supplies

Your shopping list for your puppy's mealtime is short and simple: food bowl, water bowl and food. Remember that your puppy will grow so make sure his bowls are large enough to handle his growing appetite. You should purchase the best bowls you can afford as they can last the lifetime of your puppy.

Ask your breeder about the type of food your puppy is accustomed to, the quantity and the frequency of your puppy's meals. There is probably no need to change his diet when you bring him home. Be careful not to buy more food for your puppy than you need as it can go stale before your puppy is able to finish it. You can also purchase some high-quality soft treats for your puppy to use during training. For more information on nutrition and feeding your puppy, see page 94.

Food and Water Bowls

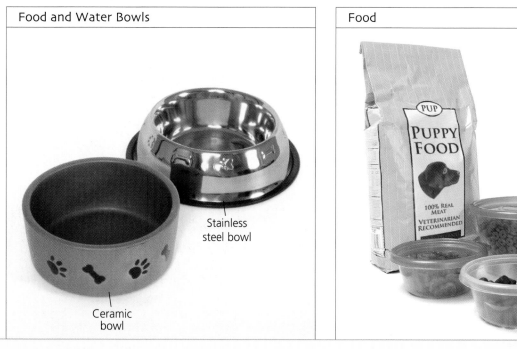

Stainless steel bowl

Ceramic bowl

Food

- You will need two bowls for your new puppy—one bowl for food and another for water.

- Heavy ceramic and stainless steel bowls are durable and easy to clean. Avoid plastic bowls, since they can be chewed and may harbor germs and bacteria.

- A bowl should have a heavy base that is wide enough to prevent it from being tipped over.

- Ask your breeder or vet whether your puppy needs a special type of bowl, such as a tapered bowl for long-eared puppies.

- Sudden changes in diet can negatively affect your puppy's digestion. At first, it is generally best to keep your puppy on the same food he is accustomed to.

- It is a good idea to purchase your puppy's food, and even some soft, high-quality treats, before bringing him home. You should also buy a sturdy storage container that will keep the food fresh.

- If you want to change the food your puppy eats, ask your breeder or veterinarian about a suitable alternative.

Leashes

Leashes are an essential tool for training as they allow you to maintain control of your puppy. You should make sure you purchase a basic leash before your puppy comes home.

The most important quality in a leash is a strong clasp. Inexpensive or flimsy clasps can break over time, so make sure to carefully inspect the clasp when you are shopping for leashes.

Leashes come in a variety of styles, colors and materials, but nylon and leather are the best choices for a puppy's first leash. As puppies grow, they may need a heavier, stronger leash. Your veterinarian or breeder can help you decide which type of leash would best suit your puppy.

Basic Leashes

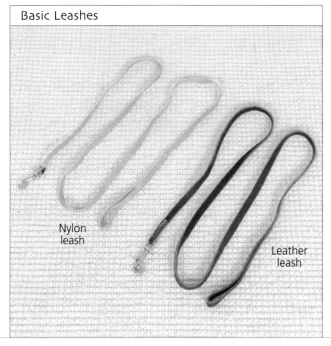

Nylon leash

Leather leash

Long Leashes

Nylon long leash

Retractable leash

- You will need to purchase at least one basic leash for walking and training your puppy.

- A good leash should be four to six feet in length and made of nylon, cotton or leather.

Note: Avoid chain leashes. This type of leash may hurt your puppy or you if you become entangled in it.

- A basic leash and its clasp should be strong enough to restrain your puppy as he grows into an adult dog.

- Long leashes give your puppy freedom to explore and are essential for working with your puppy in large spaces, such as parks and fields.

- A long leash may be a 25- to 30-foot length of nylon or a retractable leash.

- A long leash and its clasp should be strong enough to restrain your puppy as he grows into an adult dog.

- Retractable leashes can extend from just a few feet to as long as 30 feet and then automatically wind back into the handle.

Houselines and Yardlines

In addition to a basic leash and a long leash (see page 43), houselines and yardlines are essential puppy training tools. Houselines and yardlines allow an owner to easily gain control of their puppy without having to chase the puppy around. They are also useful for discouraging unwanted behavior, such as stopping a puppy from jumping up or from running out the door.

When a puppy is wearing a houseline or yardline, he should never be left unsupervised, especially outside. Also remember that puppies should not wear houselines or yardlines around young children. When a puppy is wearing a houseline or yardline around older children, he should be closely supervised. You should also instruct children never to touch the houseline or yardline.

Houselines

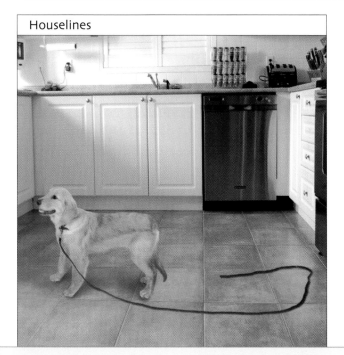

Yardlines

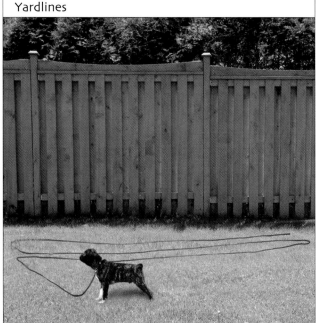

- A houseline is a six- to ten-foot long training leash that is designed to loosely drag behind a puppy that is being trained when he is inside the home.

  Note: The smaller your home is, the shorter your houseline can be.

- Unlike a leash, a houseline has no loop at the end. You can step on or pick up the houseline when you need to stop your puppy from running off or guide him away from something inappropriate, such as trying to jump up on the furniture.

- A yardline is a 16- to 20-foot long training leash that is designed to loosely drag behind a puppy that is being trained when he is outside in a fenced area.

- Unlike a leash, a yardline has no loop at the end. You can step on or pick up the yardline when you need to stop your puppy from running off or guide him away from something inappropriate, such as digging in the garden.

Is there another way to make my own houseline or yardline?

An easy way to make your own houseline or yardline involves altering a store-bought leash. First, purchase a long, lightweight nylon leash of the appropriate length for a houseline or yardline. Pet supply stores sell leashes that are up to 25 or 30 feet in length. Next, cut off the looped end of the leash to make a houseline or yardline. For more information on long leashes, see page 43.

 When can I remove the houseline or yardline from my puppy?

The best way to decide whether you should shorten or remove your puppy's houseline or yardline is to pay attention to his behavior. As your puppy matures and his training progresses, you can gradually shorten both the houseline and yardline until they are only short tabs hanging from your puppy's collar. Once you no longer need the houseline or yardline to redirect your puppy's behavior, you can completely remove it.

Making a Houseline or Yardline

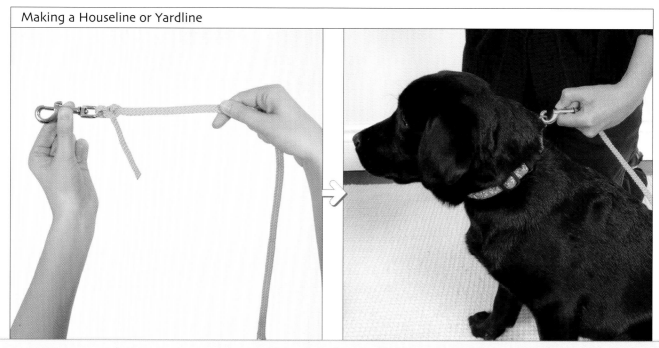

- You can easily make your own houseline or yardline from materials you purchase at a hardware or pet supply store.
- You will need a length of lightweight nylon line and a sturdy metal clip.

Note: If you cannot find nylon line, you can also use light cotton rope for the houseline or yardline.

1 Tie one end of the nylon line securely to the clip.

2 Attach the clip to your puppy's collar and allow the houseline or yardline to drag behind the puppy.

- Your puppy may chew the houseline or yardline. If the houseline or yardline breaks, simply tie a knot to reconnect the two pieces.

Note: After you have tied 3 knots in the houseline or yardline, replace it with a new houseline or yardline.

Collars and Harnesses

When choosing a collar or harness, you have a variety of styles, colors and materials to consider. The best material for a collar or harness is nylon, which is not as heavy or as expensive as leather. In addition to style, color and material considerations, the collar or harness must fit the current size of your puppy. You may have to replace an outgrown collar or harness, depending on how fast your puppy grows and how adjustable the collar or harness is.

Flat collars with a snap are a good choice for a puppy as you can put them on quickly. Head halters are helpful with excitable puppies as they often provide a relaxing effect. Whatever collar or harness you choose, remember to never leave your puppy with the collar or harness on unsupervised.

Flat Collars

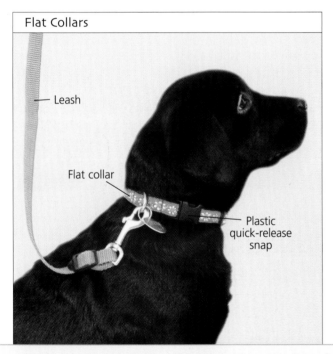

Leash

Flat collar

Plastic quick-release snap

Martingale Collars

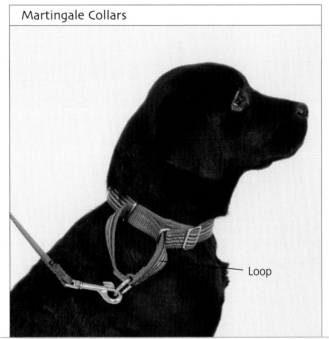

Loop

- The first collar you buy for most young puppies should be a flat collar made out of nylon with either a plastic quick-release snap or a traditional metal buckle.

- Leashes and identification tags are normally attached to your puppy's flat collar.

- When fitted properly, flat collars should not normally slip off or be too tight on your puppy.

  Note: For information on fitting a flat collar, see the top of page 47.

- Martingale collars are loose-fitting, nylon collars that have no buckles but feature a loop that tightens to make the collar fit more snugly if a puppy pulls at his leash.

- The snug fit of a martingale collar means there is very little risk that the collar will slip over your puppy's head while the leash is attached.

- You may want to purchase a martingale collar if you have a puppy who is prone to pulling out of his flat collar.

How do I know if a collar fits my puppy correctly?

The fit should be loose enough to be comfortable but tight enough to prevent your puppy from slipping out of the collar. A good guide is to fit two fingers flat beside each other between the collar and your puppy's neck. Make sure to test the fit by gently trying to pull the collar over your puppy's head. The collar should not come off. This is especially important for puppies with heavy or fluffy coats.

What information should I put on my puppy's identification tag?

Your puppy's collar is the ideal location to place your puppy's identification tag, which can be helpful should your puppy become lost. For your security, you should not include your puppy's name or your address on the tag. Simply include a contact phone number and a short sentence, such as "I'm lost – 312-555-8917," so that whoever finds him can get in touch with you.

Head Halters

Body Harnesses

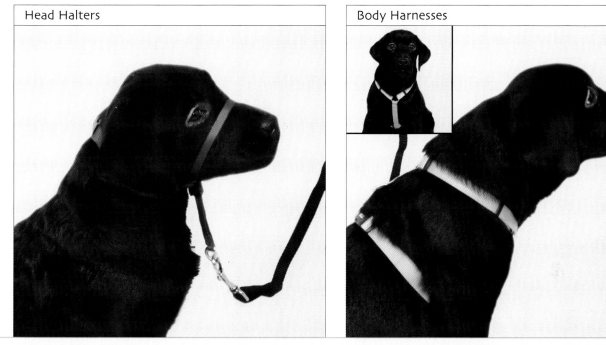

- A head halter is a type of collar that is used to handle puppies that need some extra control.

- Head halters fit around a puppy's muzzle and neck and put pressure on the muzzle when the puppy pulls on his leash.

- While they look restricting, puppies can still eat, drink and even bark while wearing a head halter.

- Head halters should not be used on puppies under 4 months of age and must be fitted with the guidance of a trainer or veterinarian.

- A body harness fits around your puppy's neck and body. If the puppy pulls on his leash, pressure is put on his body instead of his neck.

- Some smaller breeds, such as Chihuahuas, need a body harness initially to avoid injuring their delicate necks. Your breeder or veterinarian can tell you if your puppy needs a harness.

Note: Body harnesses can actually encourage unwanted leash pulling in some large breeds, such as Siberian Huskies.

Toys

A basic set of toys for your puppy includes two or three food-holding chew toys, one or two teething toys, a nylon bone, and a stuffed toy. You should avoid giving your puppy toys that are made for children or that will break into pieces that he could swallow.

Toys are very useful for playing games with your puppy and can help decrease behavioral problems by giving your puppy something fun and active to do. Chew toys are an excellent outlet for your puppy's instinctual desire to chew. Providing chew toys will also help to prevent your puppy from chewing on inappropriate objects around your house, such as your shoes or the legs of your coffee table.

Toy Guidelines

- Every puppy needs a number of toys for mental stimulation and to relieve boredom. A toy can keep your puppy happily occupied for hours.

- It is natural for puppies to chew as their teeth develop. Providing your puppy with chew toys will help prevent him from chewing on items that are not toys.

- Giving your puppy too many toys may cause him to think that everything is a toy. Do not provide your puppy with more than one or two toys at a time.

Good Toy Choices

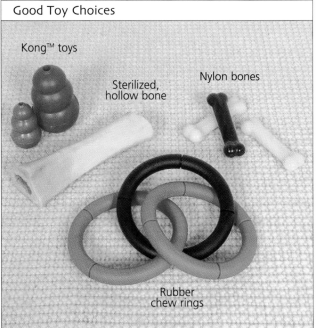

Kong™ toys

Sterilized, hollow bone

Nylon bones

Rubber chew rings

- Toys that can be stuffed with food, such as the popular Kong™ toys or sterilized, hollow bones, make excellent toys. Extracting food from a toy is a very natural and relaxing pastime for puppies.

- Teething toys, like rubber chew rings and nylon bones, are important for a puppy's developing teeth and help relieve boredom.

- These types of toys are safe to leave with your puppy unsupervised.

Tip *Why does my puppy love playing with food-stuffed chew toys?*

Puppies love food-stuffed chew toys because they are a rewarding challenge. In the wild, dogs spend a lot of time chewing and biting meat from bones. Domesticated puppies have their dinner brought to them, so once they've eaten, they have a lot of free time to find other things to chew. Extracting food from a Kong™ or other chew toy is a natural behavior that can help puppies relax.

Tip *Is a flying disc a good toy for my puppy to play with?*

Flying discs in any setting are not a good idea, offering too many risks to your puppy's immature skeletal system. Awkward jumping, twisting to catch and landing heavily can put too much pressure on his fragile neck and spine. Also, if the disc has been chewed, a jagged edge could injure his mouth. Save the flying disc for when your puppy is mature and in very good physical condition.

Toys Requiring Supervision

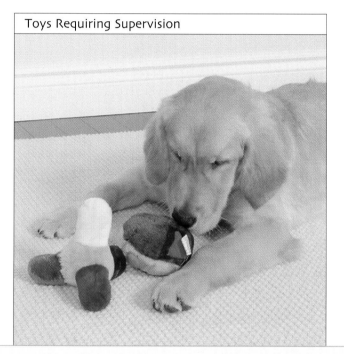

- Stuffed toys and toys with squeakers should be simple and durably constructed. Since they are often ripped apart, only allow your puppy to play with these toys under your supervision.

- Tennis balls are good for playing fetch with your puppy. However, tennis balls can break into pieces if used as a chew toy. Never leave your puppy alone with a tennis ball.

- Puppies over 6 months old can be given rawhide bones with supervision.

Poor Toy Choices

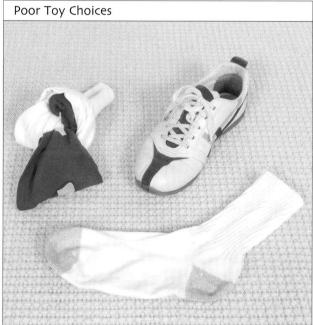

- Avoid using old household items, such as knotted shirts, shoes or socks, as toys. Playing with these items will encourage your puppy to view all household items as toys.

- Many stores carry dried animal parts, such as pig ears, for dogs to chew on. These are not recommended as they can bring out possessive behavior and cause stomach upset in some puppies.

Grooming Supplies

It's important to groom your puppy regularly so that his coat stays healthy and shiny. You can visit a local pet supply store to purchase grooming supplies before your new puppy comes home. Essential grooming tools include a brush or comb for your puppy's coat, a pair of nail clippers and a toothbrush and toothpaste. Some grooming supplies are better for specific breeds, so consult your breeder, veterinarian or a professional groomer for advice on which grooming tools you should purchase.

The first brush you purchase for your puppy should have soft bristles, since most puppies do not have much fur. When your puppy matures, you can look for a brush that's better suited for his breed.

Brushes and Combs

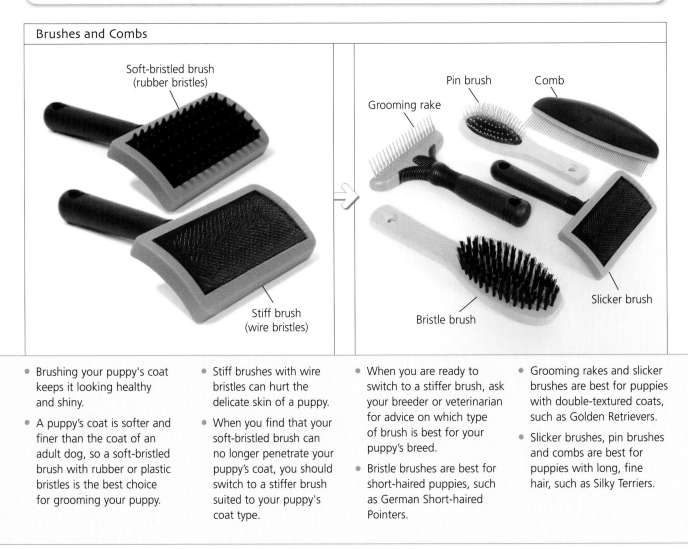

Soft-bristled brush (rubber bristles)

Stiff brush (wire bristles)

Grooming rake

Pin brush

Comb

Bristle brush

Slicker brush

- Brushing your puppy's coat keeps it looking healthy and shiny.

- A puppy's coat is softer and finer than the coat of an adult dog, so a soft-bristled brush with rubber or plastic bristles is the best choice for grooming your puppy.

- Stiff brushes with wire bristles can hurt the delicate skin of a puppy.

- When you find that your soft-bristled brush can no longer penetrate your puppy's coat, you should switch to a stiffer brush suited to your puppy's coat type.

- When you are ready to switch to a stiffer brush, ask your breeder or veterinarian for advice on which type of brush is best for your puppy's breed.

- Bristle brushes are best for short-haired puppies, such as German Short-haired Pointers.

- Grooming rakes and slicker brushes are best for puppies with double-textured coats, such as Golden Retrievers.

- Slicker brushes, pin brushes and combs are best for puppies with long, fine hair, such as Silky Terriers.

Tip *Can I use human shampoo to wash my puppy?*

Your puppy's skin is different from that of humans, so human shampoo can cause your puppy's skin to start itching or scaling. A pH-balanced shampoo designed for dogs is the best choice for washing your puppy. Ask your veterinarian to recommend a shampoo that is best suited to your puppy's breed. Your vet's clinic may even sell dog shampoo.

Tip *What should I use to clean my puppy's ears?*

You should use cotton balls and a cleanser specifically designed for dogs' ears to clean your puppy's ears. To avoid injuring your puppy's ears, you should never use cotton-tipped swabs. For information on cleaning your puppy's ears, see page 103.

Nail Clippers and Grinders

Guillotine-style nail clipper

Scissor-style nail clipper

Toothbrushes and Toothpaste

Soft-bristled toothbrush

DOG TOOTHPASTE

Fingertip toothbrush

- Guillotine-style nail clippers can be used for most puppies to keep their nails an appropriate length.
- If your puppy has large, thick nails, scissor-style nail clippers may be more suitable.

- You can also trim your puppy's nails with an electric nail grinder, which uses a spinning, sandpaper-like tip to quickly trim nails and give them smooth edges.

Note: It may take your puppy a little while to become accustomed to the noise of a grinder.

- Brushing your puppy's teeth helps maintain healthy teeth and can prevent gum disease.
- Several types of toothbrushes are available for puppies, including soft-bristled brushes and fingertip brushes that resemble bristled rubber thimbles.

- Toothpaste specifically formulated for dogs is available at pet stores. You should never brush your puppy's teeth with toothpaste intended for humans.

Choosing a Name

You will use your puppy's name thousands of times during his lifetime, so it's important to put some careful thought into your puppy's name. Take some time and include your entire household in the decision so that when your puppy comes home, you can welcome him by name.

Once you've picked a name, you should stick to it. Calling your puppy by different nicknames can confuse him and may prevent him from learning his name. You should also be aware that some names, like Bruiser, can make people react negatively to your puppy.

If you purchase a puppy from a breeder, they may require that the puppy's registered name includes the name of the kennel. For example, the registered name Llanfair Maria includes the kennel name, Llanfair, and the puppy's name, Maria.

Choosing a Name

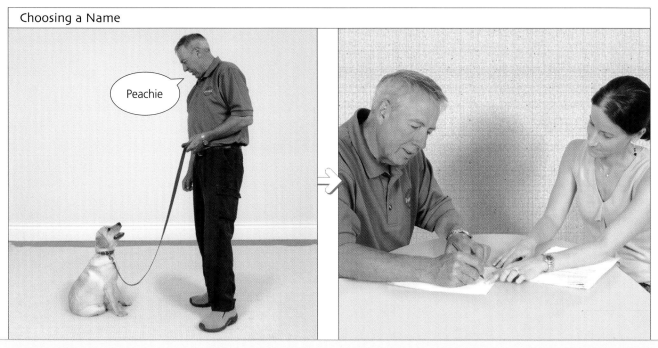

- A good puppy name will be easy for you to pronounce and easy for your puppy to distinguish from other words.

- Avoid names that sound like training commands and words commonly used in conversation. For example, Flo could be mistaken for the word "No," while May sounds very similar to the command "Stay."

- When choosing a name for your puppy, try to find a two-syllable name that ends with a vowel sound, such as Peachie or Vera.

- If your puppy is a purebred, the breeder may ask you to choose a registered name that will appear on the puppy's official papers.

- The breeder's kennel name usually makes up the first part of the registered name, followed by the name you want to use for your puppy.

- You can call your puppy by his registered name or choose one nickname that you will always use to call your puppy.

- The breeder can instruct you on any guidelines you need to follow when choosing a registered name, such as the number of letters the name can have.

Choosing a Veterinarian

To care for the health needs of your puppy, from preventative shots and checkups to treatment for an illness, you need to select a veterinarian for your puppy. If possible, take the time to interview several veterinarians before you choose the one you would like to use. You should feel comfortable enough with him to discuss any concerns you have about your puppy's health and nutrition.

Your veterinarian is also an important resource for you as a dog owner. For example, the veterinarian will be able to answer questions related to your puppy's breed and to advise you on your puppy's diet. In addition to choosing a veterinarian, you should also find out the location of the nearest emergency after-hours clinic.

Choosing a Veterinarian

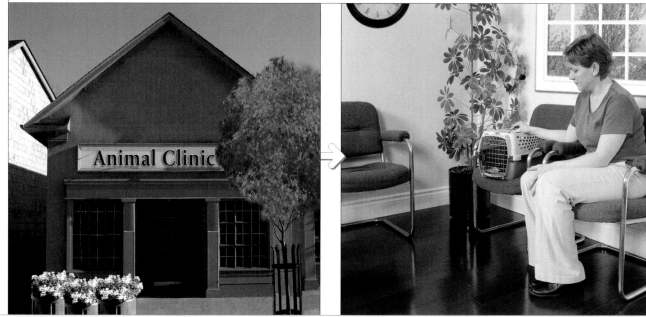

- It is your responsibility to take your puppy to a veterinarian for annual checkups and for any required vaccinations or treatments.

- You should choose a veterinarian a few weeks before you bring your puppy home.

- To find a good veterinarian, ask your pet-owning neighbors and relatives who they use. If your breeder lives close by, you should ask the breeder also.

- Once you have a short list of recommended veterinarians, call and arrange a visit to meet the veterinarians and possibly tour the clinics.

- When visiting a potential veterinary clinic, look around to see if the office and waiting room are clean, organized and free of unpleasant odors.

- Ask the veterinarian a few questions, such as how long he has been practicing and if there are any conditions or procedures that he refers to other veterinarians instead of handling himself.

- If you feel comfortable in the clinic and with the veterinarian, you have likely found a new, valuable member of your puppy-raising team.

Finding a Puppy Training Class

Investing in a puppy training class run by a qualified trainer can help your puppy build good habits and can prevent mistakes you may make in training your puppy on your own. Many training classes do not accept puppies until they are 12 weeks old and have had the appropriate vaccinations. Check with your veterinarian to ensure your puppy is up to date with his vaccinations when you are ready to enroll in a class.

Take the time to meet with and observe a trainer before you sign up for a class. If the trainer is approachable and motivating, you are more likely to follow through with practice exercises and ask questions to solve problems you may encounter during training.

Finding a Puppy Training Class

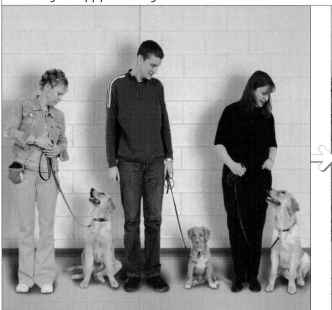 

- Puppy training classes can benefit both you and your puppy and can strengthen your relationship.
- Your puppy will learn basic commands, such as Sit and Come, how to respond to you even with distractions and how to socialize and communicate with other dogs.

- You will learn proper techniques for training your puppy, how to deal with behavioral issues and how to understand the way your puppy thinks.

- To find a good training class, ask your friends, breeder or veterinarian for referrals.
- If you see someone walking down the street with an obedient, happy and well-mannered dog, ask them where they trained.

- You can also contact the Association of Pet Dog Trainers (www.apdt.com) to obtain a list of certified dog trainers in your area.

Tip

What type of credentials should a puppy trainer have?

When researching puppy training classes, look for a trainer who is a member of a professional dog trainers association or who has taken the Certification Council for Pet Dog Trainers competency exam. You should also find out from prospective trainers how much experience they have with training a wide variety of breeds. Finally, ask trainers for references and take the time to check those references.

 Tip

What should I avoid when looking for a puppy training class?

You should avoid classes that do not require proof of vaccinations, that take place in a big and noisy environment or that make you feel uncomfortable or unsure of your puppy's safety. You should also avoid classes where the trainers encourage the use of choke chains or prong collars. A negative experience with a class may hurt your puppy's training and even your relationship with your puppy.

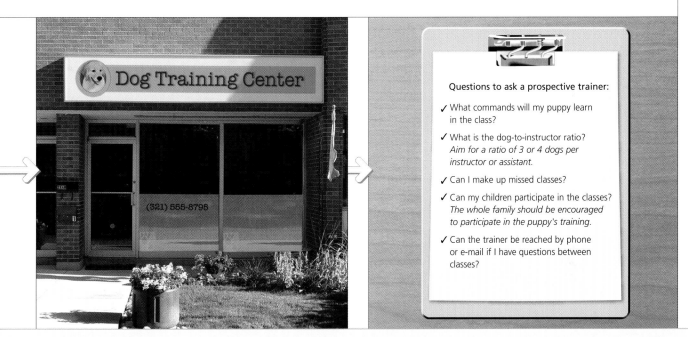

Dog Training Center

(321) 555-8795

Questions to ask a prospective trainer:

✓ What commands will my puppy learn in the class?

✓ What is the dog-to-instructor ratio? *Aim for a ratio of 3 or 4 dogs per instructor or assistant.*

✓ Can I make up missed classes?

✓ Can my children participate in the classes? *The whole family should be encouraged to participate in the puppy's training.*

✓ Can the trainer be reached by phone or e-mail if I have questions between classes?

- Before you join a puppy training class, you should go to a few different classes and observe.

- Puppy training classes should use a reward-based method, such as giving treats, to motivate and train the puppies.

- The class should not be a constant play session for the puppies. Play time, if included, should be only a small part of the training session.

- Asking questions about a training class will help you determine if this is a good class for you and your puppy.

- When looking for a puppy training class, trust your instincts. If you like the trainer and find the trainer easy to communicate with, there is a better chance that you and your puppy will succeed in the class.

Puppy-Proofing Your Home

Just as you would baby-proof your home to protect curious infants and toddlers, you should puppy-proof your home to prevent your puppy from harming himself or your belongings. Position yourself at your puppy's level by getting down on your hands and knees to look for inappropriate items that your puppy may want to chew, such as plants, shoes or kids' toys.

To further protect your puppy, consider setting up a child-safety gate to keep him with you in a smaller space that you can supervise more easily. In case your puppy does get into something that is harmful or even toxic, keep the telephone number for your local after-hours emergency veterinary clinic nearby.

Chewable Objects

Hazardous Situations

- For a puppy, virtually any object is chewable. You should put away any items that could be damaged or that would cause injury to your puppy if chewed.

- You can purchase a bitter-tasting spray from your local pet supply store to deter your puppy from chewing. You can spray this product on objects that cannot be moved, such as wooden furniture.

- Electrical cords and computer cables can be very hazardous if chewed. Cords and cables should be removed or coiled and sprayed with a bitter-tasting spray.

- Since your home will be unfamiliar territory, your new puppy must be kept safe from potentially hazardous situations.

- Toilet seats should be kept closed to prevent your puppy from climbing up and falling into the toilet.

- Swimming pools present a drowning hazard for a new puppy and should be off limits.

- Never allow your puppy to climb on high objects, such as bunk beds. His curiosity and lack of coordination could lead to a serious fall.

How can I keep my puppy out of the garbage?

Tip

Without question, your puppy will be curious about the garbage. Your best bet is to hide it or otherwise put it out of reach. Keep garbage cans under the sink, in a pantry or in other places that your puppy is unable to access. If this is not possible, use a garbage can that has a tight-fitting lid or a tall can with a swing lid or pedal-operated lid.

What are some other hazardous situations I should consider?

Tip

Indoors, make sure all cabinets are properly secured. Secure bookcases to the wall and keep tempting books, magazines and newspapers out of reach. Also, the combination of a waterbed and puppy paws can be damaging to your home and life threatening to your puppy. Outdoors, make sure your deck is puppy friendly. Do not allow your puppy on an unfenced deck or a deck that is higher than ground level as he could easily fall off the deck and hurt himself.

Toxic Substances

Household items that are toxic to dogs:

- ✓ antifreeze
- ✓ chocolate, onions, grapes, raisins
- ✓ cleaning products, bleach
- ✓ deodorant sticks
- ✓ gasoline, kerosene, lighter fluid
- ✓ medications
- ✓ paint, paint thinner, turpentine
- ✓ pesticides and fertilizer
- ✓ rubbing alcohol
- ✓ shampoo, soap, shaving cream

Plants

Some plants that are toxic to dogs:

- ✓ amaryllis
- ✓ azalea and rhododendron
- ✓ boxwood
- ✓ cactus
- ✓ castor bean plant
- ✓ columbine
- ✓ crocus
- ✓ daffodil
- ✓ delphinium
- ✓ dieffenbachia
- ✓ foxglove
- ✓ hemlock
- ✓ hydrangea
- ✓ iris
- ✓ ivy
- ✓ laurel
- ✓ lily
- ✓ lily of the valley
- ✓ lupine
- ✓ morning glory
- ✓ oleander
- ✓ tulip
- ✓ yew

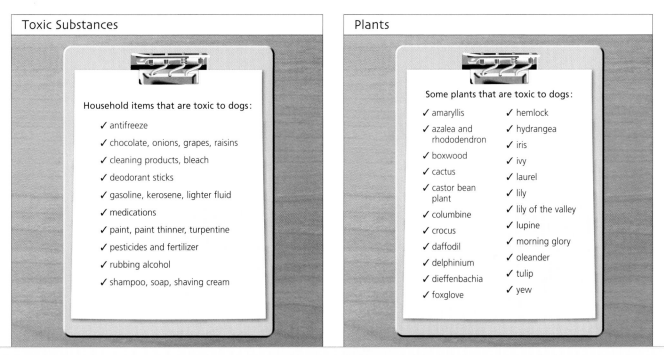

- There are many substances in the average home that are toxic to dogs. Before your puppy arrives, you should remove potentially toxic items from the areas he will have access to.

- Puppies are attracted to items with a strong fragrance. Be sure to keep cleaning supplies, perfume, soap and other toiletries away from your puppy.

- Garages, basements and garden sheds often contain extremely toxic chemicals, such as automotive fluids, fertilizers and pesticides. Keep your puppy out of these areas.

- Many common plants and flowers found around the house and garden are toxic to dogs.

- If you have houseplants on or near the floor, you should move them out of your puppy's reach. Your puppy should also be closely supervised if you have gardens in your yard.

Note: For more information on plants that are hazardous to your puppy, check with your veterinarian.

Setting Up Your Puppy's First Space

All puppies need a space to call their own—a place in your home where you can supervise while they relax and explore. You should set up a safe space for your new puppy before you pick him up from the breeder. When you bring him home for the first time, take your puppy to his own space. A new puppy will need lots of interaction with his owner, which you can provide for him in his very own safe space.

Your puppy's space should be in a central location, such as the kitchen, and not somewhere out of the way like a bathroom or bedroom. It should also be comfortable and free from dangerous items like cleaning products.

Setting Up Your Puppy's First Space

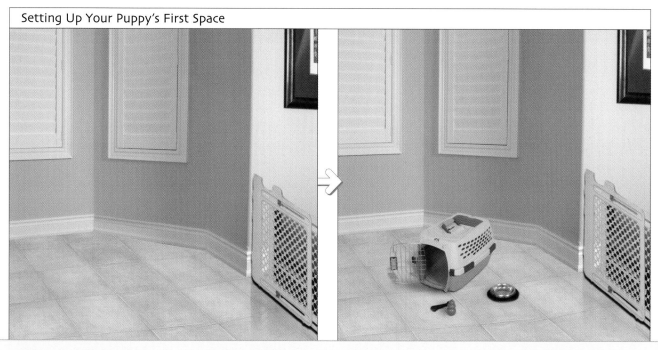

- Before you bring your puppy home, you need to set up a safe space where you can spend time with him.

- Choose an area that is close to the action in the house, such as the kitchen, so the puppy can get used to his new family and the sounds in his new home.

- The floor should be a surface that is easy to clean.

- Set up a child-safety gate to restrict your puppy's access to other areas of the house.

- Place the puppy's crate, with the door open, inside the space you set up.

- You should also place a chew toy and the puppy's water bowl in the space.

- Make sure any items that could be a choking hazard are moved out of the puppy's reach and any cabinets are closed securely.

- Electrical cords should be moved out of the puppy's reach if possible.

  Note: For more information on puppy-proofing, see page 56.

Know Your Local Dog Laws

When you own a puppy, you must accept the responsibility to obey local licensing and leash regulations. Find out what regulations exist in your area and practice good manners by always cleaning up after your puppy when you are out in public.

Before you decide on the breed of puppy you want, you should find out whether your area has any additional restrictions. For example, some municipalities have banned specific breeds of dogs.

Some cities have designated off-leash parks where puppies can play without having to wear a leash. You should wait to take your puppy to an off-leash park until he is at least six months old and will come when you call him.

Know Your Local Dog Laws

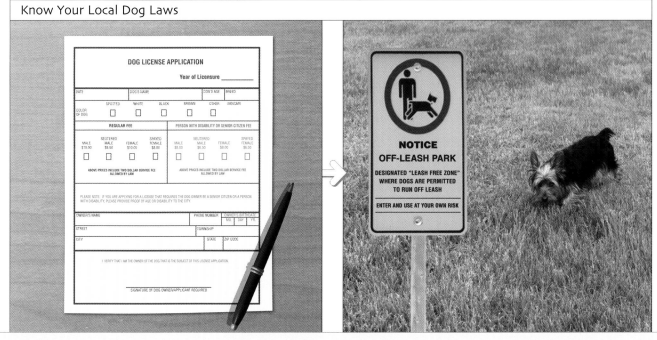

- Most cities and municipalities require that you purchase a dog license annually and clip the license tag to your puppy's collar.
- You can usually purchase a license from your local animal shelter.

- The license tag is a good form of identification in case your puppy gets lost and also offers proof of licensing. If you are caught with an unlicensed dog, you could be fined.
- Some areas require proof of a rabies vaccination before providing you with a license.

- Most cities and municipalities also have leash laws that specify that dogs must be leashed and under your control at all times when out in public.
- One exception to leash laws is an off-leash park.

- An off-leash park is a controlled space in which dogs can socialize with you, other dogs and other dog owners without a leash. Check with your local animal shelter or city hall to find out the locations of off-leash parks or parks with designated off-leash areas.

The First Week

The First Car Ride

When you bring your puppy home, it may be the first time he will be in a moving car. Your priorities are that he is safe, calm and comfortable. Whatever you do, there is no getting around the fact that you will be dealing with a worried little dog. To get your trip off to a good start, allow your puppy to eliminate immediately before the trip.

Ideally, young puppies should ride in a crate in the back seat. An older puppy or dog may use a seatbelt harness designed for his size and weight. Your puppy should not ride in a seat with an airbag, should never ride with his head out the window and should not ride on a passenger's lap or roam around in the vehicle.

Transporting a Young Puppy

- Bringing your puppy home may be your new puppy's first ride in a car.

- Keep in mind that the puppy may whine, cry, eliminate or vomit during the ride. Do not correct the puppy during the ride. Simply try to keep him calm and distracted.

- Being in a crate or travel carrier secured by tie-down ropes or a seatbelt in the vehicle is the safest option for a young puppy.

- Place an old blanket or towel and a puppy-safe chew toy inside the crate.

- Bring along an extra blanket or towel as well as some paper towels and a plastic bag, in case the puppy eliminates or vomits during the ride. If this occurs, you will need to pull the vehicle over and clean up the mess inside the crate.

- Before you head for home, if the puppy seems overly anxious, take a few short practice rides around the block to help the puppy get used to riding in the car.

Can puppies experience car sickness?

Tip If your puppy drools excessively, vomits or has diarrhea during a car ride, he may be experiencing car sickness caused by the vehicle's movement. To minimize potential car sickness, try not to feed your puppy for several hours before a trip and partially cover his crate with a blanket to block out some of the moving landscape from his view. You should also watch your puppy closely for signs of distress while in the car.

After the first car ride, how can I make my puppy comfortable riding in the car?

Tip Have your puppy in the car early and often. Short, regular car rides, always on an empty stomach and with an empty bladder, will help prevent motion sickness and get your puppy used to traveling. Make sure he rides to some fun destinations, such as friends' or relatives' houses. If you only take him for car rides to the veterinarian, he may want to avoid the car.

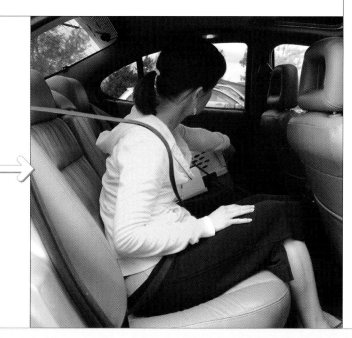

Transporting an Older Puppy or Dog

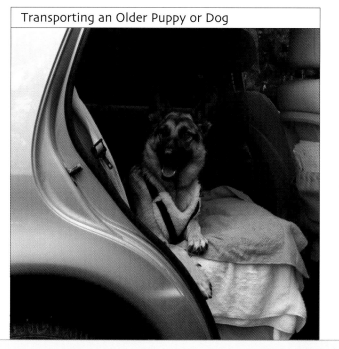

- Try to keep the car ride as relaxed and calm as possible.
- Have another person sit with the puppy during the drive so you can concentrate on driving.
- The person riding with the puppy should talk quietly to the puppy and place a hand against the crate door to provide distraction and comfort for the puppy during the ride.

- Properly restraining an older puppy or dog will help keep him settled, prevent you from becoming distracted by him and keep everyone safe in the vehicle.
- Many pet supply stores sell seatbelt harnesses that are specially made to keep older puppies and dogs properly restrained while riding in a car.

Note: You should not use a seatbelt harness to restrain a young puppy in a car.

- Make sure that the seatbelt harness you choose fits your dog and has a wide chest strap.

Making Your Puppy Feel at Home

Your puppy's first few days in his new home are important for his development. You can help your puppy to feel safe and comfortable by keeping your home calm. Maintain a normal household routine, such as running the dishwasher or microwave, to help your puppy get used to the sounds and activity around his home.

During these first few days, you should establish your puppy's mealtimes and introduce him to new people. Rather than leaving food and water out all the time, you should give your puppy three to four meals each day. Make sure you offer water frequently throughout the day, until a couple of hours before bedtime. For information on feeding your puppy, see page 94.

Let Puppy Explore

Keep Things Calm

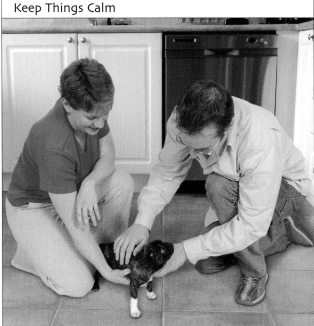

- When you first bring your new puppy into your home, take him to the safe place you have created for him (see page 58) and allow him to explore.

- If your puppy seems timid and sits in a corner, stay close by but do not pet him or try to coax him out. Do pet and praise him as a reward for coming out on his own though.

- Remember that puppies need their sleep. If the puppy just wants to find a quiet place and sleep, let him.

- Keep your home and family members calm to avoid frightening or over-stimulating the puppy.

- If your puppy has a fearful reaction to something, do not console him. Simply remove him from the situation and then reward more confident behavior with praise or a treat.

- Puppies between 8 and 10 weeks of age require extra patience. During this period, puppies can be easily frightened and it can take months for a puppy to recover from an unpleasant experience during this time.

Tip

What is the first thing we should do when arriving at home for the first time?

Even before you go inside the house, take your puppy to the spot where you want him to eliminate and then stay there until he goes. When he eliminates, praise him enthusiastically, give him a treat and then take him inside. You can now continue with housetraining your puppy. For more information on housetraining, see pages 76 to 83.

Tip

Should I try to teach my puppy anything on the first day?

With a new puppy, learning goes on all the time. It's never too soon to encourage appropriate behavior, such as coming to you, or discouraging behavior you don't want, such as jumping up on people. You can also begin teaching him his name by holding eye contact while cheerfully saying his name.

Mealtime

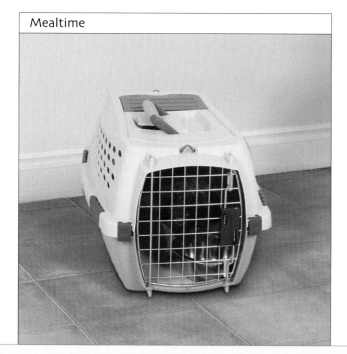

- At mealtime, put the puppy and his food bowl into the crate and let him eat.

  Note: If the puppy does not finish or seems disinterested, remove the food after about 15 minutes and offer a bowl of water outside of his crate. You can offer food again at your puppy's next mealtime.

- When the puppy is finished, remove the food bowl and offer a bowl of water outside of his crate.

- When the puppy is finished drinking, remove the water bowl and then take the puppy outside to his potty area.

Meeting New People

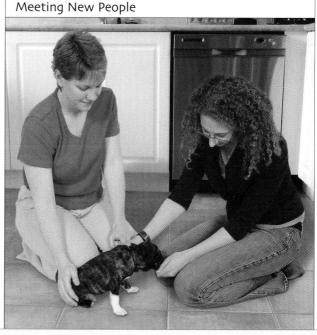

- After the puppy has had some time to explore and get settled, you can invite one or two friends at a time to meet your puppy.

- When meeting the new puppy, visitors should be calm and sit on the floor or in a low chair.

- If the puppy is too excited, ignore him, but visitors can pet the puppy when he is calm.

- Introducing your puppy to lots of calm, friendly people early on will help him to grow up to be confident about meeting new people.

The First Night Home

Your puppy's first night in his new home may be difficult for him considering it is probably his first time sleeping without his littermates. Remember though, that whining, fidgeting, sleeplessness and frequent trips to the potty area are normal for your puppy for the first few nights at home. Your puppy will soon get into a routine and sleep for longer periods during the night.

During the first few nights at home, keep his crate beside your bed to help him feel more comfortable. He will also be close by so you can hear him whine when he needs to eliminate during the night. When transporting your puppy to the potty area, make sure you do not play with him or speak more than necessary. Instead, quietly praise your puppy after he eliminates and then place him back in his crate.

Before Bed

- There are several things you can do to help make your puppy's first night in his new home a little easier on both of you.

- Feed your puppy his dinner no later than about 6:00 p.m. and give him his last drink of water a couple of hours before bed.

- Right before you go to bed, take your puppy out to his potty area so he can empty his bowels and bladder. You may also want to quietly walk with him in the yard to tire him out before bed.

Where Puppy Should Sleep

- Place your puppy's crate close by your bed so your puppy will be able to hear you breathing. This will help prevent him from feeling too lonely.

- The puppy may whine, but he will feel more secure with you close by than if he was alone in another room.

- If your puppy whines, you may want to put a finger or two inside the crate to soothe him.

- Do not, under any circumstances, allow your new puppy to sleep in your bed with you.

Tip

Are there any other tips for making the first night a bit easier?

Fill a hot water bottle with warm water and place the bottle outside his plastic crate, against the crate's side. When your puppy feels its warmth through the crate, it will remind him of his mother and littermates and help him feel a bit more secure. Also, place any necessary outerwear, such as slip-on shoes, by the door or in another easy-to-find place for when you have to take your puppy out to the potty area in the middle of the night.

Tip

Where should my puppy sleep after the first few nights?

If you don't want your puppy sleeping in your bedroom permanently, you should gradually move the crate toward his regular sleeping place each night. Start this process after about a week in your room. After you move him, you may have some restless nights because he does not want to be further away from you. If he has recently been out to eliminate, do not go to him if he whines, or he will learn that whining brings you to him.

Potty Area Visits

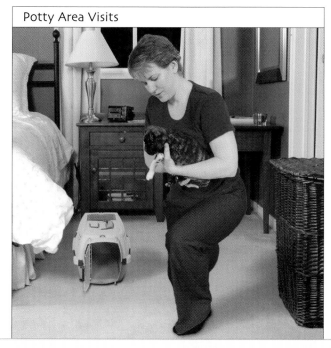

- If your puppy begins to cry or whine after having been quiet for several hours, he probably needs to eliminate.

- Take your puppy out of his crate, carry him outside to his potty area and quietly praise him after he eliminates.

- Take him back to his crate and give him a small treat before going back to bed.

  Note: Keep in mind that your puppy will soon be able to hold his bladder and bowels. You will not have to get up through the night forever.

In the Morning

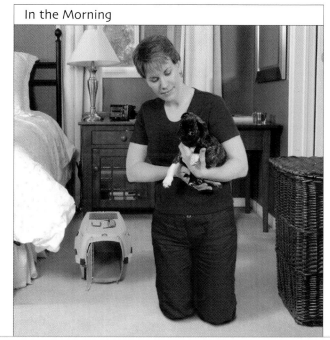

- As soon as you wake in the morning, immediately take your puppy out of his crate and carry him to his potty area.

- Remember that puppies will sometimes eliminate several times first thing in the morning. Wait to make sure he is done, then praise him and return indoors.

  Note: Once your puppy is 10 to 12 weeks old, his bladder should be mature enough that he can walk all the way to his potty area without being carried.

Introduction to Crate Training

A crate is a useful tool, both for housetraining and for preventing unwanted or inappropriate behavior. For more information on housetraining, see page 76. A crate can also become a safe place for your puppy—somewhere for him to take a nap or relax on his own. Also, going to the vet in a familiar crate helps your puppy to be less distressed in the waiting room and traveling in a familiar crate makes car and airplane travel more enjoyable.

When you are unable to supervise your puppy, a crate is a safe place for him to stay. When he is secure in his crate, he will not be able to do the things that can get him into trouble, such as chewing furniture or eliminating in the house.

Introduction to Crate Training

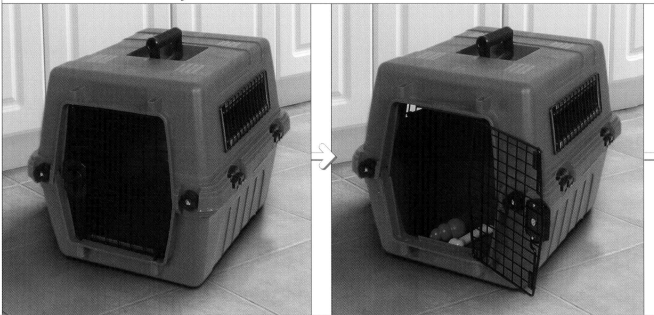

- A crate is a box made of plastic, fibreglass or metal and has a door you can close to keep your puppy inside.

- A crate should be large enough for your puppy to stand up, turn around and lie down.

- Crates are portable, which makes them ideal for taking your puppy to the veterinarian or for traveling with your puppy.

- You can place items in the crate to provide a more comfortable environment for your puppy. For example, you may want to put a soft, washable blanket in the bottom of the crate to provide some padding for your puppy.

Note: For younger puppies, it's best not to include bedding in the crate as they may chew the bedding.

- You may also want to include a favorite toy inside the crate. Avoid over-filling the crate with items for your puppy.

Tip

Should I discipline my puppy when he is in his crate?

You should never punish your puppy while he is in his crate because you want him to have a positive association with his crate. You should also avoid scolding your puppy when you place him in his crate. However, calmly placing your puppy in his crate as a response to unacceptable behavior, such as chewing on furniture, is appropriate. The punishment is in taking your puppy away from his family and social environment, not putting him in his crate, which remains a place where he feels safe.

Tip

Do I need to buy a puppy-sized crate for my new puppy?

No. You can buy an adult-sized crate and allow your puppy to grow into the crate. This prevents you from having to buy more than one crate for your puppy. However, if the crate is too big, your puppy may eliminate in the crate. If you purchase a crate that will fit your puppy when he is full-grown, you should also purchase a crate divider, which creates a smaller space in the crate while your puppy is little.

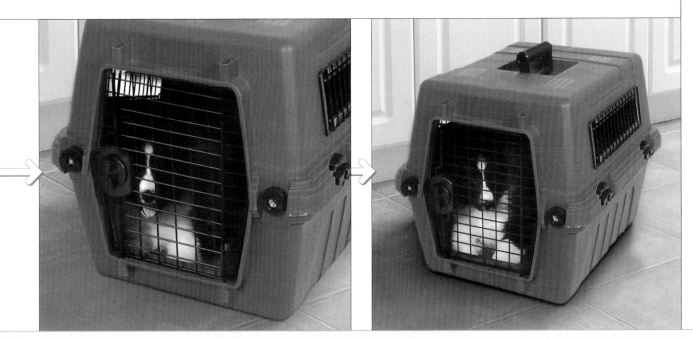

- A crate is a safe place where your puppy can go to relax or sleep.

- When training, most puppies will consider moderate lengths of time in the crate to be pleasurable.

- When you are not training your puppy to be in the crate, you can leave the crate door open. This allows your puppy to enter and leave the crate when he wants to.

- A crate is also a location where you can place your puppy to keep him safe when you are unable to supervise him.

  Note: You should always remove your puppy's collar before leaving him unsupervised in his crate.

- Crates are ideal for teaching your puppy appropriate behavior. For example, if your puppy chews inappropriate items, you can place him in his crate with a stuffed Kong™. This allows your puppy to satisfy his need to chew in a controlled environment.

Crate Training Your Puppy

When crate training your puppy, you are working to make his crate a place that he associates as happy and comfortable, where he can go to relax and where you can leave him when you cannot supervise him.

In addition to the training method shown below, you can also reward your puppy for being curious about the crate. When he is outside the crate, keep the door open and place goodies inside the crate when he is not looking. Finding a surprise treat or toy provides a good association with going inside the crate.

Your puppy's age determines the maximum length of time he should remain in his crate. To calculate the maximum amount of time in hours, add your puppy's age in months plus one. For example, a three-month-old puppy should not stay in a crate for more than four hours.

Crate Training Your Puppy

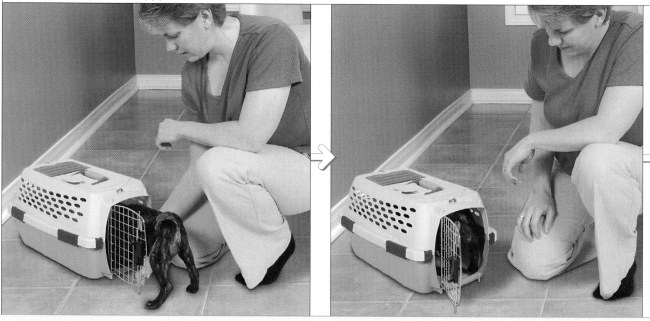

- When your puppy has been crate trained, you can leave your puppy in the crate when you are unable to supervise him. You must be patient as crate training takes time.

1 Set up the crate and leave the crate door open.

2 Place treats just inside the crate to encourage your puppy to approach the crate.

3 When your puppy approaches the crate to take the treats, praise him.

4 When your puppy is comfortable approaching the crate, gradually toss treats further inside the crate so he has to enter the crate to take the treats.

5 When your puppy goes inside the crate, praise him.

6 Continue giving your puppy treats and praising him as long as he stays inside the crate.

My puppy barks when he is in his crate. What should I do?

Tip If your puppy barks when he is in his crate, you should just ignore him provided you are sure he doesn't need to relieve himself. You can try draping a towel over the front of the crate, which will help reduce the activity he sees around him. If you decide to take your puppy out of the crate, wait until he has been quiet for 5 to 10 seconds before you let him out. If you let your puppy out of the crate when he is barking, he will most likely continue to bark in his crate in the future because he knows you will pay attention to him when he does.

What else can I do to encourage my puppy to like his crate?

Tip Feeding your puppy his meals in the crate is a great way to establish a positive association with the crate. When you feed your puppy all of his meals in the crate, it helps to strengthen your puppy's feeling that it is his special place and good things happen there. However, to prevent spills, do not place a water bowl in the crate. Instead, offer your puppy water regularly outside of the crate throughout the day.

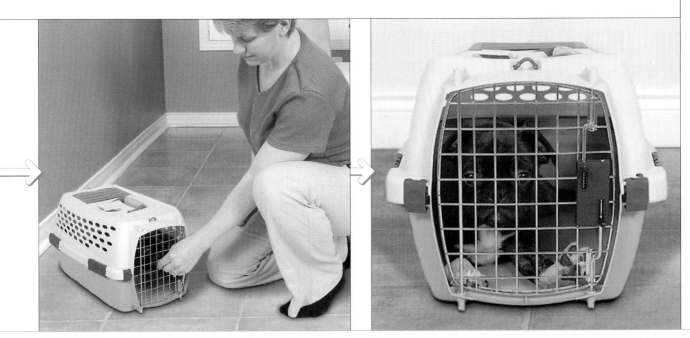

7 When your puppy is comfortable being inside the crate for a few moments, gently close the door of the crate.

8 Give your puppy a treat, praise him and open the door.

Note: Do not open the door if your puppy whines or makes noise. Only open the door when he is quiet.

9 Gradually increase the time that the crate door is closed.

10 When your puppy is comfortable with the crate door closed for several minutes, begin leaving the room for short periods.

• Begin by leaving the room for 1 minute, then gradually increase the time you are out of the room.

11 When you re-enter the room, keep your attitude low-key so you do not excite your puppy.

Note: If your puppy stays quietly in his crate while you are out of the room, give him a treat and praise him before allowing him to leave the crate at the end of the training session.

Introducing the Puppy to Your Children

When you bring a puppy into your home, you want him to be a part of your family. Your puppy should be comfortable around and even happy to be with your children. For the first introduction, you want your kids to be as calm as possible when greeting the puppy. Too much attention, even the playful and loving kind, can overwhelm the puppy.

If your kids are too young to understand the importance of staying calm, give them a new game or toy to distract them from the newness of the puppy, allowing the puppy some quiet time to get used to his new home. Eventually, the puppy will become less of a novelty to your children and more of a friend. For more information on establishing a good relationship between your children and puppy, see pages 86 to 91.

Set Rules

Puppy Rules

✓ Pet the puppy quietly and gently. Roughhousing and shouting are forbidden.

✓ Walk, don't run.

✓ Do not pet the puppy when he jumps up. Instead, turn around and walk away.

✓ The puppy is not to be disturbed when he is sleeping or in his crate.

✓ Keep your toys and possessions off the floor. The puppy will chew and damage them and he may injure himself or become sick.

✓ Do not pick up the puppy.

Meet the Puppy Game

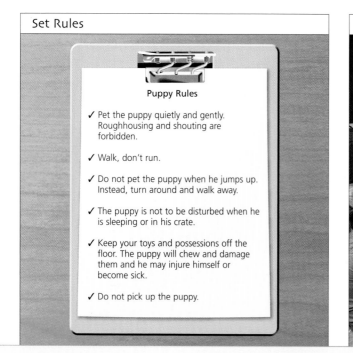

- A new puppy is a big event for any child. No matter the children's ages, you must be responsible for keeping both your children and your puppy safe and happy from the first moment your puppy comes home.

- **You must supervise all interaction between children and your puppy.** You must be ready to step in if either your children or puppy start to misbehave.

- Establish rules for your children's interaction with your new puppy. Children need to know what is expected of them.

- The Meet the Puppy Game keeps children sitting quietly and allows the puppy to explore each person on his own.

1 All the family members sit on the floor and spread their legs apart so that their feet touch the next person's feet, creating an enclosed circle.

2 Place your puppy in the center of the circle and allow him to explore. Each person can gently pet and quietly praise the puppy when he visits them.

3 Be sure to end the game within about 10 minutes, before your puppy gets too excited.

The First Vet Visit

A pleasant first visit to the veterinarian will help prepare your puppy for future visits for care that includes shots, check-ups and treatment. The first visit will also give you the opportunity to ask your veterinarian some important questions, such as how to minimize your puppy's exposure to disease, when to start training classes, how to prevent heartworm and other parasites and even whether to buy pet insurance.

After a successful first visit, take the time for a few "happiness drop-ins" at the vet clinic. A few minutes to eat treats and be greeted by staff will help your puppy become familiar with the clinic, making return trips easier. Before dropping in, be sure to contact the veterinarian's office to make sure they are not busy or treating animals that may have contagious diseases.

The First Vet Visit

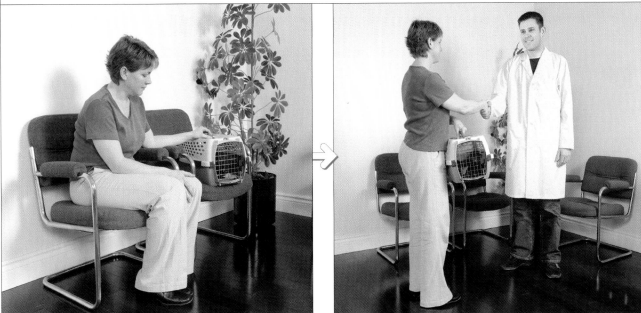

- Your puppy will have to visit the veterinarian throughout his life, so you should try to make the first visit as pleasant as possible.

- Schedule an appointment for your new puppy to occur within the first few days after you bring your puppy home.

- Since your puppy will not yet be fully vaccinated, he will be susceptible to catching diseases from other dogs. Carry your puppy in his crate or in your arms to prevent his feet from touching the waiting room floor where sick dogs may have been.

- During the first visit, the veterinarian will make sure your puppy is free from health defects and set up a vaccination schedule for you.

- Bring a sample of your puppy's stool with you so your veterinarian can check for parasites.

- To help your puppy have a positive experience, remain calm and upbeat. Praise your puppy for calm behavior during the examination and keep him occupied using treats or toys.

- If your puppy seems stressed or upset, avoid consoling him, but reward any confidence with a treat.

Housetraining

Housetraining Fundamentals

You should start housetraining as soon as your new puppy comes home. The goal of housetraining is to make sure your puppy always eliminates outdoors, in his potty area, not inside your house.

The Outside command and the "Do Your Business" command are useful tools for housetraining. These commands help to teach your puppy that when he eliminates in the proper area, he will be rewarded.

The Outside command also helps to stop your puppy from eliminating inside your house.

You should not punish your puppy when he eliminates in an inappropriate area. Punishing your puppy only teaches him that it makes you angry to see him eliminate. Your puppy will not understand that you are angry because he eliminated inside the house.

Establish a Potty Area

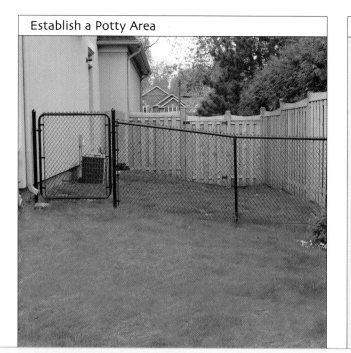

Age Specific Potty Breaks

Age of Puppy	Average potty breaks per day
6 to 14 weeks	8 to 10
14 to 20 weeks	6 to 8
20 to 30 weeks	4 to 6
30 weeks and beyond	3 to 4

- You should establish a specific potty area for your puppy in your yard. Having a specific potty area for your puppy will make cleanup easier.

- The area you choose should be separated from the rest of your yard by a fence or by plants. Separating the potty area from the rest of your yard helps to keep children out of the potty area and hides the area from the rest of your yard.

- The ground of the potty area may be completely covered by grass or may have a section of patio stones or sand.

- To make housetraining easier, try to set up a schedule for your puppy so you feed him and take him to his potty area at the same times each day.

- Take your puppy to his potty area when he wakes up in the morning, before and after every meal, before and after playtime and before you go to bed.

Note: When housetraining, you may find it useful to make written notes of your puppy's potty habits. Written notes allow you to see any patterns that are developing and help with the housetraining process.

What should I use to clean up mistakes that may happen indoors when housetraining?

Tip You can purchase special cleaning solutions at pet supply stores that are non-toxic and specifically designed to remove the scent of dog urine and feces. It is very important to thoroughly clean the indoor area where your puppy eliminated to remove the scent as much as possible, as puppies tend to sniff out and eliminate where they have eliminated before.

 Why does my puppy sometimes urinate when he meets new people or dogs?

Tip If your puppy releases a small amount of urine when he meets new people or dogs, it means he is anxious to make a good first impression. This is your puppy's way of being polite and submissive. If you punish your puppy for this behavior, you can actually make it worse. To lessen the likelihood of excitable urination, ask people to greet your puppy in a calm and matter-of-fact way. As your puppy matures and gains confidence, this behavior should taper off naturally.

The Outside Command

1 Say the command "Outside" in a firm, urgent tone if you see your puppy eliminating in an inappropriate area.

• The tone of your voice will startle your puppy and cause him to stop eliminating.

2 Quickly walk your puppy to his potty area so he can finish eliminating there.

3 When your puppy has finished, praise him enthusiastically.

Note: Do not punish your puppy for eliminating in an inappropriate area.

The Do Your Business Command

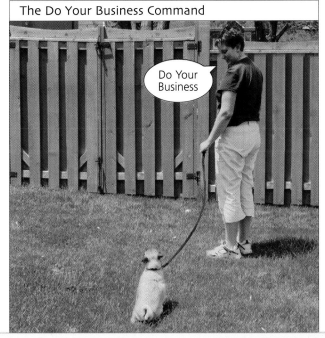

• You can teach your puppy to eliminate on command. This is useful when you do not want to be outdoors for a long time.

1 Each time you take your puppy to his potty area, say the command "Do Your Business" as soon as he squats.

2 Praise your puppy quietly while he eliminates.

3 When your puppy has finished, praise him enthusiastically and give him a treat.

• Eventually, your puppy will be able to eliminate whenever you say "Do Your Business."

Housetraining Using a Crate

All puppies have a natural instinct to keep their homes clean and not eliminate where they sleep. Once you have crate trained your puppy and he is comfortable using it as a place to sleep, you can begin housetraining using a crate. See pages 68 to 71 for information on crate training.

Puppies should be taken to their potty area before and after eating, sleeping and playing, or every hour.

Until your puppy is housetrained, he should always be under direct supervision or in his crate.

If your puppy is not reliably housetrained and you have to be away for more than two and a half hours, you should set up a long-term confinement area for your puppy. For more information on long term confinement areas, see page 80.

Housetraining Using a Crate

1 When housetraining your puppy, place your puppy in his crate with a chew toy. You can have the crate in the same room with you so your puppy does not feel isolated.

2 After your puppy has been in the crate for an hour, allow him to leave the crate.

Note: If your puppy shows signs of needing to eliminate, such as circling or sniffing, allow him to leave the crate before the hour is up and continue with steps 3 to 8.

3 Attach a leash to your puppy's collar.

4 Walk quickly with your puppy to the potty area you have designated for him.

Note: Walking quickly prevents your puppy from eliminating on his way to the potty area.

5 Wait for five minutes for your puppy to eliminate.

6 After your puppy has finished eliminating, give him a treat and praise him enthusiastically.

- If your puppy does not eliminate after five minutes, walk him back to his crate and leave him inside the crate for another 10 to 20 minutes. Then repeat steps 3 to 6.

What can I do to make housetraining successful during the night?

Tip

To make housetraining go as smoothly as possible during the night, feed your puppy dinner before 6:00 p.m. and give him his last drink of water a couple of hours before bedtime. This will give your puppy's bowels and bladder more time to process any food and water before bedtime. You should also take your puppy out to his potty area right before you go to bed. For the first few nights at least, keep the crate beside your bed so you can hear your puppy whining and take him to his potty area when he needs to relieve himself.

When I walk my puppy to his potty area, he eliminates on his way there. What can I do?

Tip

If your puppy is very young, such as younger than 10 weeks, you can pick your puppy up from the crate and carry him to his potty area. This will prevent him from eliminating on his way to the potty area. After approximately 10 weeks of age, a puppy should be able to hold his bladder and bowels on his way to the potty area.

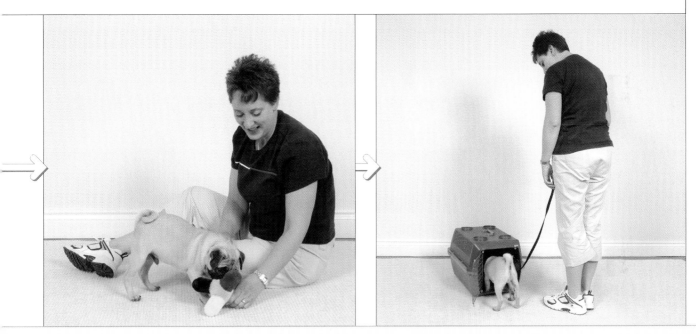

7 After your puppy has eliminated in the potty area, allow him to play in a very limited area inside the house for approximately 30 minutes.

Note: You must closely supervise your puppy during playtime to watch for signs that he needs to go to the potty area, such as circling and sniffing.

8 After playtime, return your puppy to his crate to relax.

9 Repeat steps 2 to 8 throughout the day.

• Each week, increase the time your puppy remains in his crate by 15 minutes until he reaches two hours. You can also increase his playtime by 15 minutes.

Housetraining While You Are Away

If you work full time or plan to go out for an evening, you can continue to housetrain your puppy without disrupting your essential day-to-day activities. Although you should not frequently leave your puppy alone for long periods of time, you can set up a long-term confinement area if leaving him alone is necessary. A long-term confinement area can accommodate your unhousetrained puppy's need to eliminate when you are not home.

When setting up a long-term confinement area, make sure the area is safe and puppy-proofed. For information on puppy-proofing, see page 56. You should also be aware that placing your puppy in a long-term confinement area on a regular basis can increase the time it takes to housetrain your puppy.

Housetraining While You Are Away

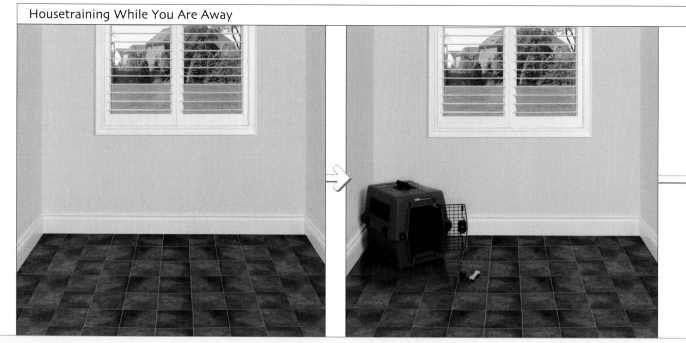

- If you have to leave your unhousetrained puppy alone for a long period of time, such as when you are away all day at work, you should set up a long-term confinement area for him.

- Confining your puppy while you are away for an extended period prevents your puppy from eliminating in inappropriate areas in your house and restricts his access to areas where he can get into trouble.

- A long-term confinement area can be any room with easy-to-clean floors.

- Place your puppy's crate in one part of the long-term confinement area. Leave the door of the crate open so your puppy can enter and exit the crate as he pleases.

- Setting up your puppy's crate in the long-term confinement area gives him access to his sleeping area.

- Make sure your puppy has appropriate chew toys to play with while you are gone.

What should I do when I arrive home?

When you first greet your puppy, try to make the encounter as low key as possible, as an excited greeting may cause him to accidentally eliminate. Then take your puppy out to his potty area. While being away from home may be unavoidable at times, especially for work, try to keep lengthy absences to a minimum during the housetraining period.

What should I do if I don't have a room in my house that I can use as a long-term confinement area?

If you do not have a room available in your house for a long-term confinement area, you may want to consider purchasing an exercise pen. Pet supply stores sell ready-made exercise pens of various heights and sizes. You can use a pen to section off a safe area for your puppy for long-term confinement during the housetraining period. Make sure the exercise pen is large enough to fit a crate and an area where your puppy can eliminate.

- Puppies naturally do not want to eliminate in their sleeping area, so if your puppy is not yet housetrained, you must set up a potty area for him to use within the long-term confinement area.

Note: You can use newspapers or a dog litter box for your puppy's potty area. For more information on dog litter boxes, see page 82.

- The potty area should be away from the puppy's crate and water bowl.

- You can gradually increase the size of the long-term confinement area. For example, you can use a baby gate to block off a doorway of a larger room for your puppy.

- For each month that your puppy does not have any housetraining accidents and does not exhibit any inappropriate behaviors, you can increase the size of the long-term confinement area.

- Eventually, your puppy will be able to be left alone in the house without being confined.

Litter Training

If you live in a high-rise building or have limited access to outdoor areas, you may choose to litter train your puppy. Litter training should always take place in the same location in your home.

When litter training, you train your puppy to eliminate in a dog-sized litter box filled with dog litter. You can purchase dog litter training supplies at a pet supply store.

Until your puppy is litter trained, he should always be under direct supervision or in his crate. If your puppy is not reliably litter trained and you have to be away for more than two and a half hours, you should set up a long-term confinement area for your puppy. For information on long-term confinement areas, see page 80.

Litter Training

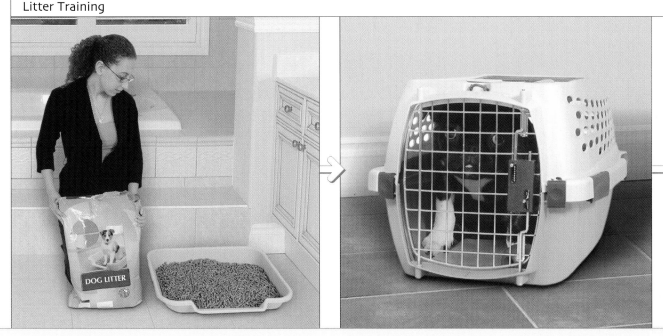

- You should set up your puppy's potty area in the corner of a low-traffic room, such as a bathroom or utility room, that has a floor that is easy to clean.

1 Place the litter box on the floor where you want to set up the puppy's potty area.

2 Fill the litter box half-way with dog litter.

3 When litter training your puppy, place him in his crate with a chew toy. You can have the crate in the same room with you so your puppy does not feel isolated.

4 After your puppy has been in the crate for an hour, allow your puppy to leave the crate.

Note: If your puppy shows signs of needing to eliminate, such as circling or sniffing, allow him to leave the crate before the hour is up and continue with steps 5 to 9.

5 Attach a leash to your puppy's collar.

How often should I clean the litter box?

When you accompany your puppy to the litter box to have him eliminate, you should remove any urine-soaked litter or feces from the litter immediately after he eliminates. If your puppy is in a long-term confinement area (see page 80) during the day, you should clean the litter as soon as you return home. To clean the litter, you can use a large litter scoop, which you can purchase at a pet supply store. You should also replace the litter and thoroughly scrub the litter box with a vinegar-water solution or non-toxic deodorizing cleaner at least once a week to keep it clean.

My puppy wants to chew the dog litter. What should I do?

If your puppy tries to chew the dog litter pellets, you may want to switch to using thick, flat layers of newspaper in his litter box. You can reintroduce the litter later by adding a layer of litter on top of the newspaper. You should supervise your puppy's behavior while he is in the litter box. If he shows little interest in chewing the litter, you can gradually add more litter and remove more of the newspaper until the box only contains litter.

6 Walk quickly with your puppy to the litter box.

7 Wait for five minutes for your puppy to eliminate.

8 When your puppy has finished eliminating, give him a special treat and praise him enthusiastically.

● If your puppy does not eliminate after five minutes in the litter box, walk him back to his crate and leave him inside the crate for 10 to 20 minutes. Then repeat steps 5 to 8.

9 After your puppy has eliminated, he can play under your supervision for 30 minutes. Then return him to his crate.

Note: During playtime, watch for signs that your puppy needs to return to the litter box.

10 Repeat steps 4 to 9 throughout the day.

● Each week, increase the time your puppy remains in his crate by 15 minutes until he reaches two hours. You can also increase his playtime by 15 minutes.

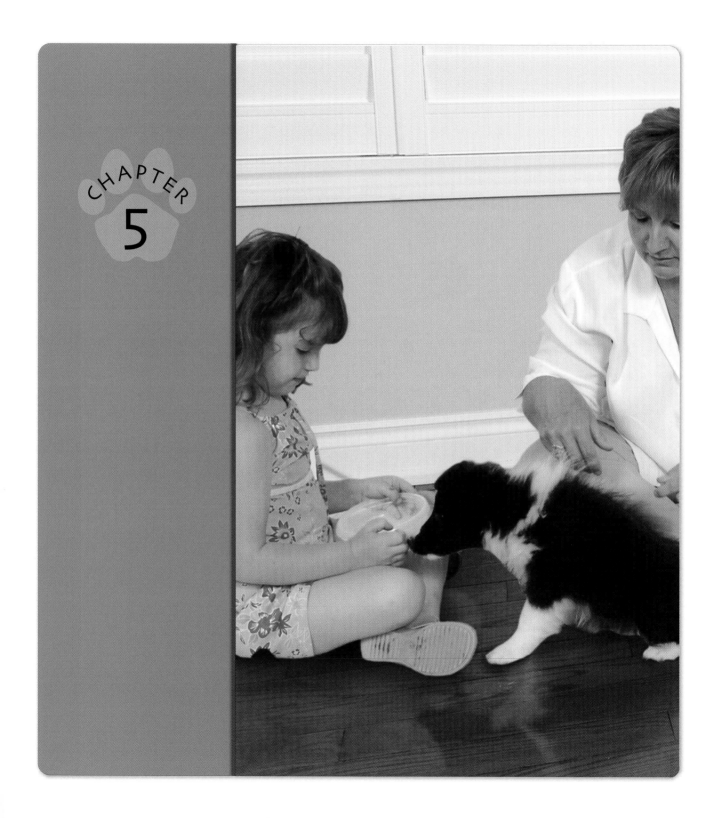

Puppies and Kids

Helping Kids and Puppies Get Along

Parental Responsibilities

Involving Kids in the Puppy's Training

Helping Kids and Puppies Get Along

With the proper guidance, the friendship between puppies and children can be special and rewarding. Caring for a puppy can help children to have a positive attitude towards animals, be considerate of animals' needs and learn to be responsible.

Puppies and children should be taught to respect each other. For children, this means learning how to behave appropriately around puppies. You should teach your children how to properly touch a puppy and read his body language, which games are appropriate to play and when the puppy shouldn't be disturbed.

You can help your puppy to feel comfortable around children by giving him many good experiences with meeting kids. For example, you can ask every child your puppy meets to feed him a couple of treats that you provide.

Helping Kids and Puppies Get Along

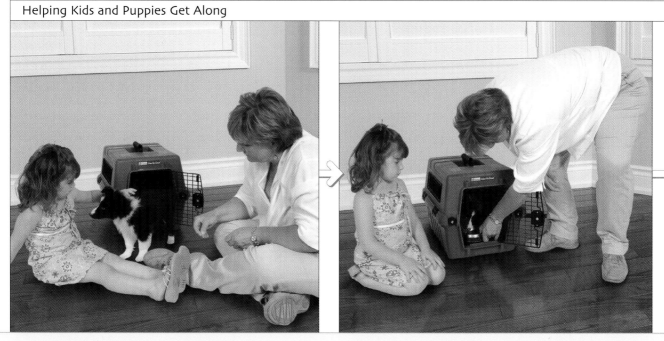

- Keeping your children and your puppy in a supervised, calm environment will help them feel secure and happy and create a good relationship between them.

- Your puppy should have a crate where he can go to rest and relax.

- The crate allows you to ensure that both the puppy and the children remain safe when you cannot be there to supervise their interaction.

- Teach your children never to bother the puppy when he is in his crate.

- Feed your puppy his meals in his crate. This will help ensure that your children cannot bother the puppy while he is eating.

  Note: Your puppy should be comfortable with people around his food bowl while eating. For more information, see page 196.

- The puppy should also go into his crate during your children's meal and snack times. This will help ensure that the puppy does not learn to beg for food from your children.

  Note: For information on preventing begging, see page 181.

Tip

What should I consider when choosing a puppy for my children?

If you have children and have never had a puppy before, you should consider a breed that is intelligent, friendly, outgoing and easily trainable, like a Golden Retriever. Having a puppy that is easy to train is very important for any busy family. Always remember that raising a puppy is a lot of work, whatever breed you choose. However, it's well worth the effort if you are consistent with your training and how you treat your puppy.

Tip

Can my children play in the yard with the puppy?

Your children can play in the yard with your puppy if you are watching them. Whenever your children are interacting with your puppy, you should be supervising to ensure everyone stays safe. When you are unable to supervise your puppy in the yard, he should never be left alone tied up. Children may unintentionally tease a puppy that is tied up, which could cause the puppy to act aggressively.

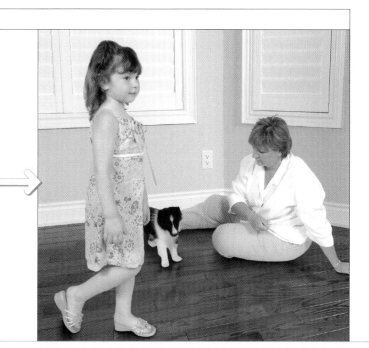

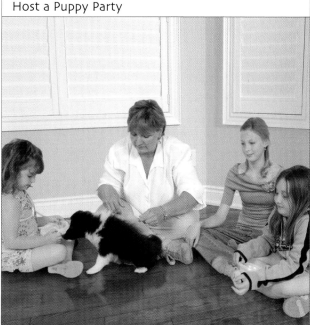

Host a Puppy Party

- Children should walk and stay calm when they are near the puppy. An overexcited child can create an overexcited puppy, who may grab or nip at the child's clothes or hands.

- Children can play many games and tricks with a puppy with adult supervision (see pages 154 to 177).

- No one should play any tug-of-war games with an untrained puppy. A puppy who learns to tug on a toy may think that tugging on a child's clothing is acceptable too.

- Have a puppy party to introduce your child's friends to the puppy.

1 Invite two or three of your child's friends to your home.

2 Divide the puppy's food for one meal into separate containers, with one container for each child.

3 Have the children sit on the floor and take turns hand feeding the puppy.

- Take this opportunity to educate your child's friends about the importance of being calm around the puppy and not rewarding him for unwanted behaviors, such as jumping up.

Parental Responsibilities

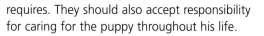

Although helping to raise a puppy can be a wonderful learning experience, children should never be solely responsible for a puppy's care. Puppies are completely dependent on their owners for their basic needs, so they should be cared for by an adult who can make sure these needs are met.

Parents should be fully prepared for the energy, financial commitment and time that raising a puppy requires. They should also accept responsibility for caring for the puppy throughout his life.

When puppies and children are playing, parents should always supervise to make sure the children treat the puppy gently and the puppy does not nip or jump up. Parental supervision is essential to ensure that all interaction between children and puppies is safe, fun and rewarding.

Taking Care of the Puppy

- You should encourage your children to help with taking care of the puppy, but as the parent, you must accept all responsibility for ensuring the puppy's needs are met.

- If your children are mature enough to help feed, groom, train and exercise the puppy, you can create a puppy chores chart to help the children remember what needs to be done.

- You can give your children small rewards for completing the chores assigned to them.

Handling the Puppy

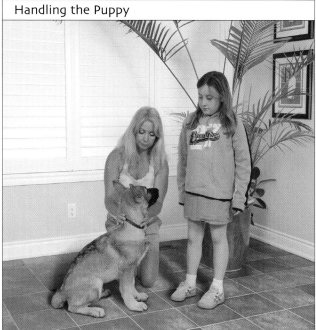

- You must give your children guidelines on handling the puppy.

- Show your children how to handle the puppy with a gentle, assured touch.

  Note: For information on handling exercises you can perform with your children, see page 117.

- Teach your children never to put their faces near the puppy's face and never to squeeze the puppy around his neck.

- Make sure your children know that they must never pick up the puppy. A child may drop a wiggling puppy and accidentally injure him.

How can I teach my children to be responsible caregivers for our puppy?

Children learn by example. If you always treat your puppy with kindness, your children should do the same. It's a good idea to teach your children how to do some simple puppy care tasks, like giving your puppy a drink of water, under your supervision. Try to teach your children that they should respect the puppy and treat him the same way they would like to be treated.

Can my children take our puppy for a walk?

Once your puppy has learned proper leash manners, you can supervise your older children while they take your puppy for a walk. Older children should outweigh your puppy before they are allowed to hold the leash and younger children should not walk the puppy at all. You may want to attach both a leash and a yardline (see page 44) to your puppy's collar so that while your child holds the leash, you can walk behind and hold the yardline.

Supervision

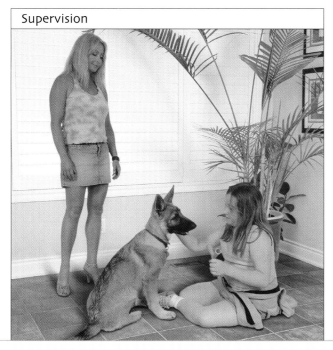

- The most essential job of a parent in a household with a new puppy is supervision. The puppy must never be left alone with a child under any circumstances.

- You must supervise all interaction between the puppy and your children to ensure that the puppy and children stay safe.

Separation

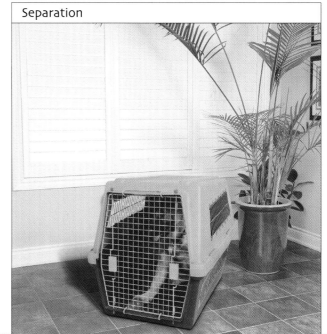

- When you cannot supervise your puppy and children together, it is your responsibility to separate them.

- Your puppy's crate is an ideal tool for separating your puppy and children when you are not able to properly supervise them.

  Note: You must ensure that your children do not bother the puppy when he is in his crate.

- You can also use child-safety gates to create a safe space for your puppy and puppy-free areas for your children and their toys.

Involving Kids in the Puppy's Training

When deciding how to involve your children in training your puppy, you should use common sense and consider the maturity of your children and puppy. Puppies usually see children as playmates, rather than leaders, since children often use passive body language and have high-pitched voices. The sooner your children help with training, the easier it will be for them to gain the puppy's respect.

Children should learn how to give training commands with parental supervision. Parents should also supervise training sessions to ensure their children are considerate of the puppy's needs. For example, you should make sure your children do not ask your puppy to perform commands when he is tired.

Involving Kids in the Puppy's Training

- You can have your children involved in training your puppy to help strengthen the bond between them.

- Practicing training commands will help your children learn how to control the puppy and help the puppy learn his place in the family.

- You must supervise all interaction between your children and the puppy. You must be ready to step in if either the children or the puppy start to misbehave.

- Before your children train the puppy, attach a houseline to the puppy's collar.

  Note: For information on houselines, see page 44.

- When your children are training the puppy, the training sessions should last no more than a few minutes.

- Your children should take turns so only one person trains the puppy at a time, with adult supervision.

- Ensure that your children use only a specified amount of food rewards when training to avoid overfeeding the puppy.

What other things can I do to involve my children in the puppy's training?

You can help your children practice tricks and games with your puppy. Tricks and games are a fun way to have your children involved in training. For more information on tricks and games that your children can play with your puppy, see pages 154 to 177.

How can I help my younger children become involved in the puppy's training?

You should use a hands-on approach when helping younger children train your puppy. You should stand beside or behind your children and physically guide their movements when training. It's a good idea to have young children practice commands that you have already taught your puppy. You can also have your children come with you to the puppy's training classes, but make sure to discuss this with your trainer ahead of time.

- In addition to practicing obedience commands with the puppy, children, with adult supervision, can also help in diminishing unwanted puppy behavior, such as jumping up.

- When unwanted behavior begins, the children should stand, cross their arms and look away from the puppy. When the puppy is calm, the children can return their attention to him.

- The puppy will soon learn that the children will interact with him only if he is calm.

- Children can also learn to help prevent unwanted behavior, such as possessiveness.

- Children can play the Give and Take (see page 156) or Targeting Tricks (see page 168) games with the puppy, with adult supervision.

- Older children can also help an adult with the exercises discussed on page 196 to help prevent food possessiveness.

CHAPTER

6

Puppy Care

Feeding and Nutrition

Exercising

Brushing

Eye and Ear Care

Dental Care

Nail Care

Bathing

Feeding and Nutrition

Feeding your puppy is no longer a matter of simply putting down a bowl of dry kibble at mealtime. There are now numerous dietary options for your puppy.

Fortunately, your breeder will recommend the type of food you should feed your puppy when you bring him home. Your veterinarian will also be happy to discuss any dietary issues during your first visit.

TYPES OF FOOD

There are a number of different types of food you can feed your puppy. Your choice will largely depend on your budget and philosophy. As long as your puppy's nutritional needs are met and your veterinarian is pleased with your puppy's health and growth, the diet you choose should be fine.

Dry and Canned Food

Nutritionally speaking, good-quality dry and canned foods are the same. They both include the essential nutrients your puppy needs to grow.

Puppy Formula

Puppies grow at a significant rate so they need more nutrients than an adult dog. Because of this, many foods come in puppy formulas to help build muscles and strong bones. To avoid growing too quickly, however, some breeds may need to switch to adult formulas before they are a year old.

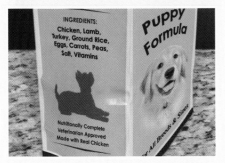

Ingredients

You should pay attention to the ingredient list on the foods you consider for your puppy. The higher an ingredient appears on the list, the more of that ingredient there is in the food. Meat proteins, such as chicken, lamb or beef, should appear at the top of the list. Grains, such as rice and wheat, should also be near the top of the list. Vegetable proteins are harder for your puppy to digest and should make up a smaller amount of the food.

TYPES OF FOOD continued

Home-Cooked and Raw-Food Diets

As an alternative to dry and canned foods, you can also choose nutritionally complete home-cooked or raw-food diets. Both typically include balanced amounts of meat, vegetable and grain ingredients. Preparing these diets requires careful research and can mean a fair amount of extra work. To spare you the preparation time, some pet supply stores offer high-quality frozen raw foods for dogs.

Snacks and Treats

Treats are an important form of reward for your puppy. However, you need to remember that treats are generally not as nutritious as his regular food. Feeding your puppy too many treats can disrupt the balance of his diet. If you find that you need a lot of treats for training, consider using a portion of your puppy's regular food as treats.

Treats should be about the size of a large pea or the fingernail on your pinky finger. You should also use soft treats that will allow your puppy to eat with his head up and maintain eye contact with you. Both high-quality hot dog slices and freeze-dried liver are good soft treat choices.

Water

Puppies need to drink a lot of water. This is especially true in warm weather since puppies drink to cool off. It is a good idea, however, to control your puppy's access to water by offering it to him often rather than leaving a full water bowl on the floor at all times. This prevents him from gulping huge amounts of water, which can cause housetraining problems. By giving your puppy access to water only once every hour or so, you help to regulate how often he needs to relieve himself and reinforce your role as leader. Typically, you should offer water at mealtimes, before and after outings, every time your puppy comes out of his crate and often throughout the day.

FEEDING SCHEDULE

Puppies need to eat more often than adult dogs. Generally, it's a good idea to feed your puppy three times a day—in the morning, at midday and in the evening—until he is about 4 months old. After that, you can gradually decrease the amount of food you feed in the middle of the day until that meal is eliminated. Your puppy should continue to eat two meals a day for the rest of his life.

Meals should be of equal size as this helps to regulate digestion and housetraining. At mealtime, put down the dish of food and allow your puppy to eat. If your puppy has not finished the meal after 10 minutes, pick up the bowl. You can offer your puppy the food again at his next meal. If you are feeding canned, home-cooked or raw food, keep it refrigerated until the next meal.

There are many benefits to feeding your puppy on a schedule rather than allowing him access to his food all day. When you feed him at specific times, you make housetraining easier and reinforce your role as the provider and leader. Scheduled feedings also allow you to quickly spot any changes in your puppy's eating habits.

CHANGING FOODS

Sudden changes to your puppy's diet can cause digestive upset. You should initially serve your puppy the same food he received from the breeder. If you do change the type of food you feed your puppy, do so gradually. For example, you could start with three parts old food and one part new food and continue to gradually blend the foods until you are just feeding the new food. Remember that you should consult your breeder or veterinarian before making major changes to your puppy's diet.

ADDING WATER TO DRY FOOD

You may find it helpful to add some water to your puppy's meals if he is on a diet of dry food. Moistening dry food by pre-soaking it with water will make it easier for a young puppy to eat. As your puppy matures, you can eliminate the pre-soaking and add just enough water so the food floats. Floating food can help to slow down the eating of overly enthusiastic puppies.

OVERFEEDING

Your puppy should be well-fed, but never overweight. In general, you should be able to feel your puppy's ribs but not see them. Remember that puppies go through stages as they grow. If your puppy seems a little plump, keep an eye on him for a couple of weeks without changing anything. If he remains plump, visit your veterinarian for a weigh-in and consultation on your puppy's diet.

FEEDING "PEOPLE FOOD"

Giving your puppy a taste of what you are eating is asking for trouble. This may create fussy eating habits in your puppy and can also cause him to beg for scraps whenever you are eating. To keep your puppy's behavior from becoming disruptive during mealtimes, you should put him in his crate when you eat. Once he has learned the Down command (page 140), you can have him stay in the Down position while you are eating. For information on preventing begging, see page 181.

DRY FOOD FRESHNESS AND STORAGE

The vitamins in dry foods tend to diminish over time, so it is best to buy food in small amounts that can be finished within a couple of weeks. If you buy huge bags of dry dog food, your puppy may not be able to finish it before it goes stale. You should keep dry food in an airtight container and store it in a cool, dry location. If you suspect that your puppy's food has gone stale, you should discard the food.

Exercising

Exercising your puppy is both an indoor and outdoor activity. Outdoors, try to keep exercise sessions on the grass. Avoid pavement, which puts stress on your puppy's delicate bones and tissues. Whether you are in a park or in your backyard when exercising outdoors, keep your puppy on a leash or yardline so that you can better manage his behavior. For information on yardlines, see page 44.

Indoor exercise may include games you play with your puppy and short training sessions, which keep your puppy mentally and physically active. Another good outlet for your puppy's energy is chewing on a food-stuffed toy, such as a Kong™. Be careful to ensure that he does not exert himself too much just before or after eating and drinking.

You should talk to your breeder or veterinarian about how much exercise is appropriate for your puppy as he grows.

Exercising

- Exercise is a basic need for puppies, just like food and water. Exercising your puppy, both physically and mentally, is not an optional activity.

- While you should not exercise your puppy to the point of exhaustion, helping him burn off his energy each day will keep him content.

- Be careful when exercising your puppy. Puppies are normally awkward and more susceptible to injury until they are fully grown because their muscles and bones are still developing.

- Providing your puppy with both physical and mental exercise is important.

- Practicing obedience training and playing games are good ways to provide physical and mental exercise.

- See pages 154 to 177 for games and tricks that you can play with your puppy.

- Chewing on a chew toy, such as a food-stuffed Kong™, is also a good form of physical and mental exercise.

What games and activities should I avoid?
Take care not to engage in activities that will frustrate or confuse your puppy. Anything that encourages unwanted behavior, such as nipping, should definitely be avoided. These types of activities will also communicate to your puppy that you are more of their playmate than the head of the pack. A few examples of activities to avoid include roughhousing, chasing games and tug-of-war.

Can I go jogging with my puppy?
If you are looking forward to your puppy joining you on your evening jog, you should wait until his skeletal structure has fully matured. This generally occurs when dogs are about 14 months old, depending on their breed. The repetitive pounding on hard pavement can cause damage to your puppy's growing bones and tissues.

Energy Level	Example Breeds	Daily Exercise Guideline
Very High	Labrador Retriever, German Short-Haired Pointer	40-80 minutes
High	Beagle, Soft-Coated Wheaten Terrier	30-60 minutes
Medium	Bernese Mountain Dog, Scottish Terrier	20-30 minutes
Low	Pekingese, Newfoundland	5-20 minutes

- If you do not give your puppy an adequate amount of exercise, he will find other, less-acceptable ways to occupy himself.
- Lack of exercise can lead to many behavior problems, including excessive barking, hyperactivity and destructive chewing.
- Remember that your puppy needs you to help him exercise. A puppy that is left alone to amuse himself in a fenced yard will develop unacceptable behaviors such as digging and excessive barking.
- Puppies need different amounts of exercise depending upon their breed, age and personality.
- Younger puppies need less exercise than older puppies. Always monitor your puppy for signs of fatigue.
- You should break up the amount of exercise your puppy needs each day into several exercise sessions throughout the day.
- You can vary the length and number of exercise sessions each day, as long as your puppy gets an appropriate total amount of exercise each day.

Brushing

For puppies, being brushed is the equivalent of receiving a doggie massage. You should introduce your puppy to brushing gradually by making sure that your first brushing sessions are gentle, brief and fun. Speak softly and calmly while you brush your puppy to help him relax. You should also make sure you use a soft brush to avoid scraping your puppy's delicate skin.

Whether your puppy has a short, wiry coat or fluffy poodle curls, brushing him every day can help prevent matted fur. Careful brushing can also help you keep track of your puppy's health by making you aware of health problems, such as fleas and ticks. Puppies with dense coats or long hair might require specialized grooming techniques. Your breeder or groomer is the best source of information for grooming advice.

About Brushing

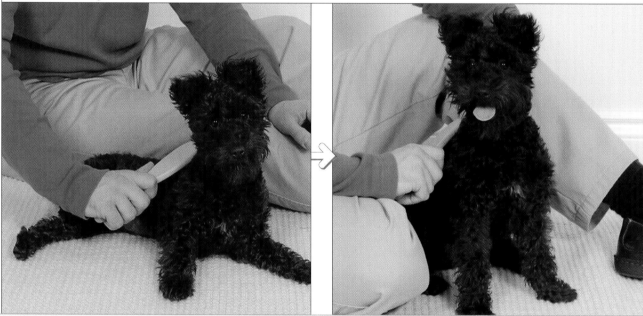

- Regular brushing is an important part of your puppy's grooming and health care.

- Brushing your puppy will help keep his coat in good condition and prevent knots and matting by removing fur that has been shed and any objects that may be caught in his coat.

- Brushing will improve the health of your puppy's skin by removing dead skin cells and increasing circulation.

- Brushing sessions also provide a great opportunity for you to bond with your puppy.

- No matter what type of coat your puppy has, regular brushing sessions are a good idea.

- Breeds with long or thick fluffy coats should be brushed daily to prevent matting and tangling. The more often you brush, the less likely it is that you will encounter these problems.

- Even short-haired breeds and breeds that do not shed should be brushed at least weekly.

- Your breeder or groomer will be the best source of advice on how to brush your puppy's coat.

Can I brush out burrs and matted sections from my puppy's fur?

Prickly plants, such as burrs, and sections of densely tangled fur, called mats, should generally be cut out rather than brushed. Trying to remove a burr or detangle a mat is frustrating and can hurt a puppy. Always remember that the longer a matted section is left alone, the heavier it will become and the more it will pull on a puppy's skin. If your puppy's coat becomes seriously matted, you should consult a groomer.

How should I care for the fur on my puppy's face?

Puppies with short fur do not need to have their faces brushed. If your puppy has a long coat, however, you should gently brush or comb the fur on his face to prevent matted fur. Take extra care when brushing around your puppy's eyes and whiskers, as these are very sensitive areas. Dogs with long fur around their mouths, such as Schnauzers, often get food stuck in the long fur. Wiping your puppy's mouth after each meal can help keep his facial fur clean.

Brushing Your Puppy

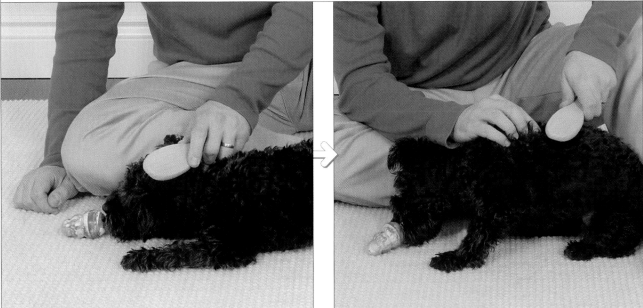

- You should use a soft brush to groom a young puppy's coat. See page 50 for information on brushes.

1 Distract your puppy with a food-stuffed chew toy.

2 While your puppy is distracted, gently draw the brush along the length of his body from the top of his head to his tail.

3 Repeat step 2 until your puppy's entire coat has been brushed. Then brush your puppy's belly and legs.

4 As you brush, examine your puppy's coat and skin. Look for scratches and cuts, as well as any swollen, discolored or hairless patches on your puppy's skin.

5 You should also look carefully for fleas and ticks. See page 204 for information on fleas and ticks.

Note: If you see anything out of the ordinary, you should contact your veterinarian.

6 When you finish brushing and examining your puppy's coat and skin, give your puppy a treat or favorite toy.

Eye and Ear Care

Keeping your puppy's eyes and ears clean and dry can help prevent infection and make your puppy feel more comfortable. You can help your puppy relax when you clean his eyes and ears by being calm and having a positive demeanor. If your puppy is still anxious, you can ask a friend to hold your puppy and distract him with a food-stuffed toy while you clean your puppy's eyes and ears.

This will help to make the process a positive experience for your puppy.

Before you bathe your puppy, place some cotton in his ears to prevent them from getting wet and always wipe his ears dry after baths and swims. Make sure you never use cotton-tipped swabs because they could damage your puppy's delicate ears.

Checking Your Puppy's Eyes

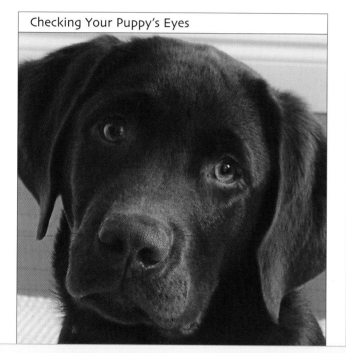

Cleaning Your Puppy's Eyes

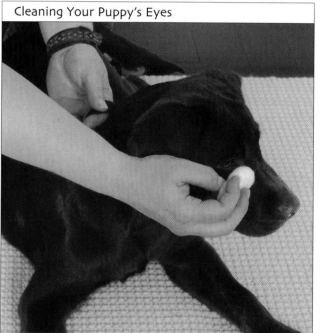

- A puppy's eyes should be clean and alert. You should check your puppy's eyes each day.

- If you notice any swelling, redness, mucus build-up or foreign objects in your puppy's eyes, you should see your veterinarian. These symptoms can be an indication of illness, allergies, irritation or parasites.

- Some breeds, such as Poodles, are prone to eye discharge that can stain their coats. Your breeder or veterinarian can suggest appropriate cleaning products.

- All breeds tend to accumulate some amount of crusty build-up around the eyes. To avoid infection, it is important to wipe away this build-up regularly.

1 Moisten a clean cotton ball or soft cloth with warm water.

2 Kneel beside your puppy and hold his collar with one hand.

3 With the other hand, gently wipe any crusty build-up from the corners of your puppy's eyes.

4 When you have finished wiping, give your puppy praise and a treat.

Tip

What are ear mites?

Ear mites can invade your puppy's ear, feeding on the skin's outer layer. If your puppy does a lot of ear scratching or head shaking or he tries to scratch his ears while walking, he may have ear mites. Mites should be diagnosed and treated by your veterinarian with prescription medication. Mites are contagious, so your puppy may pick them up from another dog that has them, even if you practice good ear hygiene.

How do I care for my puppy's nose?

Just like you, your puppy's nose can get sunburned, so avoid exposing him to too much sun. Some of the flat-faced breeds, such as Pugs and Boston Terriers, have wrinkles around their noses, which need regular wiping. If you notice that your puppy has a persistently runny nose, you should have your veterinarian check him out as it could be a symptom of a disease such as kennel cough.

Checking Your Puppy's Ears

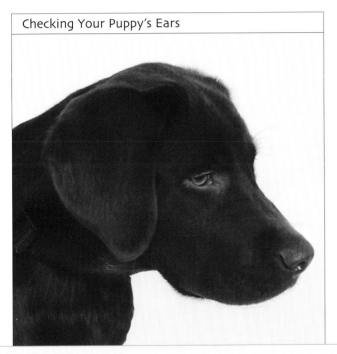

Cleaning Your Puppy's Ears

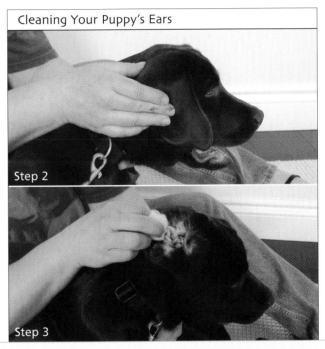

Step 2

Step 3

- A puppy's ears, whether floppy or upright, should normally be clean and odor free. You will need to check your puppy's ears every few days.

- Breeds with floppy or hairy ears are more prone to ear problems and should be checked daily.

- If you notice any swelling, redness, a bad odor or heavy build-up of brown wax, you should see your veterinarian. These symptoms may indicate illness, irritation, infection or ear mites.

- You should use a cleanser designed for dog's ears to clean out your puppy's ears on a weekly basis.

1 Apply cleansing solution to each ear.

Note: Refer to the cleansing solution's packaging for the exact amount to apply.

2 Gently massage the base of each ear for 30 seconds. Then let the puppy shake his head.

3 Using several cotton balls, wipe away the loosened dirt and wax from the outer ear only.

4 When you have finished wiping, give your puppy praise and a treat.

Dental Care

Examining your puppy's mouth on a regular basis and brushing his teeth are good habits to establish. In addition to helping curb bad doggy breath, regular dental care can add years to your puppy's life, as dental infections left unchecked can lead to more serious health problems. Introduce your puppy to brushing his teeth as soon as you bring him home, preferably when he's sleepy or in a calm mood. While caring for your puppy's mouth, make sure you examine his teeth, gums and tongue for signs of redness, swelling or decay.

For preventative care, in addition to regular brushing, include dry, crunchy dog food as part of your puppy's diet, which will help keep his teeth clean. Also, ask your veterinarian for recommendations of products that can help prevent tooth decay and tartar.

Proper Dental Care

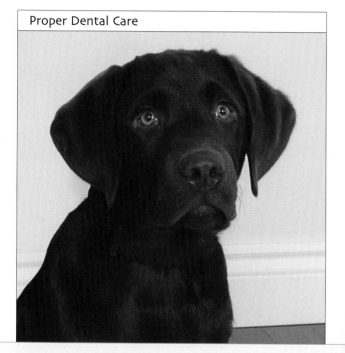

Examining Your Puppy's Mouth

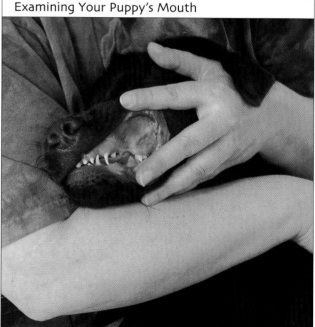

- Taking the time to examine your puppy's mouth and brush his teeth on a weekly basis will help ensure long-term health for your puppy.

- Just like humans, a puppy's teeth can form tartar and plaque which may lead to bad breath and dental infections.

- Infections of the teeth or gums can spread to other parts of a puppy's body and quickly lead to serious illness. Any signs of infection should be seen by your veterinarian immediately.

- You should examine the inside of your puppy's mouth for signs of infection and injury.

- A puppy's teeth should be bright white. Check whether any of your puppy's teeth are discolored, loose or chipped.

- A puppy's gums should be healthy looking and pink. Red, bleeding or swollen gums can be an indication of infection.

Tip *Do puppies go through a teething stage?*

A puppy's teething period begins at about 3 to 4 months of age when he starts to lose his baby teeth. When teething, your puppy will want to chew just about anything in sight, so be sure to provide him with plenty of chew toys. During this time period, it is completely normal to find a baby tooth on the floor or find blood on a chew toy. Usually by 6 or 7 months of age, all of his adult teeth have come in.

 Tip *What can I give my puppy to help with his teething?*

Considering it is natural for your puppy to want to chew when teething, you should make sure he has plenty of acceptable chewing options around. Food-stuffed chew toys can be soothing for teething puppies. You can also soak a rope toy in water or broth and then freeze it before giving it to your puppy. You should always supervise your puppy when chewing on rope toys and be sure to have him chew the frozen toy outside, as it can get messy.

Brushing Your Puppy's Teeth

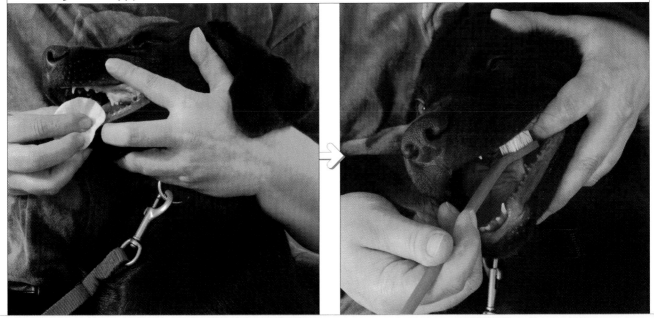

1 Sit with your puppy in your lap. Place your left arm loosely around his neck and support his head from underneath with your left hand.

2 Hold a dental wipe or wrap a piece of soft cloth around the index finger of your right hand.

Note: You can buy dental wipes at most pet supply stores.

3 With your left index finger, lift your puppy's upper lip so you can see his teeth and gently rub the surface of his teeth and gums with the dental wipe or cloth.

Note: If your puppy is bothered by the wipe or cloth, try using just your finger instead.

● Once your puppy becomes used to having his teeth rubbed with the dental wipe or cloth, you can begin brushing all of your puppy's teeth with a dog toothbrush and dog toothpaste.

● Keep your first teeth-cleaning sessions short. Initially, you should aim to work on just a few teeth at a time, such as the teeth on the upper right side of the mouth.

Note: For more information on dog toothbrushes and toothpaste, see page 51.

● Do not use human toothpaste to brush your puppy's teeth.

Nail Care

Preparing your puppy for a lifetime of monthly nail care is a gradual process. Slowly introducing your puppy to having his nails trimmed can make the difference between having a dog who lies quietly to have his nails done and a dog who runs at the sight of clippers. The steps below feature guillotine-style nail clippers, which can be used on most puppies. For a discussion of other clipper styles, see page 51. You can also ask your veterinarian, breeder or groomer about which type of clippers to use.

Some dogs have a dew claw, which is a nail located higher up on the paw that does not touch the ground. Dew claws don't get worn down by walking, so if they are not trimmed they can grow all the way around into the skin of your puppy's legs.

Overview

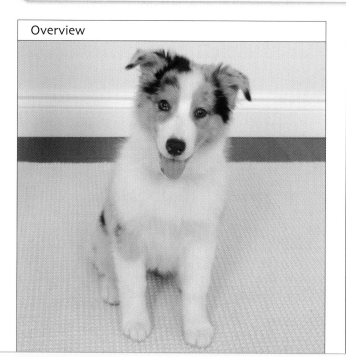

- Your puppy's nails will need regular trimming, about once a month. His nails should be even with the bottom of his paws.

- If you do not trim your puppy's nails regularly, the nails will grow too long. This can make walking extremely uncomfortable for your puppy.

- Trimming your puppy's nails will keep him from inadvertently scratching you and will help prevent damage to your floors and furniture.

Handling Paws

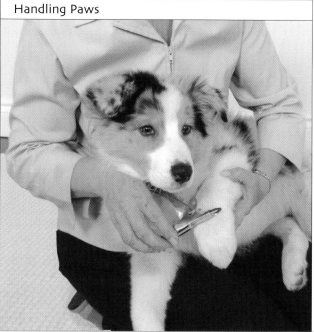

- To make trimming your puppy's nails easier, you should get him accustomed to having his paws touched and handled.

1 Spend a few minutes each day patting, holding and gently squeezing each of your puppy's paws.

2 Once your puppy is used to having his paws handled, introduce the nail clippers by gently touching them to your puppy's paws.

- You should also open and close the clippers to get your puppy used to the sound.

- After each handling session, give your puppy a treat.

Tip

What is the quick?

The quick is the soft, fleshy part of the nail near its base. You should avoid cutting the quick as it is very painful for your puppy and it will make him afraid of having his nails trimmed. On dogs with white nails, you can see the quick's darker, often pink, shading. Finding the quick on dogs with black nails is more difficult. To be safe, trim just a bit of the nail at a time to avoid cutting the quick.

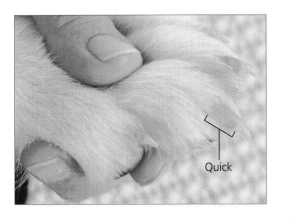

Quick

Trimming Nails

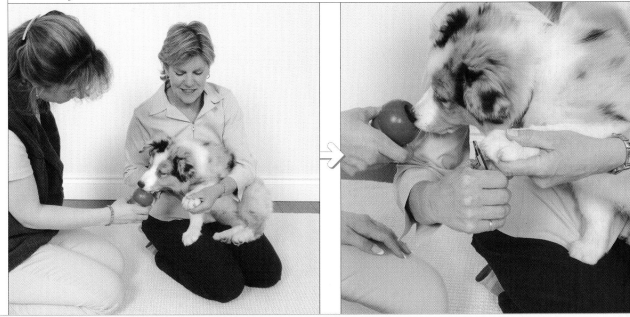

- Once your puppy is accustomed to having his paws handled and is used to the nail clippers, you can begin trimming his nails.

1 Sit on the floor and hold your puppy securely, but not too tightly, on your lap.

2 Have another person distract your puppy by offering a food-stuffed toy for him to chew.

3 While your puppy is distracted, take one of his paws in your hand and hold the base of one of his toes between your thumb and index finger.

4 Trim off just the tip of the nail. If you trim off too much of the nail, you may cut into the quick.

Note: For more information on the quick, see the top of this page.

5 Give your puppy a treat and end the trimming session.

- During the next trimming session, repeat steps 1 to 5 except trim two nails in step 4. Increase the number of nails you trim during each session.

Note: Eventually, you will no longer need a helper when trimming your puppy's nails.

Bathing

Before you bathe your puppy, you should place a pitcher of clean water close to the sink or tub that you can use to rinse him off. Next, you should brush your puppy's coat to remove any tangles. You can also place some cotton balls in your puppy's ears to keep them dry.

After your puppy's bath, you should use plenty of old, clean towels to dry him off. Remember to dry your puppy's ears and between his toes, using cotton balls if necessary. Once your puppy is clean and dry, you can brush him so that his coat is shiny and tangle-free.

Another option for drying your puppy is to use an electric hair dryer. If you decide to use a hair dryer, make sure you introduce it to your puppy gradually.

Get Your Puppy Used to Bathing

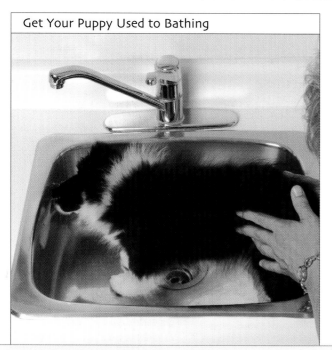

1 Spread peanut butter on the inside of the sink or bathtub and place your puppy in the sink or tub, allowing him to lick off the peanut butter.

2 Play with your puppy in the dry sink or tub for a few minutes.

3 Repeat steps 1 and 2 daily.

4 Without plugging the drain, slowly run the water while giving your puppy some treats.

5 When your puppy is comfortable with the running water, wet his back slightly and dry him with a towel. Then slowly progress to a full bath.

Give Your Puppy a Bath

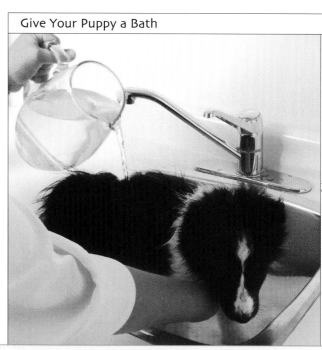

1 Place an old towel or bathmat in the sink or tub to prevent your puppy from slipping.

2 Gently place your puppy in the sink or tub, leaving the drain unplugged.

3 Using a pitcher, gradually wet your puppy's entire coat with lukewarm water.

Note: If you are bathing your puppy in the tub, you can use a removable showerhead to wet your puppy's coat.

4 Squeeze a small amount of dog shampoo, about the size of a quarter, onto your hands and rub them together.

What type of shampoo should I use for my puppy?

Tip

Human shampoo can strip away oils from your puppy's coat and dry out his skin, so you should purchase a shampoo designed specifically for dogs. You will find many dog shampoos to choose from, including some specialty shampoos designed for specific coats, for dry skin or even to achieve a whiter coat. You can also check with your veterinarian for recommendations.

How often should I bathe my puppy?

Tip

Dogs do not need to be bathed often because they do not sweat through their skin. Generally, you should bathe your puppy only when he looks or smells dirty—otherwise, not more than once a month. Washing your puppy too frequently can lead to itchy skin, dandruff and a dull, brittle coat.

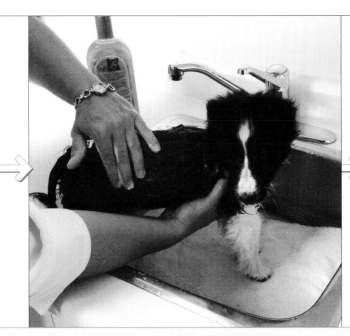

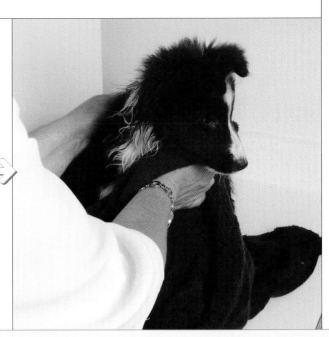

5 Work the shampoo into your puppy's coat in a gentle, circular motion, beginning at the neck and working your way to the end of the tail.

- Be sure to thoroughly wash your puppy's chest, belly and legs.

6 Very gently wash your puppy's head, ears and face, being very careful not to get any soapy water into your puppy's eyes or ears.

7 Rinse your puppy thoroughly with a pitcher of clean, lukewarm water. Be sure to completely rinse away any shampoo residue.

8 Hold up a towel while your puppy shakes himself off to get rid of most of the water.

Note: If you are bathing your puppy in the tub, you can partially close the shower curtain while your puppy shakes.

9 Using old, clean towels, thoroughly dry your puppy's coat.

Note: Any moisture left on your puppy's coat can lead to skin problems.

- If your puppy has a thick coat, you may also find it helpful to use a hair dryer to dry him.

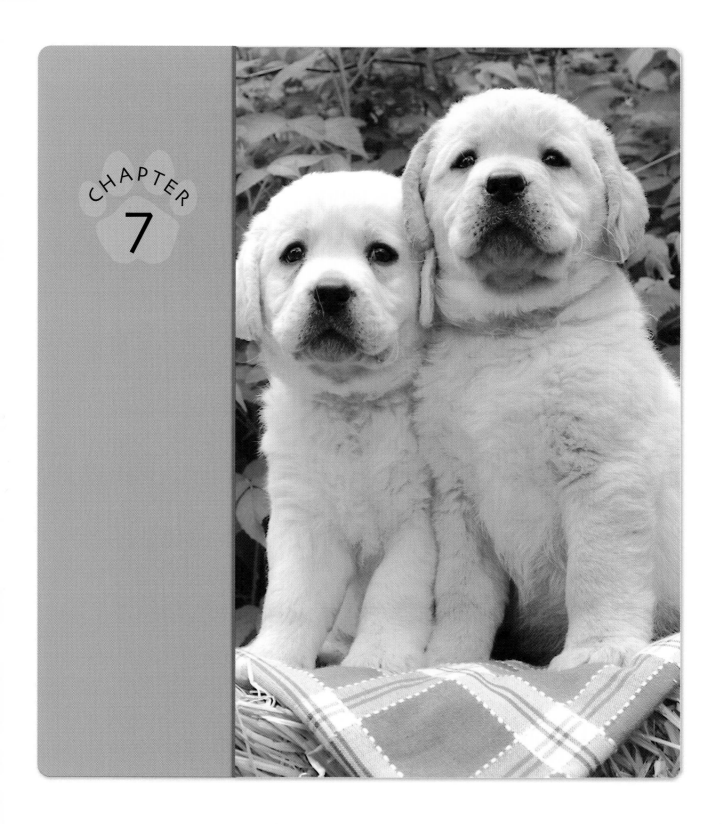

CHAPTER

7

Puppy Development

Stages of Puppyhood

As your puppy grows, he will go through various stages of development, just like a child. Understanding how your puppy matures can help you cope with the inevitable trials you will experience as you raise him.

It is very important to remember that your puppy's first year will have a lasting impact on the rest of his life. You will need to be patient in order for him to grow up to be a happy and well-adjusted dog.

The age ranges listed for each stage of development overlap because puppies mature at different rates, depending on their breed and individual personality.

BEFORE PUPPY COMES HOME (Birth to 7 weeks)

Puppies are born nearly helpless. For about the first two weeks of life, they are both deaf and blind. Sometime between the second and third week of life, their eyes open, their hearing begins to develop and they learn to walk.

Between the ages of 3 and 7 weeks, puppies discover the basics of acceptable canine behavior. They learn to interpret dog body language (see page 126) and learn how to keep from biting too hard through discipline from their mother and play-fighting with their littermates. It is best that a puppy not be separated from his mother and siblings before 7 weeks of age or he may not fully develop these proper social behaviors. Separating a puppy too early from his littermates can lead to problems in the future with aggression, biting, separation anxiety and difficulties with housetraining.

LEARNING ABOUT HUMANS AND THEIR WORLD (7 to 12 weeks)

After about 7 weeks of age, puppies should start the process of socializing and bonding with humans. A puppy learns at an astonishing rate between 7 and 12 weeks of age. How puppies learn to interact with humans at this point will have a huge impact on their future social behavior and receptiveness to training.

Puppies at this stage are eager to experience new things, places and people. You should encourage this curiosity by introducing your puppy to a wide variety of people, animals and environments. This will help him to become a confident and well-adjusted dog.

Try to be patient and keep your expectations for perfect behavior low during this stage. Concentrate your efforts on making sure that your puppy has good, safe experiences that he will remember for the rest of his life.

First Fear Imprint Period (8 to 12 weeks)

While your puppy is eager to experience new things from 8 to 12 weeks of age, he may become temporarily fearful of all sorts of objects and situations. While this is completely normal, it must be handled with sensitivity. Try to introduce new things to your puppy slowly and in a non-threatening manner. You need to protect your puppy at this time and encourage his confidence as he experiences new things.

Be sure that you do not force your puppy into scary experiences. A puppy that goes through a traumatic event during his first fear imprint period can be left with fears that will affect him for the rest of his life. Fortunately, the first fear imprint period lasts only a few weeks.

CONTINUED

BECOMING INDEPENDENT (10 to 16 weeks)

From about 10 weeks of age, your puppy begins to gain strength, coordination and self-assurance.

During this period, you will see your puppy's personality come out. He is likely to become bolder, more confident and more independent.

While your puppy may seem to be listening to you less, this is not the time to loosen up on the rules. You need to remain consistent so that your puppy will continue to see you as the leader.

Your puppy will also begin to lose his baby teeth during this period. As his adult teeth grow in, he will have an increased need to chew on objects. You must provide him with appropriate items to chew or he will chew on whatever happens to be close by.

ADOLESCENCE (4 to 8 months)

Your puppy will become a typical teenager at around 4 months of age. His hormones will surge, he will experience growth spurts and he may try to take advantage of any inconsistencies he perceives in your leadership. You will notice his actions become somewhat unpredictable—sometimes he'll obey your commands and other times he'll do his own thing. You may also notice your puppy occasionally slipping back into bad habits such as jumping up on people and furniture.

You need to remain patient with your puppy during this period. Remember that he is not intentionally defying you, but rather testing the limits of his world. Providing consistent, fair and kind leadership is more important than ever during your puppy's adolescence.

ADOLESCENCE (4 to 8 months) continued

Second Fear Imprint Period (6 to 14 months)

At some point between 6 and 14 months of age, your puppy will go through a second fear imprint period that often coincides with a growth spurt. He may again begin to show fear of objects and situations, both new and familiar.

As with the first fear imprint period, you will need to help your puppy gain confidence by rewarding him when he shows courage. To help him feel secure, be careful not to pet and comfort your puppy when he acts fearful. Your job is to ensure he is safe and to patiently let him work through his fears on his own.

GROWING INTO MATURITY (1 to 4 years)

Dogs tend to reach maturity beginning at 1 year of age, with some taking as long as 4 years to fully mature. In general, smaller puppies tend to reach maturity more quickly than larger dogs.

When your puppy reaches full maturity, he will have settled into your day-to-day routine and become established as a member of your family. You should, however, make a point of keeping up his training and continuing to expose him to new people, animals and experiences. This will ensure that he remains the happy, confident and friendly dog you have helped him to become.

Picking Up Your Puppy Safely

You will need to pick up your puppy in numerous situations. For example, you will need to pick up your puppy to get him into the car or to lift him onto the examination table at the veterinarian's office.

When picking up your puppy, hold him firmly against your chest while fully supporting his weight with your arms and hands. If your puppy feels secure when being held, he'll be less likely to squirm. If your puppy doesn't like being picked up, try simply sitting on the floor and lifting him into your lap at first. Be sure to give him treats so that he associates being held with rewards.

Never lift a puppy by placing both hands under his stomach or by pulling on his front legs, as this could injure him. Also, never drop a puppy from your arms when you are standing.

Picking Up Your Puppy Safely

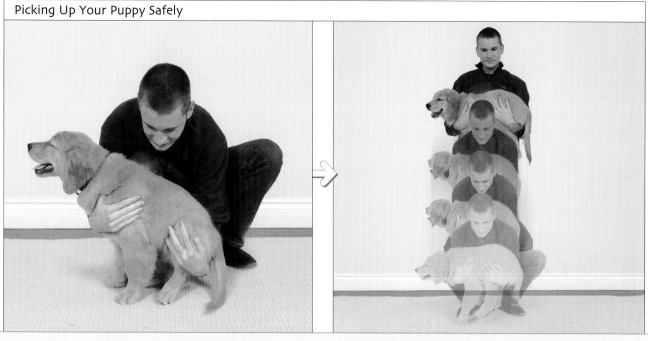

1 To pick up your puppy, crouch down facing your puppy's side.

2 Place one hand under your puppy's chest, just in front of his front legs. Your fingers should be curved around your puppy's body.

3 Place your other hand under your puppy's hind end, just behind his back legs. Your fingers should be curved around your puppy's body.

4 Lift your puppy slightly and pull him close to your chest.

Note: Depending on your puppy's size, you may need to reposition your hands on the side of your puppy's body that faces away from you.

5 Keeping your back straight, slowly stand up while cradling your puppy.

- When carrying your puppy, keep him close to your chest to help him feel secure.

- To put your puppy down, slowly crouch down and release him when his paws touch the ground.

Handling Your Puppy

Some puppies are sensitive about having their mouths, paws or other parts of their body handled. You can help your puppy to feel more comfortable with being touched by practicing handling exercises a few times daily. Try to do this at different times each day and keep the sessions short at one or two minutes.

You should always stroke your puppy slowly and calmly. Give your puppy gentle verbal praise and reward him with a treat when he allows you to handle a different part of his body.

Once your puppy has become accustomed to being handled, you can supervise children or friends while they handle your puppy. Having a variety of trusted people handle your puppy can help him to feel more comfortable when he encounters different people in the future.

About Handling Your Puppy

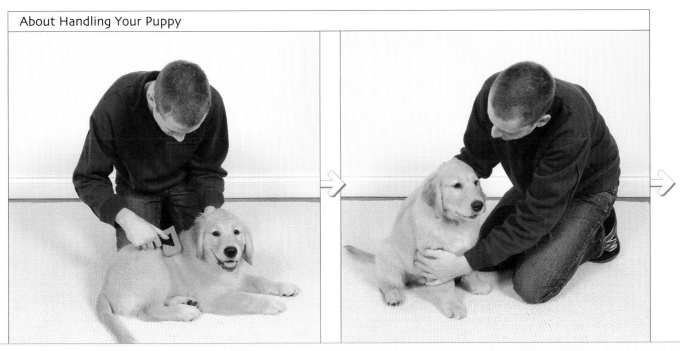

- Teaching your puppy to accept being touched prepares him for grooming activities, such as brushing and nail clipping, as well as veterinary examinations.

- You should gently handle different areas of your puppy's body daily.

- Since young puppies tend to accept handling more easily than older puppies, you should start handling your puppy from the day he comes home.

- You should keep handling sessions short and calm.

- If your puppy squirms excessively when you touch a certain part of his body, do not scold him. Try touching areas that are close by and gradually move back toward the sensitive area.

- If your puppy growls during handling, stop immediately. Call a trainer or veterinarian to determine whether your puppy is worried, uncomfortable or in pain.

CONTINUED

When handling your puppy, you should move slowly and work in stages. For example, since your puppy may dislike having his lips lifted, you should start touching the area around your puppy's mouth before you examine his teeth.

You may find it challenging to perform these handling exercises while holding onto treats. If this is the case, try placing a dab of peanut butter on the door of your refrigerator. While your puppy licks the peanut butter off the door, you can use both hands to perform the handling exercises on your puppy.

You should keep practicing these exercises occasionally even after your puppy is an adult, as this will help ensure he continues to be comfortable with being handled.

About Handling Your Puppy (continued)

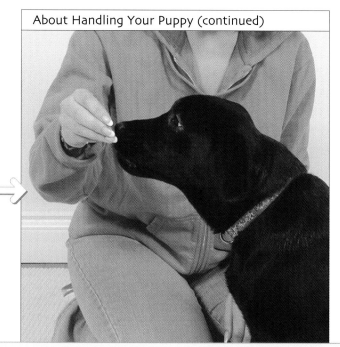

- Your puppy may be sitting, lying down or standing throughout these handling exercises.

- You can kneel or sit on the floor close to your puppy during handling sessions.

- With the exception of handling the mouth, hold a treat close to your puppy's nose as you perform these exercises. You will give him the treat after you handle each of his body parts.

  Note: At first, you should handle only one area of your puppy's body per session.

Handling the Ears and Eyes

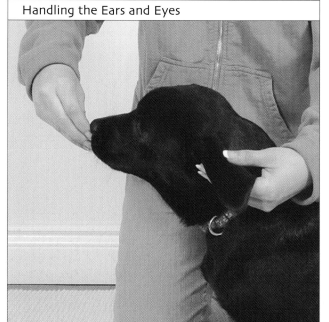

1 Gently touch the areas around one of your puppy's ears or eyes.

- If you are handling an ear, you can also massage the flap of the ear and then gently place one of your knuckles just inside the ear.

2 Give your puppy a treat immediately and praise him.

3 Repeat steps 1 and 2 for the other ear or eye.

Tip

How can I prepare my puppy for being handled by the veterinarian?

To help prepare your puppy for veterinary examinations, place him on top of a clothes dryer that isn't running and conduct a simulated exam. This is useful because the dryer's metal surface is similar to the surface of a veterinarian's examination table. Once your puppy is comfortable being handled on top of a clothes dryer, you can have a friend that your puppy hasn't met perform some of the handling exercises.

Tip

What else can I do to help my puppy become accustomed to being touched?

You can try playing fun games like "Puppy Dress Up" (page 176), "Pass the Puppy" (page 158), "Collar Hold Game" (page 154) and "Where's Your Tummy?" (page 164) to help your puppy feel comfortable with being handled. However, you should always make sure that you don't handle your puppy roughly when playing games. Rough play may teach your puppy bad habits and could even cause him to get hurt.

Handling the Mouth

1 Gently touch the area around the outside of your puppy's mouth.

2 Gently lift your puppy's upper lip and open his mouth.

3 Gently touch your puppy's teeth, gums and tongue.

4 Give your puppy a treat immediately and praise him.

Handling the Legs and Paws

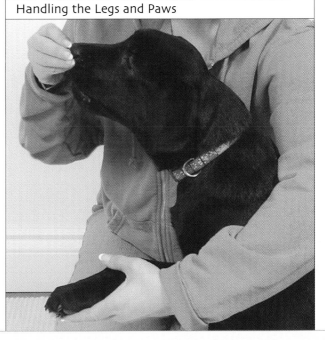

1 Run your hand gently down one of your puppy's legs to his paw and then take his paw in your hand.

2 Apply gentle pressure on each of your puppy's toes to extend his nails.

3 Gently touch the area between each toe.

4 Give your puppy a treat immediately and praise him.

5 Repeat steps 1 to 4 for each leg and paw.

The Importance of Socialization

The best way to raise a confident, happy puppy is to start socialization as soon as you bring him home. Socialization involves introducing your puppy to a variety of safe and enjoyable experiences. Before your puppy is three months old, you should expose him to anything you want him to encounter when he is older—different people, places, sights and sounds. The objective is to teach your puppy the world is a happy place.

A puppy's first impressions of the world, good or bad, will influence him throughout his life. You should do your best to avoid having your puppy encounter any frightening experiences during socialization. Proper socialization can help a puppy to be happy and calm, which benefits both the puppy and the owner.

The Importance of Socialization

- To help your puppy grow into a happy, confident dog, you must provide him with lots of good learning experiences in the first 12 weeks of his life—a process called socialization.

- You must provide your puppy with experiences that stimulate all of his senses.

- Introduce your puppy to as many new sights, sounds, smells and experiences as possible.

- As your puppy gets older, he will become more cautious of things he has never encountered before. To maintain his confidence, you must help him to safely encounter a wide variety of new things before he matures.

- A well-socialized dog will usually have fewer anxiety issues and a higher comfort level around people, places and other animals.

Tip

What is the breeder's role in my puppy's socialization?

Your breeder should start to socialize your puppy when he is still with his littermates. Your puppy will be with the breeder for approximately the first eight weeks of his life, so you should make sure that you are dealing with a reputable breeder who will take care to properly socialize your puppy. The socialization process is more effective when it begins with the breeder and is then continued by you when the puppy is brought home.

Tip

Why is it important to socialize my puppy?

If a puppy is not properly socialized in the first twelve months, he may become shy, frightened of new experiences and unpredictable. Under-socialized puppies are more likely to bite and can have problems interacting with other dogs or people. They can also be difficult to train as they may be prone to anxiety, aggression or excessive barking.

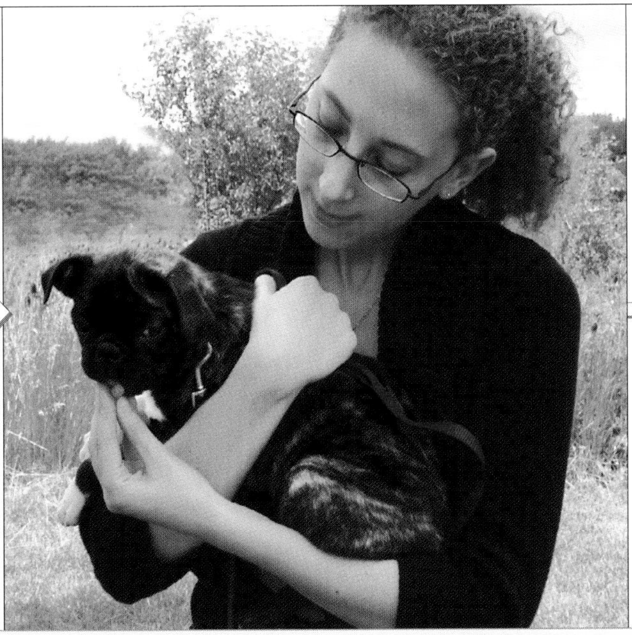

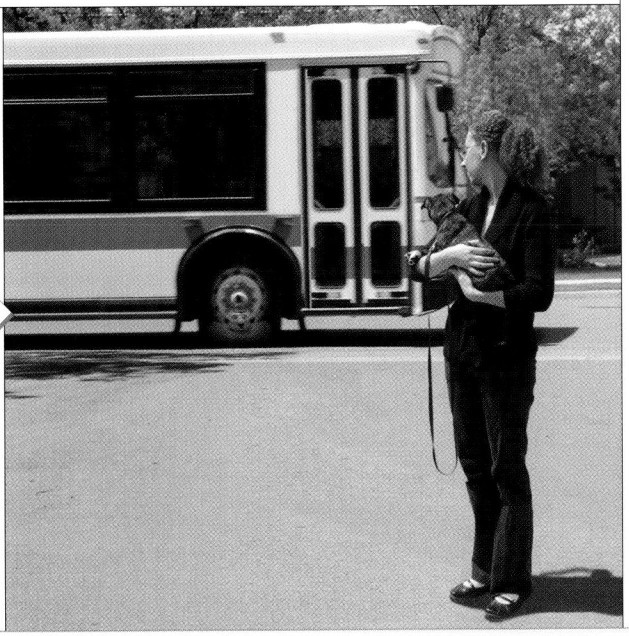

- Every new experience you introduce your puppy to should be safe and happy so as to create a positive association with the experience.
- Give your puppy lots of treats and praise for showing acceptance of new things and experiences.
- Do not try to soothe or calm your puppy if he acts fearful of new things or experiences. To help calm your puppy, simply remain calm yourself.
- The main periods for socialization are from 2 to 4 months and from 7 to 9 months of age.
- In addition to the main socialization periods, you should continue to socialize your puppy on an ongoing basis into adulthood.
- For more information on how to socialize your puppy, see page 122.

How to Socialize Your Puppy

Proper socialization can help puppies to be confident and relaxed in new situations. To socialize your puppy, introduce him safely and pleasantly to a wide variety of new people and new experiences. This is especially important when your puppy is 2 to 4 months old and again at 7 to 9 months old. Try to stimulate your puppy's senses with different sights, smells, textures, tastes and sounds.

Your puppy's early experiences in life, good or bad, will leave a lasting impression, so do your best to control what happens during socialization. Watch your puppy closely to ensure he is enjoying the new experiences and try to encourage him with plenty of treats and praise. When outside of the house, always keep your puppy on a leash and only take him into situations that you can control or easily leave.

People

- When socializing your puppy, you should try to have your puppy meet as many people as possible.

- Begin with meeting one person at a time. When your puppy is confident meeting people one at a time, you can have him start meeting groups of people together.

- Allow each new person to give your puppy a treat and pat him. Make sure that no one accidentally rewards unwanted behavior such as jumping up.

- During socialization, your puppy should come into contact with every type of person that he is likely to encounter as a mature dog.

- He should meet all kinds of people—tall and short, young and old, male and female.

- He should also meet people wearing hats, wearing sunglasses and carrying bags, as well as those in wheelchairs and using canes.

What precautions should I take before my puppy is fully vaccinated?

Tip

When puppies have not been fully vaccinated, they may be vulnerable to diseases spread by other dogs. Although it's important to start socializing your puppy before he's fully vaccinated, you should take precautions to limit his exposure to diseases. For example, keep your puppy away from places where unfamiliar dogs frequently play or eliminate. Also, try to carry your puppy in public so that his feet don't touch the ground and ask guests to remove their shoes before coming inside your house.

What should I do if my puppy seems fearful of a new experience or situation?

Tip

The best way to soothe a frightened puppy is to remain calm and demonstrate with your body language that there is nothing for him to fear. Although you can use treats to encourage your puppy during new experiences, don't force him into anything he's worried about. Let your puppy discover on his own that the new situation or person is perfectly safe. Keep in mind that puppies normally are a bit apprehensive at first in new situations.

Dogs and Other Animals

- You should have your puppy meet other dogs and animals during the socialization period.

- Invite your friends and relatives to your home with their healthy, vaccinated dogs to meet and play with your puppy.

Note: You should know these dogs and have seen their behavior with other dogs before allowing them to meet your puppy.

- Keep a close eye on your puppy when he is with an older dog to make sure that the visit goes smoothly.

- Your puppy should also meet dog-friendly cats.

- If you live in the city, you may also want to drive to the country and allow your puppy to see animals, such as cows, horses and sheep, from a distance.

- Be prepared to give your puppy lots of treats and praise when he shows confidence around new animals.

CONTINUED

How to Socialize Your Puppy continued

During socialization, you should introduce your puppy to as many different people, places and animals as possible. If you show your puppy that you enjoy meeting new people and having new experiences, he will be more likely to follow your lead and enjoy socialization.

You should reward your puppy when he is confident in new situations by giving him treats or praise and by patting him or playing with him. Try to ignore any anxiety or fear your puppy displays to help discourage these behaviors.

Try to avoid introducing your puppy to too many new experiences at once as this can be overwhelming. The best strategy is to socialize your puppy frequently for short periods of time. Remember that puppies tire easily and need a lot of rest.

Objects, Sounds and Situations

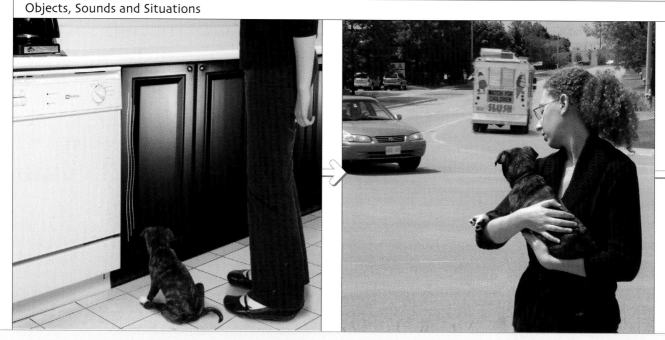

- Allow your puppy to become comfortable with any type of object that he is likely to encounter as a mature dog.

- Make sure you have a supply of food treats with you any time you are with your puppy.

- You should get your puppy used to the noises made by dishwashers, vacuum cleaners, washing machines, lawnmowers and hair dryers.

- Take your puppy to a street with traffic and, from a safe distance, let him become comfortable with the sights and sounds of different types of vehicles.

- When your puppy is accustomed to many different objects, try making familiar objects new. For example, turn a chair upside down for your puppy to explore.

- Give your puppy lots of treats and praise when he shows confidence investigating new objects.

Tip

How can I stimulate my puppy's sense of touch during socialization?

You can stimulate your puppy's sense of touch by teaching him how different types of surfaces feel under his feet. For example, you can let your puppy walk on different types of floors, on carpet, grass, doormats, cement or fallen pine needles. Introducing your puppy to different surfaces can help him feel confident when he encounters new surfaces in the future. However, try to make sure your puppy stays away from areas that unfamiliar dogs frequent before he is fully vaccinated.

Tip

Is there an easy way I can familiarize my puppy with new noises?

You can play a sound effects CD to safely familiarize your puppy with different sounds. For example, a CD with the sounds of a baby crying may help prepare your puppy for the arrival of a new baby. Pet supply stores and music stores should have a variety of CDs available or you could download sound files from the Internet. Start out by playing the CD at a low volume and gradually increase the volume as your puppy becomes comfortable with the sounds.

- Take your puppy for frequent rides in the car to get him accustomed to the car and to view the outside world.

- When you are out in the car with your puppy, stop in a parking area and let your puppy look out the window to take in all the sights.

- Take your puppy with you everywhere you safely can during the socialization period, such as your friends' homes, outdoor shopping malls, schools and the beach.

- When you go to a new place that has a lot of people and activity, watch from a safe distance until your puppy is comfortable.

- You should carry your puppy in public places to keep him safe from disease until he is fully vaccinated.

Body Language and Your Puppy

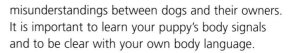

Have you ever seen the excited bow a dog makes when he wants to play? This action is part of the intricate body language dogs use to communicate. In fact, dogs communicate more through body language than they do verbally.

While humans also use body language, it is different from the body language used by dogs. This difference can often lead to misunderstandings between dogs and their owners. It is important to learn your puppy's body signals and to be clear with your own body language.

Your puppy's eyes, ears, tail, mouth and body are all used to convey body language. You should also take into account what your puppy is doing and what is going on around him when interpreting his body language.

Your Own Body Language

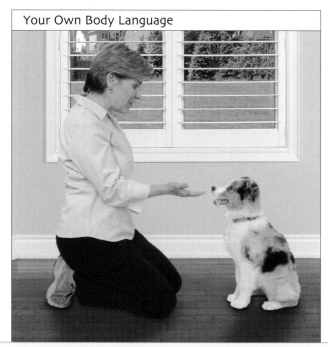

- You can use your own body language to communicate with your puppy and develop a better relationship with him.

- When giving your puppy a command, keep your posture relaxed and confident.

- To make your puppy feel welcome, crouch down and open your arms to him.

- If your puppy starts playing too rough, turn your side or back to him, fold your arms and look away until he calms down.

Body Language to Avoid

- If a puppy seems unsure or fearful, do not make direct eye contact with him. Instead, turn your head slightly away from him to help calm him.

- Looming over your puppy and staring down at him may make him feel threatened. Instead, stand relaxed and upright when near your puppy.

PUPPY BODY LANGUAGE

Signals of a Happy Puppy

There are many body language signals your puppy may use to let you know that he is feeling happy and at ease. Look for your puppy's mouth to be slightly open and soft-looking and for his ears to be positioned forward or slightly back. His nose will be down and his tail will be relaxed and may be wagging.

When your puppy wants to play, he will do a little bow in which he lowers his front legs, elbows and chest to the ground. His hind end will be high in the air with his tail wagging wildly, ears up and mouth open and sometimes barking.

Signals of Tension or Insecurity

Dogs and puppies will often use body language to express insecurity or a desire to calm a tense situation. Look for the following signs.

- Turning his head away from a situation signals vulnerability or discomfort.
- Licking his lips signals nervousness.
- Yawning signals confusion or insecurity.
- Panting often signals nervousness.
- Turning the side of his body towards a person or another dog is a calming signal and indicates he wants to calm the situation down.

Warning Signals

There are a number of distinctive signals a dog or puppy will display when he feels threatened. Always use caution whenever a dog or puppy shows the following warning signals:

- Flattened ears or ears that are stiff and forward.
- Lowering shoulders and turning head.
- Tension around the mouth or curled lips that expose teeth.
- Growling.
- Crouching and/or crawling away.
- Fur raised up on the neck and back.
- Tail pointing up and quickly wagging in small circles or tucked between legs.
- Stiff body posture or freezing in place.

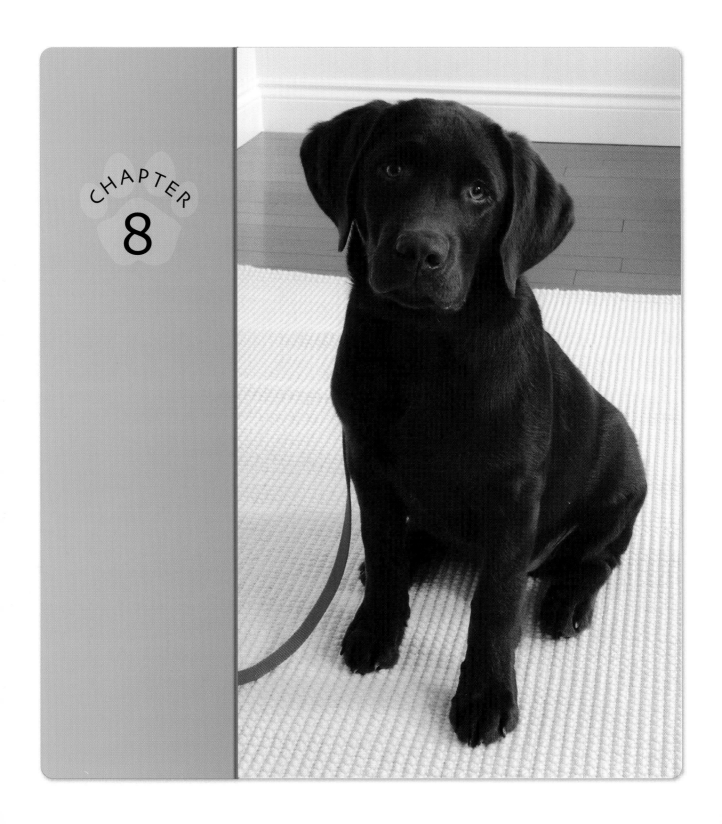

Training Basic Commands

Puppy Training Basics

Many dog trainers use the principles of positive reinforcement to teach puppies how to behave. With positive reinforcement training, you use treats and praise to reward the behaviors you want from your puppy, encouraging him to repeat those behaviors. For example, if you give your puppy a treat for correctly performing the Sit command, he will be more likely to respond to that command in the future.

Your puppy is never too young to learn using positive reinforcement techniques. You can start training your puppy as soon as he comes home.

For the best success when training your puppy, try to be consistent, but most of all be patient. Avoid training your puppy when you are feeling impatient or have had a bad day. If a training session is stressful or unpleasant for your puppy, he will be less likely to remember what he has learned.

Positive Training Methods

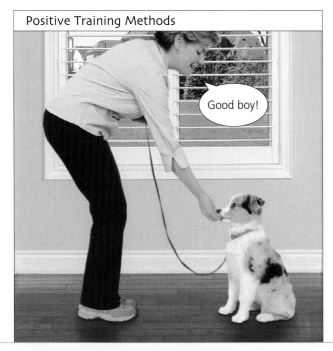

Good boy!

- Using positive training methods means you reward your puppy when he does the right thing instead of punishing him when he does the wrong thing.

- Positive training allows your puppy to associate specific behaviors with receiving a reward. For example, when you say "Sit" and your puppy sits, you praise him and give him a food treat.

- With practice, when your puppy hears you say "Sit," he will more likely sit again since he will expect a food treat and praise.

Training Sessions

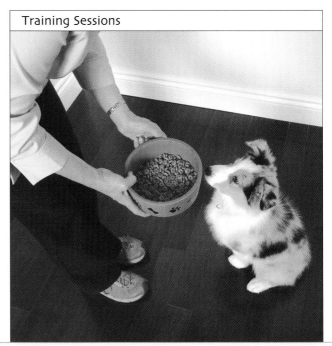

- Training sessions should be short and occur frequently throughout the day. Every time you are with your puppy, it is a potential time to train.

- Start with training sessions of 2 to 5 minutes each. As your puppy gets older, his attention span will get longer and you can gradually extend the length of your training sessions.

- Try to incorporate training into your puppy's daily routine. For example, practice the Sit command before you put down his food bowl.

How many commands should I work on during each training session?

Tip

During each training session, you should work on only one or two commands. The first command should be one that your puppy can perform successfully. You can then follow up by introducing a new or less familiar command. You should make sure you end each training session with an activity your puppy enjoys.

What should I do if my puppy is misbehaving?

Tip

You can either ignore him until he stops the behavior on his own or redirect him to appropriate behavior. You should always try to supervise your puppy so that you can redirect his behavior before he gets into trouble. If ignoring your puppy or redirecting his behavior does not work, try removing him from the situation and place him in his crate for 10 minutes or so, giving him time to settle down.

No Distractions

Giving Commands

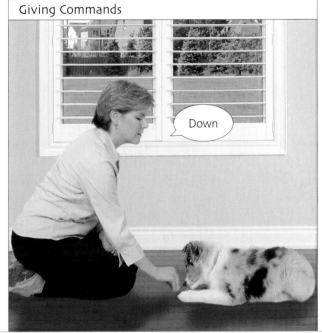

- You should begin your training sessions in an area with few distractions, such as a quiet room in your house.

- Removing distractions from your training area makes you the most interesting item in the room so your puppy's attention will be on you.

- As your puppy becomes comfortable with the commands, you can begin adding distractions, such as having other people in the room.

- When giving a command, use a calm, confident, normal speaking voice. Do not yell, use a questioning tone or use the excited tone that you would use for praise.

- Make sure you use each command consistently. For example, use the Down command only when you want your puppy to lie down.

- Use one command for each action you want your puppy to perform. For example, if you say "sit down," your puppy will not know if he should sit or lie down.

- Only say a command once. For example, saying "down, down" will confuse your puppy.

CONTINUED ▶

A basic tool you need for training is a lure to guide your puppy into position for whatever task you are training. The lure can be either a food treat or a favorite toy. Using a lure also introduces your puppy to the idea of hand signals for commands. How you hold the treat in your hand and move the treat when guiding your puppy into position will be similar to the hand signal for that command.

If you are not using a treat to guide your puppy into position, you can use a food treat as a reward after your puppy performs a command. Whether you use a food treat as a lure or just as a reward, make sure your training sessions occur before your puppy's mealtimes to ensure he is hungry.

Using Lures

- When you first start training your puppy to perform a command, you can use a lure to guide your puppy into position. You will most often use a food treat as a lure.

- A lure shows your puppy what to do without using your hand or leash to push or pull him into position.

- To lure your puppy into position, hold a treat in your hand so that he can see or smell it. Then use the treat in your hand to lure your puppy into position. The puppy will follow the lure into position. Then, give your puppy the treat.

Rewards

- You can use food treats, such as kibble or hot dog pieces, as rewards when your puppy performs the appropriate task. When you are using lures, the lure will be the puppy's reward.

- For best results, you should try to reward your puppy at the exact moment he performs a task.

- You should keep your puppy's rewards handy, but in a location that is not obvious to your puppy. For example, you may want to keep your rewards in a waist pouch so you can retrieve them quickly.

Tip

How can I be sure my puppy is not getting too much food when I train with food treats?

In the morning, measure out your puppy's entire ration of food for the day. You can then divide the amount into portions you need for each meal, as well as a portion for your training sessions.

Tip

What types of food treats are best for puppies?

In addition to his regular food, try some creative treats, such as freeze-dried liver, cheese cubes or dry cereal. Keep treats soft and small to reduce the risk of choking and to prevent your puppy from becoming full too quickly. Introduce one new treat at a time, leaving a couple of days between new treats to monitor how he tolerates the treats. Never give your puppy chocolate, grapes, or onions, which can be fatal even in small amounts.

Praise

Good boy!

- Puppies also love your praise. Your happy compliments let them know they are doing something you like.

- When praising your puppy, use a warm, upbeat tone of voice.

- You can use praise in combination with other rewards, such as food treats.

- Most puppies also enjoy physical contact as a reward for good work during training. For example, you can quickly scratch behind his ears or on his chest.

Life Rewards

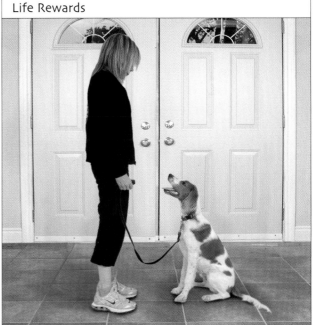

- You can also give your puppy life rewards. A life reward can be any item or activity that your puppy enjoys, such as a walk, car ride, playing a game or chewing a favorite chew toy.

- For example, before you take your puppy out the door for a walk, give him the Sit command. Going for a walk becomes your puppy's reward for sitting.

- Using life rewards helps you gradually move away from constantly giving your puppy food treats for good behavior.

Beyond Puppy Training Basics

Successful training requires slow and steady progress to ensure your puppy completely understands each command. Before trying the training concepts below, make sure you and your puppy are familiar with the training techniques covered on pages 130 to 133.

When training your puppy, break down each task into smaller components and build your puppy's understanding of these different components gradually. For example, you should not expect your puppy to sit for a period of time in a new environment right away. Instead, allow him first to understand the command and then you can introduce sitting for a period of time. After he has grasped these two components, you can try the command in a new environment. Remember that one of the most important aspects of training is to always praise and reward your puppy for behaving correctly.

Train in Small Steps

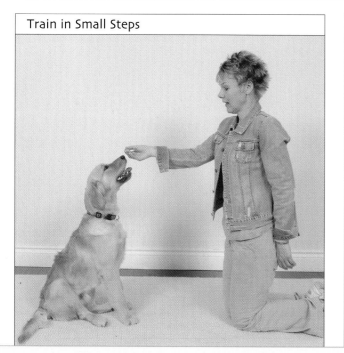

- As a general rule, when your puppy consistently responds to a command, you can move forward a step in your training. For example, you can stop using a treat to guide your puppy into position.

- If your puppy is unsuccessful at the new step after three attempts, you have moved forward too quickly and you should go back to the previous step in your training.

Stopping the Lure

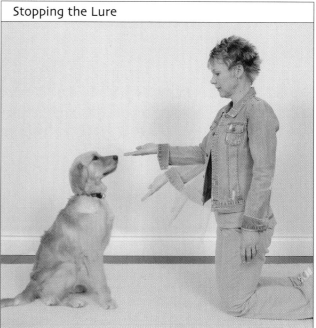

- After your puppy responds reliably when lured with a treat, you can stop using the treat to guide your puppy. You use a treat only as a reward after your puppy performs the command.

- When you begin training a hand signal, the signal is often a large movement. As your puppy becomes accustomed to the hand signal, you can begin to reduce the hand signal movement until it is as subtle as you would like.

- You can use the voice command and hand signal together or only use one or the other.

Tip

Will I have to continue giving my puppy food rewards forever?

Once your puppy is consistently obeying your commands, you can gradually begin to replace food rewards with praise or pats when he successfully performs a command. You can also start to substitute food rewards with life rewards, such as chewing a favorite toy or going for a walk. You should continue to randomly reward your puppy with food treats throughout his life. Your puppy will be more likely to obey commands if he knows that it's possible to earn a food reward.

Tip

What can I do if my puppy has trouble with a command?

If your puppy is having trouble learning a command, break the action down into smaller steps, rewarding your puppy for each small success. For example, if your puppy is having trouble with the Down command (page 140), use a treat to lure your puppy's head toward the ground and reward that action, gradually progressing until he is able to move his whole body into the Down position.

New Situations

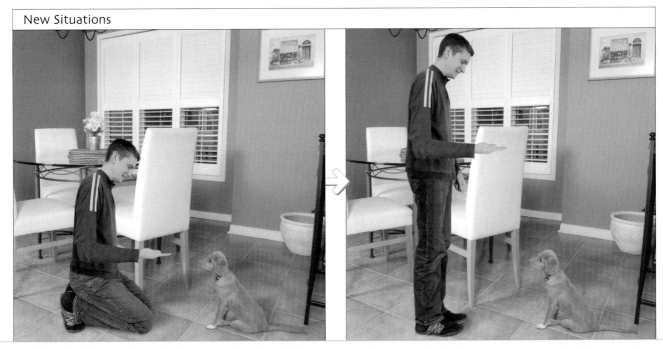

- As your puppy becomes comfortable with a command, you should begin giving the command in a variety of situations.

- With time, you can move your training to other rooms in your house and outdoors with your puppy on a leash. When you change the training location, your puppy learns that a command means the same thing no matter where he is.

- Remember that each time you move to a new location, you may need to go back a few steps in your training.

- You should also vary how you give the command, such as saying the command while you are standing or sitting.

- You should also begin giving the command when your puppy is in different places relative to you, such as when he is to your left and to your right.

- Using different situations in your training will help your puppy learn that the command means the same thing no matter where you are or what you are doing.

Teach Your Puppy His Name

The goal of teaching your puppy his name is to have him make eye contact with you. Establishing eye contact builds your relationship with your puppy and can be useful for getting his attention before giving commands and teaching him proper behavior.

Start by teaching your puppy his name as soon as you bring him home by saying his name in a pleasing tone whenever he looks at you. Make sure to reward all eye contact that you initiate, as long as your puppy is behaving while making eye contact. For example, do not reward him if he is begging for food at the same time he is making eye contact.

Teach Your Puppy His Name

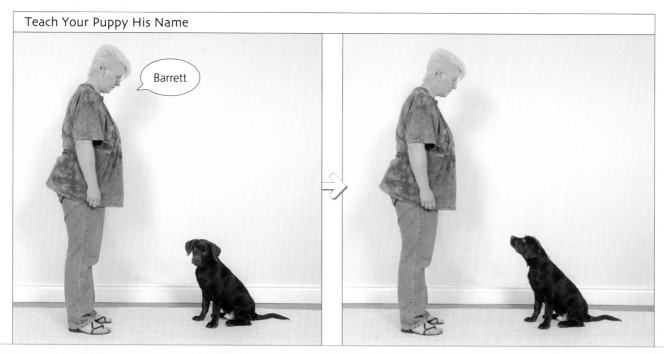

Barrett

- You should work on teaching your puppy his name a few times every day. Eventually, your puppy should look at you each time you say his name.

  Note: Be sure you do not overuse your puppy's name when playing with him. Your puppy's name should be a signal that you want him to look at you and wait for instructions.

1 When you are with your puppy, look at your puppy and say his name in a cheerful tone of voice.

2 As soon as your puppy looks up into your eyes, immediately praise him and give him a treat.

  Note: You can also pat or play with your puppy instead of giving him a treat.

- If your puppy does not look up when you say his name, make a small noise, such as a clucking noise with your tongue or a soft whistle. Do not say the puppy's name again. When he looks at you, praise him and give him a treat.

The Release Word

Many training commands, such as Sit, require your puppy to remain in position for a certain length of time. After your puppy has completed a command, you can say your release word to tell him that he has finished the command and can move out of position.

"All done," "Well done," and "Release" are some common release words. It doesn't matter which word you choose, as long as you use it consistently.

You should try to avoid words that are used in everyday conversation, such as "okay."

Each time you perform steps 1 to 3 below, increase the time your puppy has to remain in position by one second. However, if your puppy frequently breaks position before hearing the release word, you should decrease the length of time he remains in position before releasing him.

The Release Word

1 Use the command you want your puppy to perform, such as Sit. For information on the Sit command, see page 138.

2 After your puppy has been in the position you asked for, such as sit, for one second, say the word you have chosen to release your puppy from the command.

Note: In this example, we say "alright."

3 Encourage your puppy to move around by clapping gently or petting him. Then give your puppy a treat.

Note: If your puppy moves out of position before you say the release word, do not give him a treat. Repeat steps 1 to 3.

Sit Command

The Sit command is one of the first commands you should teach your puppy. At first, you should train the Sit command in a zero-distraction environment and when your puppy is hungry. This command will help you maintain control of your puppy in any situation, from sitting before crossing a busy street to greeting new people.

You should start working on the Sit command as soon as you bring your puppy home, but no more than five times per training session. You can also use the Sit command in everyday life with your puppy. For example, you can have your puppy perform the Sit command before mealtime and before opening doors. Your puppy will learn that by sitting, he receives rewarding things like his meal and going outside.

Sit Command

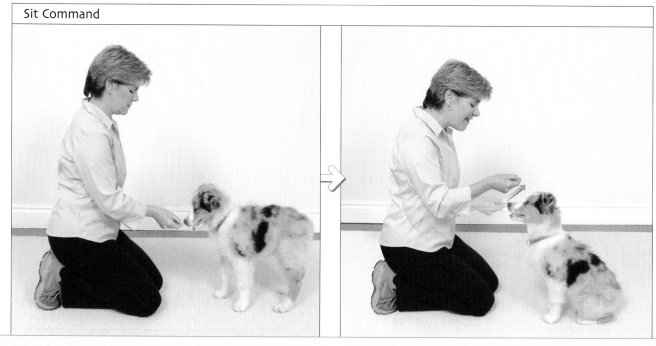

1 Kneel on the floor facing your puppy.

2 Hold a treat in your right hand, with your palm facing your puppy.

Note: For information on using treats to lure your puppy into position, see page 132.

3 Hold the treat close to your puppy's nose.

4 Move the treat up above your puppy's head, between his eyes, toward the back of his head.

Note: Be sure not to raise the treat too high or the puppy may jump up to get the treat. Try to keep the treat within easy sniffing distance of the puppy's nose.

- As your puppy's nose follows the treat, his head will move up and back and he will sit.
- When the puppy sits, praise him calmly and give him the treat.

How long should my puppy sit?

You want your puppy to sit and remain in position until you release him. When your puppy is sitting consistently without being lured with a treat, you can then work on building the amount of time he spends in the Sit position. Once he is sitting, praise him quietly, wait for one second and then give him the treat only if he remains sitting until you say the release word. With each time you practice, add a few seconds to his sit time. For information on release words, see page 137.

What is the next step?

Train your puppy to sit in different situations and environments so that he knows to sit whenever you give the command, no matter where he is. After he has mastered the basics of sitting, start moving around. For example, give the command while you are standing or sitting instead of kneeling or when you are beside him and not in front of him. Train in different rooms of the house and increase distractions, such as having the television on.

The Command and Hand Signal

- When your puppy is easily following the treat lure and moving into the Sit position, you can repeat steps 1 to 4 on page 138 and begin saying the command "Sit" at the same time as you move the treat in step 4.

- When your puppy is rèliably responding when you lure him with a treat and the Sit command, you can stop using the treat to guide your puppy into position. You can use just the Sit command and the hand signal instead.

1 Kneel on the floor facing your puppy.

2 Say the command "Sit."

3 With your right hand flat, palm facing the puppy, bend your elbow and raise your right hand so it is parallel to the floor. This is the hand signal for Sit.

4 When your puppy sits, praise him calmly and give him a treat.

Note: If the puppy does not sit, do not give him a treat and repeat steps 1 to 4. After three unsuccessful attempts, return to training with the treat lure.

Down Command

You can use the Down command when you want your puppy to lie down. Be sure not to confuse your puppy by using the command when you want him to get off furniture or to stop jumping up on you. In addition, you should not use the Down command with another word, such as "Sit down," "Lie down," or "Get down." You can begin working on the Down command after your puppy has mastered the Sit command (page 138). Puppies are usually full of energy and easily distracted, so try to train this command in a zero-distraction environment and when your puppy's energy is low. Also, praise your puppy calmly when he performs the Down command because if your praise is in an excited tone, he may pop right up out of the Down position.

Down Command

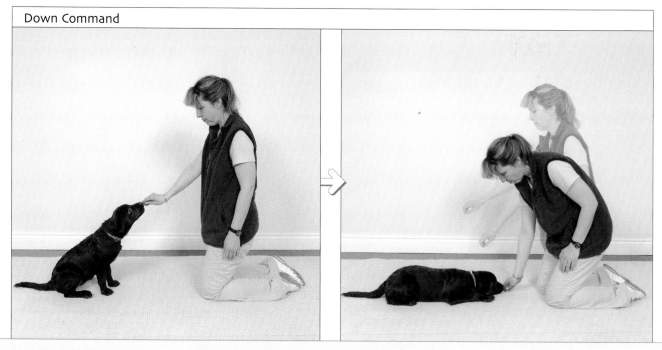

1 Kneel on the floor facing your puppy, with your puppy in the Sit position (see page 138).

2 Hold a treat in your right hand, with your palm facing the floor.

Note: For information on using treats to lure your puppy into position, see page 132.

3 Hold the treat close to your puppy's nose.

4 Move the treat down to the floor, slightly in front of your puppy's front paws.

Note: Try to keep the treat within easy sniffing distance of your puppy's nose.

- As your puppy's nose follows the treat, his head will move down and he will lie on the floor.

Note: Your puppy's abdomen should be on the floor. His back legs may tuck underneath him or may rest out to the side.

- When your puppy lies down, praise him calmly and give him the treat.

Tip

How long should my puppy stay in the Down position?

When your puppy consistently responds to the Down command, you can begin working with him to stay in the position for a longer period of time. After your puppy is in the Down position, withhold his treat for one second and then say your release word. Only give your puppy the treat if he stays down until you give the release word. Start him off by staying in the Down position for one second and then add a few seconds at a time with each time you practice. For information on release words, see page 137.

 Tip

What is the next step?

You should train in different situations and environments so your puppy knows that Down means Down no matter where he is. After he has mastered the basics of the command, start moving around. For example, practice the Down command while you are standing or sitting instead of kneeling or when you are beside him and not in front of him. Train in different rooms of the house and increase distractions, such as having another person in the room.

The Command and Hand Signal

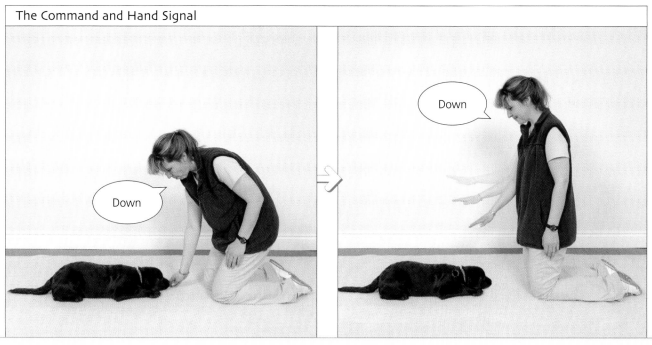

- When your puppy is easily following the treat lure and moving into the Down position, you can repeat steps 1 to 4 on page 140 and begin saying the command "Down" at the same time as you move the treat in step 4.

- When your puppy is reliably responding when you lure him with a treat and the Down command, you can stop using the treat to guide your puppy into position. You can use just the Down command and the hand signal instead.

1 Kneel on the floor facing your puppy, with your puppy in the Sit position.

2 Say the command "Down."

3 With your right hand flat, palm facing down, move your lower arm toward the floor. This is the hand signal for Down.

4 When your puppy lies down, praise him calmly and give him a treat.

Note: If your puppy does not lie down, do not give him a treat and repeat steps 1 to 4. After three unsuccessful attempts, return to luring your puppy with a treat (steps 1 to 4, page 140).

Come Command

You can start practicing the Come command with your puppy from day one with some success, because very young puppies naturally want to follow you and be with you. Starting early will lay a solid foundation for your puppy to come when called that will continue when he is older and more independent. The goal of the Come command is for your puppy to develop an instinctive reaction to immediately come to you when he hears the command, no matter what he is doing.

Perfecting this command requires a lot of practice with many repetitions and gradually increasing distractions. Also, you must always reward your puppy for responding to the command. Give enthusiastic praise or a tasty treat while he is learning and for the rest of his life thereafter.

Come Command

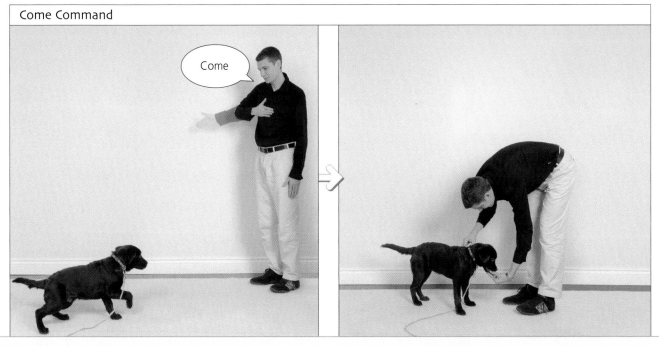

Come

1 Attach a houseline (see page 44) to your puppy's collar. Allow the houseline to drag on the floor behind your puppy.

2 Stand within five feet of your puppy and call "Come" in a clear and cheerful voice.

3 Make a large sweeping movement with your right arm, bringing the palm of your right hand to the middle of your chest. This is the hand signal for Come.

4 When your puppy looks at you and/or starts moving toward you, back away a few steps and praise him enthusiastically until he reaches you.

5 When your puppy reaches you, give him more praise and a treat and lightly hold his collar for a moment.

6 Say your release word (see page 137) and let go of his collar.

• If your puppy does not come toward you, do not call him again. Pick up the end of the houseline and gently guide your puppy toward you. Do not drag the puppy. As soon as the puppy takes a single step in your direction, perform steps 4 to 6.

Tip

How long should I continue training the Come command?

Continue to practice this command throughout your puppy's life. For example, when you take him to the park, ask him to come to you periodically and not just when it is time to go home. Each time he comes to you, give him a treat and release him again to play. Whenever you are training, never give your puppy the opportunity to ignore you or choose not to come when called.

Tip

What else do I need to remember when teaching the Come command?

Make it fun and rewarding for your puppy to come when called. For example, never have him come to you so you can scold him for bad behavior or to do something with him that is not fun and rewarding, such as trimming his nails. Using the Come command in these situations will only teach your puppy to ignore you.

Increasing Distractions and Distance

Practicing Outdoors

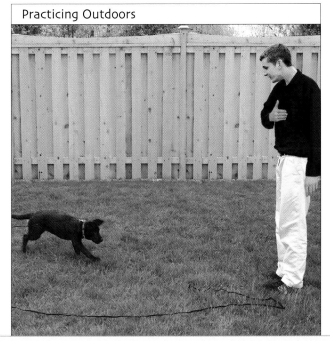

- When your puppy is running enthusiastically to you every time you call, start adding some small distractions, such as having other people in the room or having the television on. Gradually work in more distractions until you can call your puppy even when he is absorbed in something else.

- You should also start calling him from greater distances, such as from the next room.

- When your puppy is coming reliably with distractions and from farther distances within the house, you can move the training to a fenced area outdoors.

1 Attach a yardline (see page 44) to his collar and then perform steps 2 to 6.

- Start your outdoor training with very few distractions and gradually work in more distractions, such as other people in the yard.

Note: If you do not have a fenced area outdoors, you can still practice outside, but keep the end of the yardline in your hand instead of letting it drag on the ground.

Relax Command

Teaching your puppy to relax is an important skill he can use to stay calm when facing a new environment or a strange situation, such as a friend's house or a veterinarian's waiting room.

To practice, you need a regular leash to attach to your puppy's collar.

You will also need a chair to sit on. When you are just starting, you should keep the sessions short and the distractions to a minimum. With time, you can practice this command when you are sitting just about anywhere, such as when watching TV or talking with friends.

Relax Command

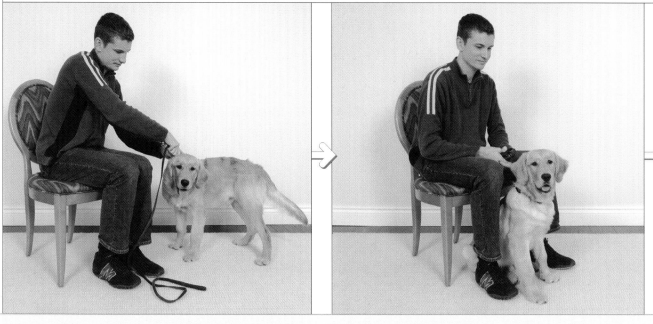

1 Attach a leash to your puppy's collar.

2 Sit in a chair with your feet on the floor in front of you.

3 Help your puppy to move into a Sit position between your feet, facing away from you.

Note: Do not use the Sit command when moving your puppy into position. For information on the Sit position, see page 138.

• Make sure there is no tension on the leash, but do not allow the leash to be too slack.

What if my puppy starts to chew the leash or my shoes?

Tip When starting out with this command, your puppy may find the leash or your clothing tempting to chew. If he behaves in this way, gently grasp his collar, take whatever he is chewing out of his mouth, place him in the Sit position again and then release his collar. If this behavior continues or if he is extremely restless, a food-stuffed chew toy may help him to relax.

What is the next step when practicing the Relax position?

Tip If your puppy is consistently remaining in the Relax position until you release him, you can gradually extend the length of time he remains in position during future training sessions. As he continues to stay in the position for longer time periods, you can then begin practicing at locations with distractions, such as on your front porch, on a park bench, at a strip mall or at the vet clinic.

4 Say the command "Relax."

5 Sit, relaxed and calm, for about 30 seconds. Do not talk, pat or give treats to your puppy.

Note: Your puppy should be able to get comfortable when in this position, whether he is lying down or sitting.

• If your puppy stands up or tries to move away, help him back into the Sit position between your feet without saying anything.

6 Say the release word, such as "alright," as you get up and move from the chair. For information on release words, see page 137.

• Each time you successfully practice this exercise, have your puppy stay in the Relax position for a few seconds longer than the previous time.

Good Leash Manners

A puppy who knows how to walk nicely on a leash is much more pleasant to walk with than one who persistently pulls on his leash or tries to take off in another direction. Until your puppy learns how to walk properly on a leash, practice with very short "walks," perhaps only 10 or 20 feet.

You should start by helping your puppy get accustomed to wearing a collar and leash (see page 148). Then begin training in an area with few distractions, such as inside your house. After he understands the basics, you can walk at a brisk pace, as if you are late for a meeting. Remember that good leash manners apply to you as well, so always take a plastic bag on your walks to clean up after your puppy.

Good Leash Manners

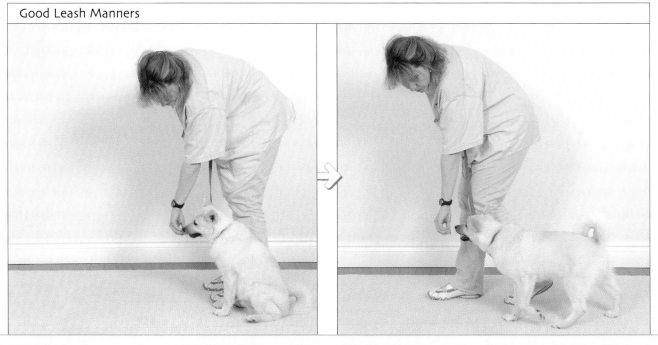

1 Attach a leash to your puppy's collar and stand with your puppy on your left side.

2 Hold the leash in your right hand and place your right hand against your stomach.

- The leash should not be tight, but should not be so loose that the puppy can trip over it.

3 Hold a treat in your left hand, slightly in front of and below your puppy's nose.

Note: You may have to bend down to position the treat near your puppy's nose.

4 Keeping the treat slightly in front of and below your puppy's nose, walk forward a few steps at a pace your puppy can comfortably keep up with. As your puppy walks with you, praise him.

- If your puppy becomes distracted and pulls on the leash, stop walking and praising immediately. Try to get his attention with the treat and then repeat step 4.

5 After a few steps, stop walking. Raise the treat up between the puppy's eyes to lure him into the Sit position (see page 138).

6 When your puppy sits, give him the treat.

My puppy is very tiny. What if I can't reach his nose when practicing good leash manners?

To hold a treat in your very small puppy's line of vision, try using a wooden spoon smeared with a little bit of peanut butter. As your puppy improves with walking on a leash, you can gradually raise the spoon so the treat is at waist level.

 What is the most important thing to remember when teaching my puppy good leash manners?

Be consistent with your puppy whenever he is on leash, not just when going for walks. Even if you are just taking him to the car, do not allow him to pull on his leash. If you are inconsistent with your expectations of your puppy, you will teach him that pulling on his leash sometimes works.

Moving On

- When your puppy is easily following the treat lure and walking beside you on the leash, you can repeat steps 1 to 6 on page 146 and begin saying the command "Let's Go" at the same time as you start walking in step 4.

- When your puppy is reliably responding when you lure him with a treat and the "Let's Go" command, you can stop using the treat to guide your puppy. You can use just the "Let's Go" command.

1 Hold a few treats in your left hand at waist level instead of near your puppy's nose as you perform steps 1 to 6. Say "Let's Go" at the same time as you start walking.

2 After a few steps, give your puppy the treat and continue walking.

Note: Keep the distance you walk before giving your puppy a treat fairly short. If you go too far, your puppy may stop responding.

- As your puppy becomes better at walking nicely beside you, you can gradually increase the distance your puppy walks between receiving a treat. Then begin gradually substituting praise for treats.

Before Your First Training Class

It's never too early to start training your puppy. For the first two to three months, puppies focus on eating, sleeping and playing. If your training sessions are fun, your puppy will view them as play and will learn more easily.

Learning helps puppies to build their self-confidence and confident puppies are more eager to learn. Always remember that puppies are very similar to babies as they are sensitive and have short attention spans. You should keep all training sessions stress-free and don't let your puppy get overtired.

Aside from familiarizing your puppy with a collar and leash and getting enough physical activity, it is also important to start socializing your puppy as soon as possible. For more information on socialization, see pages 120 to 125.

Overview

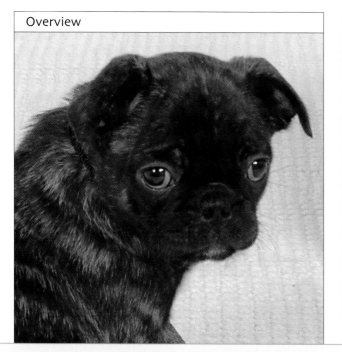

Getting Used to a Collar and Leash

- Many training classes do not accept puppies younger than 12 weeks because before that time most puppies are not yet fully vaccinated.

- Just because your puppy is too young for a training class, however, does not mean you shouldn't work with your puppy from the day you bring him home.

- There are many ways you can work with your puppy before he is old enough to attend his first training class.

- Start getting your puppy used to his collar and leash as soon as you can. See pages 46 and 43 for information on collars and leashes.

1 To get your puppy used to his collar, put the collar on him before doing something the puppy likes, such as just before you play with him. Leave the collar on for about 15 minutes and then remove it.

- Gradually extend the length of time you leave the puppy's collar on him.

  Note: Never leave your puppy unsupervised or in his crate with his collar on.

148

Tip

How can I start working on good habits with my puppy?

The way you interact with your puppy on a daily basis can shape his behavior for years to come. You can start to train your puppy as soon as he comes home by rewarding good behavior, such as coming to you when called, and ignoring unwanted behavior, such as barking for attention. You can also start teaching your puppy all of the basic training commands covered in this chapter.

 Tip

Should I work on mentally stimulating my puppy too?

Mental stimulation is a great way to help your puppy learn. Play games that will challenge his mind and teach him to problem solve. For example, hide a Kong™ stuffed with food and let your puppy find the toy. Appeal to all of your puppy's senses by introducing him to new and interesting sights, smells, sounds, tastes and textures. For example, hearing vacuum cleaner sounds and playing with different types of toys will help your puppy learn about the world around him.

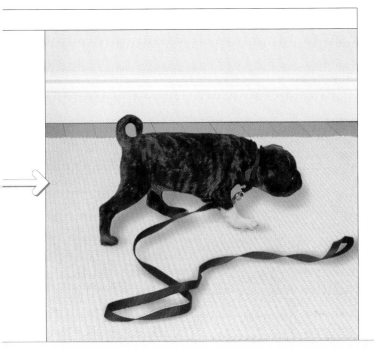

Physical Activity

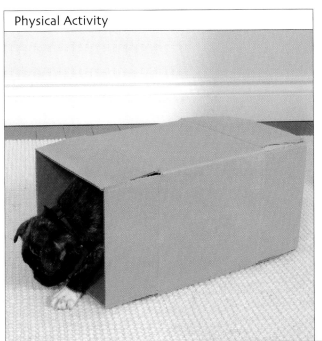

2 When your puppy is comfortable wearing his collar, clip a lightweight leash to his collar and allow him to drag the leash around for a minute or so a few times a day.

3 When your puppy is comfortable dragging the leash, try holding the end of the leash and speaking cheerfully to the puppy.

4 Praise your puppy when he starts moving toward you and give him a treat.

Note: If the puppy pulls away from you, stop praising and remain still. Wait until he takes the pressure off the leash by moving toward you. Then praise him again.

- Physical activity can stimulate your puppy's mind as well as his body.

- Place a long cardboard box with the ends opened on the ground and encourage your puppy to run through the tunnel.

- Lay a ladder on the ground and help your puppy walk over the rungs to develop his coordination.

- When working on physical activities with your puppy, avoid letting him run on slippery surfaces and be very careful when working around stairs to prevent injuries.

Games and Tricks for Your Puppy

Benefits of Playing With Your Puppy

Games and Activities to Avoid

Collar Hold Game

Give and Take

Pass the Puppy

Get It

Puppy Fetch

Where's Your Tummy?

Puppy Ping Pong

Targeting Tricks

Walk With Me

Gimme Five

Scavenger Hunt

Puppy Dress Up

Benefits of Playing With Your Puppy

Puppies are always looking to have fun. You can take advantage of this characteristic by using playtime to teach your puppy a few games and tricks. While he plays, you are strengthening your relationship and teaching him to ignore distractions and focus on you.

Playing games with your puppy is a great way to teach him new skills. Plus, the more you enjoy training your puppy, the more you will want to teach him new things!

The games you choose should encourage your puppy to be obedient and complement his other training exercises. Avoid games that reward unwanted behaviors or could interfere with your puppy's obedience training.

Benefits of Playing With Your Puppy

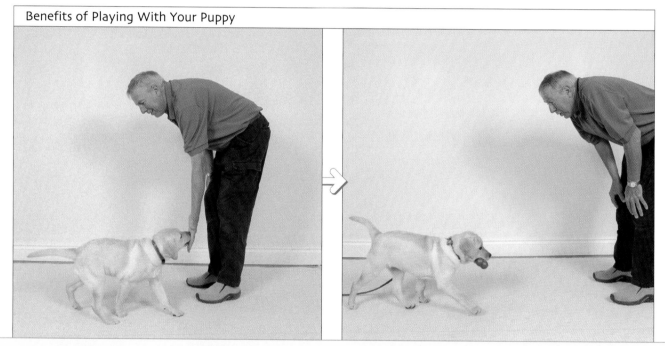

- Playing well-chosen games with your puppy and teaching him tricks are excellent ways to stimulate his growing body and developing mind.

- Puppies need a constructive outlet for their energy. Games and tricks that teach good behavior are a great way to channel their energy productively.

- Many tricks have the added benefit of helping you control your puppy more effectively.

- Games and tricks can communicate to your puppy that you are the leader in a natural, fun and non-confrontational way.

- Even the simplest games and tricks can have great benefits for a puppy. Mastering simple skills will make any puppy more confident and eager to work with his owner.

- Training your puppy with games and tricks is one of the best ways for you to bond and have fun with your puppy.

Games and Activities to Avoid

Although playing with a puppy is fun, there are certain games and activities you should avoid. For example, tugging games will encourage a new puppy to pull on objects. Teasing your puppy during games and activities is not a good idea either. It will only make him frustrated and could lead to him barking or jumping up on you to release his frustration.

Chasing games and playing roughly with your puppy are also not beneficial activities. Chasing your puppy will teach him to see you as a littermate rather than a leader and can also lead to nipping. You should avoid rough play as it rewards your puppy for behavior that you are trying to discourage.

Games and Activities to Avoid

Tugging Games
- Tugging games teach your puppy that grabbing and pulling on objects is acceptable.
- Tugging games can become a leadership challenge. Your puppy may start growling while playing with you and run off with the object if he wins the challenge.

Teasing Games
- Offering a reward, such as a treat or toy, to your puppy and then withholding the treat or toy leads to frustration and erodes trust.
- Eventually, your puppy may stop trying to earn rewards if he thinks they will be withheld.

Chasing Games
- Chasing your puppy encourages him to run away when called and to run off with objects you want.
- Allowing your puppy to chase people, especially children, teaches him that it is acceptable to jump up on people and pull at their clothing.

Rough Play
- Playing roughly with a puppy teaches him a lack of respect for humans. He will begin to think of people as littermates who can be jumped upon and nipped.
- Rough play can also create fear in insecure puppies.

Collar Hold Game

Playing the "Collar Hold Game" can help your puppy feel comfortable with having his collar touched or held. Some puppies run away when their owners reach for their collars, but you can work to prevent this behavior by playing the "Collar Hold Game." The game helps to teach your puppy that when he allows you to touch or hold his collar he will be rewarded.

You can start playing the "Collar Hold Game" after your puppy has had a few days to become accustomed to wearing his collar. Once your puppy is used to having his collar held, he should sit still whenever you reach for his collar. It should also be easier for you to put a leash on your puppy or to quickly grab his collar in emergency situations.

Collar Hold Game

- The "Collar Hold Game" teaches your puppy to become accustomed to having his collar held and will prevent him from dodging when you reach for him.

Collar Touch
- When you start playing the "Collar Hold Game," begin by simply touching your puppy's collar.

1 Kneel or sit in front of your puppy and offer him a treat.

2 Touch your puppy's collar with your other hand while he is eating the treat.

3 Repeat steps 1 and 2 three or four times.

- Once your puppy is used to having his collar touched, start touching his collar before you give him the treat.

Tip

Where is the best place to play this game?

You should play the "Collar Hold Game" in a variety of different environments. For example, you can play this game with your puppy in different rooms of your house, in your yard and eventually at the park. Practicing this game in different settings and at different times of the day will teach your puppy to look forward to having his collar held in any situation.

Tip

My puppy doesn't mind having his collar touched, but he runs away every time I take the leash off. What can I do?

You need to prevent your puppy from associating the clicking noise of the leash's clasp with its removal. Some puppies learn to recognize the sound of the leash coming off and they start to run away as soon as you take the leash off. When your puppy is wearing his leash, occasionally reach down and click the leash clasp without actually taking it off. If you do this regularly, the sound of the clasp should become meaningless to your puppy.

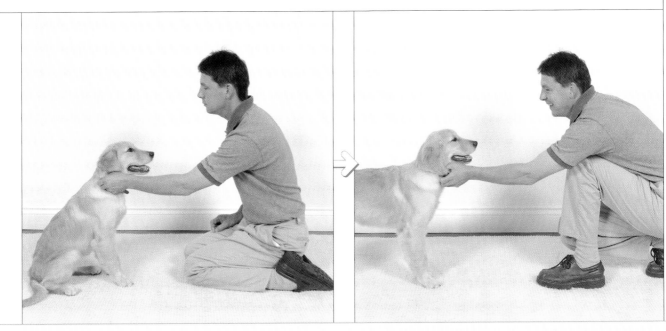

Collar Hold

• When your puppy is happy having you touch his collar, you can start to gently take hold of his collar.

1 Kneel or sit in front of your puppy and slowly reach for his collar. Then gently take hold of his collar.

2 Praise your puppy and give him a treat, holding his collar while he eats.

3 When your puppy finishes his treat, release his collar.

4 Repeat steps 1 to 3 three or four times.

• As your puppy gets used to having his collar held, gradually increase the amount of time between taking hold of his collar and offering him a treat.

• When your puppy is used to having his collar held, make the game more fun by reaching for his collar in a quicker, more playful manner.

Give and Take

Playing "Give and Take" teaches your puppy that sharing his toys is fun. Once he has mastered the game, your puppy should be willing to give you his most beloved toy without protest.

"Give and Take" helps to prevent your puppy from becoming possessive and builds his retrieving skills. Your puppy will most likely love this game as he will always win. With "Give and Take," your puppy receives a treat in exchange for his toy and then he receives the toy back. If your puppy is somewhat possessive of toys, you can start playing the game by trading him the toy he values least for a really tasty treat.

When you have finished playing "Give and Take," you may decide to put away your puppy's toy. Give him two treats in exchange for the toy before putting it away.

Give and Take

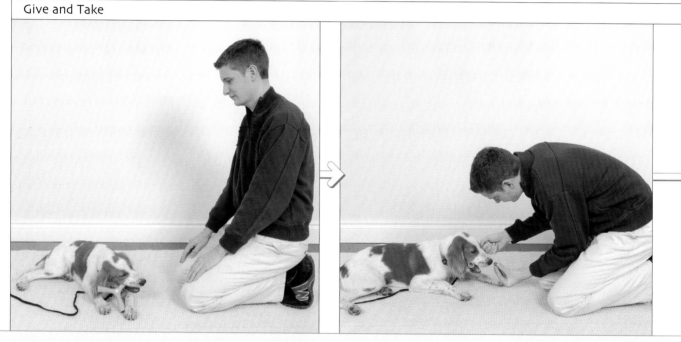

- "Give and Take" teaches your puppy to give up valued objects without protest.

1 Attach a houseline (see page 44) to your puppy's collar.

2 Give your puppy a toy that is of low value to him, such as a teething toy, and let him play with it.

3 After 10 to 15 seconds, hold a favorite treat, such as a piece of cheese or slice of hot dog, in front of your puppy's nose with one hand.

4 At the same time, take hold of the toy with your other hand.

Note: If your puppy tries to run away with the toy, step on his houseline to prevent him from getting away.

What should I do if my puppy growls when I try to take the toy?

Tip

If a puppy growls or snaps when you put your hand on his toy, even with a treat in front of his nose, walk away from your puppy and call a professional trainer. Later, when your puppy loses interest in the toy, pick it up and put it away permanently. Don't play "Give and Take" again without a trainer's advice. For more information on preventing aggressive behavior, see page 198.

Can I use "Give and Take" to have my puppy give up inappropriate objects?

Tip

If your puppy is holding an object that he should not have, you can use this game to obtain the object. If the object is small and is entirely enclosed in his mouth, be sure to hold the treat you offer below your puppy's nose. This way, when he opens his mouth to eat the treat, the small object will fall down and out of his mouth.

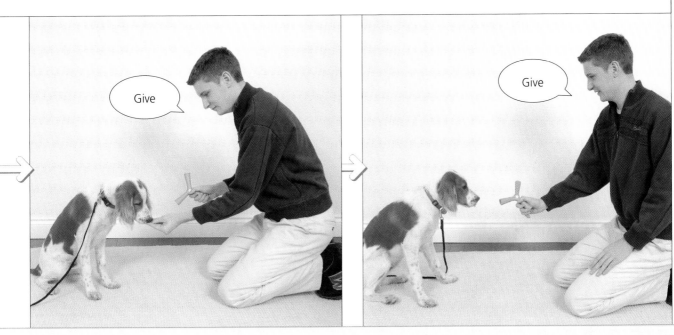

5 When your puppy releases the toy to take the treat, say "Give."

6 After your puppy has finished eating the treat, give the toy back to him.

7 Repeat steps 3 to 6 two or three more times while he is playing with the same toy.

● When your puppy gives up low-value toys easily, try playing "Give and Take" with toys he prizes more. Eventually, you can progress to playing with your puppy's favorite toys.

● Once your puppy gives up any toy easily, begin saying "Give" and take the toy without holding the treat in front of his nose in step 3. Give your puppy a treat after he releases the toy.

● Eventually your puppy will happily give up objects knowing that he will be rewarded.

Pass the Puppy

The "Pass the Puppy" game helps teach your puppy to feel comfortable being handled by many different people. You can introduce your puppy to this game a few days after he first comes home.

To play "Pass the Puppy," gather three to five people and give them lots of delicious treats. You can use dry kibble or something more exciting, like hot dog slices. During the game everyone should speak gently, act calmly and avoid reinforcing any unwanted behavior like mouthing or nipping at hands.

You can play this game with a puppy of any breed that is small enough to hold securely in your hands. It's a good idea to play this game with younger puppies—a Newfoundland puppy, for example, will be too big to pass around before too long!

Pass the Puppy

1 Have three to five people sit in a circle on the floor, facing the center of the circle.

- The people should sit very close to each other and should each have a handful of treats.

2 Attach a houseline (see page 44) to the puppy's collar.

3 Carefully lift the puppy onto your lap.

4 Give the puppy one or two treats.

5 Calmly stroke and praise the puppy for a few seconds.

6 Give the puppy another treat.

What should I do if my puppy is uncomfortable with being touched?

Tip

If your puppy objects to this game, you should practice handling him more on your own (see page 117). You can gradually introduce him to "Pass the Puppy" by starting the game with two people and then including one more person in the game each time you play. "Pass the Puppy" works well if your puppy's comfort level has not been surpassed, so try to give him a treat before he starts to squirm and make sure that you only hold him for a few seconds.

How can I advance this game?

Tip

You can advance this game by using it as an opportunity to introduce your puppy to as many different types of people as possible. For example, you could try to include people with beards or glasses. You could even ask your helpers to change their appearance by wearing different types of hats or glasses. For more information on introducing your puppy to different people, see page 122.

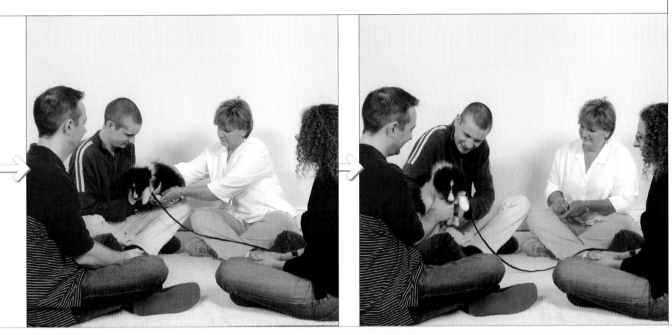

7 Gently lift the puppy and pass him onto the lap of the next person in the circle.

8 The next person should perform steps 4 to 6.

9 Continue passing your puppy from person to person around the circle until each person has held the puppy and performed steps 4 to 6 twice. This should not take more than two minutes.

Note: If your puppy begins to get overexcited or uncomfortable, place him on the floor and stop playing the game.

• If your puppy seems overly fearful of being held by people in this game, try playing "Meet the Puppy Game" instead (see page 72).

Get It

This game helps to teach puppies to take treats gently and wait for permission before eating food off the floor. You should teach your puppy the faster-moving floor version of the game only after he has mastered the in-hand version.

If you don't cover the treat quickly enough in the floor version of this game, your puppy may grab the treat, which could encourage him to snatch treats instead of wait for them. When you first start playing this game, you should use regular kibble. It will be easier for your puppy to resist dry kibble than a higher value treat like hot dog slices.

Although this game is easy to play, puppies that are possessive of their food may have difficulties. Contact a trainer if your puppy shows signs of possessiveness. For information on possessive food behavior, see page 196.

In-Hand Version

1 Attach a houseline (see page 44) to your puppy's collar.

2 Kneeling in front of your puppy, hold a treat in your hand, with your palm facing upward and your fingers closed around the treat.

3 Place your closed hand in front of your puppy's nose. Allow him to sniff and lick your hand.

- If your puppy's teeth touch your hand, take your hand away for 5 to 10 seconds. Then repeat step 3.

4 When your puppy moves his nose away from your hand, immediately open your hand and say "Get It."

5 Allow your puppy to eat the treat and praise him.

- As your puppy learns to back off from the treat, gradually increase the amount of time between opening your hand and saying "Get It." If your puppy moves toward the treat before you say "Get It," close your hand again and repeat steps 4 and 5.

How can I make this game more challenging?

You can make the floor version of "Get It" more challenging by dropping a treat onto the floor. Start 5 inches above the floor and slowly work your way up to counter height. Once your puppy is able to resist dropped treats, try practicing the game when you are making dinner by dropping some of the food you are preparing. When your puppy backs off from the food, pick the food up and reward him immediately with a tasty dog treat.

Are there any other games my puppy and I can play using the "Get It" command?

To practice the "Get It" command, you can place a row of treats on the floor and hand-feed them to your puppy one by one. When only one treat remains, you can tell your puppy to "Get It." You can also try placing a treat on top of your puppy's front paw as he is lying down. Then tell him to "Get It."

Floor Version

Get It

1 Attach a houseline (see page 44) to your puppy's collar.

2 Crouch in front of your puppy and place a treat on the floor in front of him.

3 When your puppy moves to eat the treat, cover it with your hand. Allow him to sniff and lick your hand.

- If your puppy's teeth touch your hand, pick up the treat and wait 5 to 10 seconds. Then repeat steps 2 and 3.

4 When your puppy moves away from your hand, immediately uncover the treat and say "Get It."

5 Allow your puppy to eat the treat and praise him.

- As your puppy learns to back off from the treat, gradually increase the amount of time between uncovering the treat and saying "Get It." If your puppy reaches for the treat before you say "Get It," cover the treat again and repeat steps 4 and 5.

Puppy Fetch

Although most puppies love to run after a toy you have thrown, some puppies will run off with a toy instead of bringing it back to you. "Puppy Fetch" is a great game to exercise your puppy, have fun and encourage him to bring toys back to you.

The "Puppy Fetch" game allows puppies to learn to retrieve objects in a distraction-free environment. With this game, the puppy doesn't have a chance

to run away with a toy and because he trades a toy for a treat, he is motivated to bring the toy straight back to you. For additional information on training your puppy to exchange toys for treats, see the "Give and Take" game (page 156).

As your puppy becomes more familiar with Puppy Fetch, you can add distractions and play outside with your puppy on a yardline (page 44) or long leash.

Preparing for Puppy Fetch

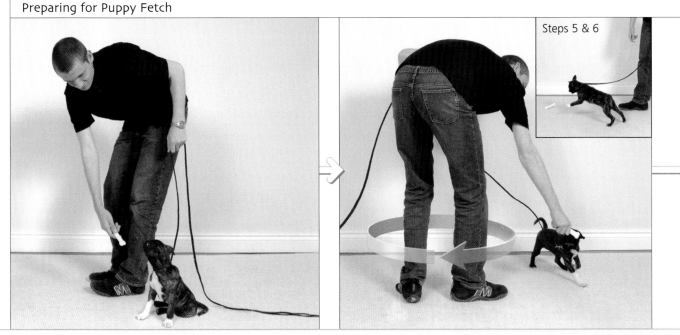

Steps 5 & 6

- To teach your puppy the "Puppy Fetch" game, you must first teach him how to pick up and give you a toy that you have thrown.

1 Attach a houseline (see page 44) to your puppy's collar.

2 With your puppy by your left side, hold one of his favorite toys in your right hand and the houseline in your left hand.

3 Get your puppy interested in the toy by holding it 6 inches in front of his nose and shaking it.

4 When your puppy moves toward the toy, turn in place to the right while continuing to shake the toy to encourage your puppy to follow it.

5 Once you complete a 360-degree turn, gently toss the toy several feet in front of you. Do not throw the toy farther than the length of the houseline.

6 Follow your puppy closely as he chases the toy so that the houseline remains loose.

How long do I have to continue following my puppy after throwing the toy?

Once your puppy has mastered "Puppy Fetch" and is bringing you the toy when you back up away from him, you can stop turning in a circle before throwing the toy and you can stop following your puppy. Simply say "Bring It" as soon as you toss the toy and allow your puppy to bring the toy back to you.

What should I do if my puppy drops the toy on the floor before I take it?

If your puppy drops the toy, nudge it with your foot—this may encourage him to pick it up again. You can also pick up the toy and offer it to your puppy. When he accepts it, take the toy back from him in exchange for a treat. This helps teach your puppy that to earn a reward he must deliver the toy to your hands. Make sure the toy is small enough for your puppy's mouth, as he may drop a toy that is too big.

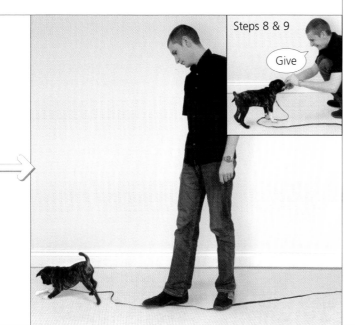

Steps 8 & 9 — Give

Puppy Fetch

Bring It

7 When your puppy reaches the toy, drop the houseline and place your foot on the houseline. The houseline should remain loose and will prevent your puppy from running off with the toy.

8 When your puppy picks up the toy, immediately say "Give."

9 Take hold of the toy with your right hand while offering a treat with your left hand.

10 When your puppy releases the toy to eat the treat, take the toy.

• When your puppy is successfully giving you the toy when you follow him, you can introduce the "Bring It" command and have him bring the toy to you.

1 Perform steps 1 to 6.

2 When your puppy reaches the toy, take a few steps backward. Make sure that the houseline remains loose.

3 When your puppy steps toward you, say "Bring It" and praise him.

4 When your puppy gets to you, say "Give" and then perform steps 9 and 10.

Where's Your Tummy?

The "Where's Your Tummy?" trick helps your puppy feel comfortable with showing his tummy and also helps to build trust between you and your puppy. A puppy usually won't expose his tummy unless he trusts the person he is with and feels safe in his surroundings, so be patient if your puppy is initially reluctant to perform this trick.

You can start teaching "Where's Your Tummy?" once your puppy has mastered the Down command (page 140). The best place to practice this trick is in a familiar environment with few distractions and carpeting to cushion your puppy's body.

Puppies that are susceptible to bloat or have spine or joint problems should avoid this trick. If you think that your puppy's health may interfere with his ability to enjoy this trick, consult your veterinarian.

Where's Your Tummy?

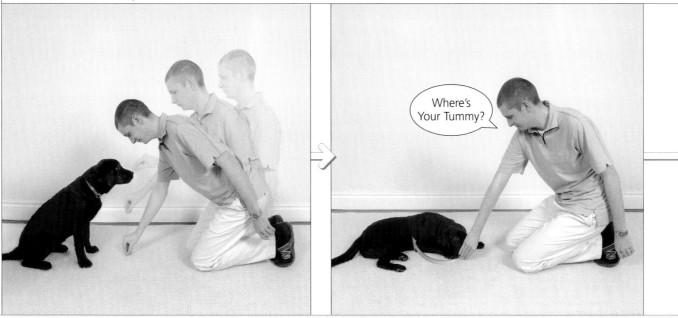

1 Kneel on the floor facing your puppy, with your puppy in the Sit position (see page 138).

2 Hold a treat in your right hand, with your palm facing the floor.

3 Hold the treat close to your puppy's nose and move the treat down to the floor, slightly in front of your puppy's front paws.

Note: Try to keep the treat within easy sniffing distance of your puppy's nose.

• As your puppy's nose follows the treat and he lies on the floor, his back legs may be positioned to one side of his body.

4 In a circular motion, move the treat back along your puppy's body on the side where his back legs are.

Note: If your puppy's back legs are tucked under him, you can move the treat along either side of his body to encourage him to shift onto one hip.

5 When your puppy turns his head to follow the treat, say "Where's Your Tummy?"

Can I use this trick to teach my puppy to roll over?

The "Where's Your Tummy?" trick is a great way to introduce your puppy to the "Roll Over" trick, which teaches your puppy to roll from one side to the other. Perform steps 1 to 8 below, but say the command "Roll Over" instead of "Where's Your Tummy?" in step 5. Also, instead of giving your puppy a treat when he is on his back in step 7, continue to move the treat around to the other side of his body. When he has finished the roll, reward him with the treat.

My puppy won't roll on his back and show his tummy. What should I do?

If your puppy is having problems learning the "Where's Your Tummy?" trick, you can break the trick down into smaller steps to make it easier for your puppy to understand what you want him to do. When your puppy successfully performs a step, like turning his head to follow the treat, reward him with a treat and move on to the next step of the trick. Keep working this way until your puppy has learned the whole trick.

Advancing the Trick

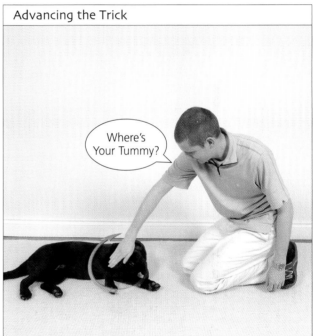

Where's Your Tummy?

6 Continuing in the circular motion, move the treat up around your puppy's head, keeping the treat close to his body.

● Your puppy should turn his head and shoulders to try to reach the treat.

7 When your puppy rolls over onto his back, give him the treat and rub his tummy with your other hand.

8 Give your puppy the release word (see page 137) and allow him to get up.

● Once your puppy can easily roll onto his back by following a treat, start making the hand motions in steps 2 to 6 without a treat in your right hand. When your puppy rolls onto his back, give him a treat from your left hand.

● When your puppy is reliably following your hand signals, gradually increase the length of time your puppy lies on his back before you give him the treat.

Puppy Ping Pong

Puppy Ping Pong is a fun way to practice the Come command (see page 142) and reinforce your puppy's ability to find you. This game is appropriate for all breeds and temperaments.

In this game, your puppy is like a canine ping pong ball going back and forth between two people. This game is tons of fun to play, but if your puppy becomes overexcited, such as barking excessively or jumping up on you, you should wait until he calms down before continuing.

You can start playing this game once your puppy has learned the Come command. Puppy Ping Pong can be played once or twice a day, but make sure that you don't play on hard or slippery surfaces.

Puppy Ping Pong

- Puppy Ping Pong strengthens your puppy's response to the Come command and helps to expend some of your puppy's energy. See page 142 for information on the Come command.

1 Attach a houseline (see page 44) to your puppy's collar. Allow the houseline to drag on the floor behind your puppy.

2 Stand on one side of a large, carpeted room.

3 Have a helper take your puppy to the opposite side of the room.

4 Call your puppy with the Come command.

5 Praise your puppy as he comes running toward you.

- If your puppy does not respond to the Come command, try whistling or talking to him excitedly. Do not repeat the Come command.

6 When your puppy gets to you, reward him with a treat.

What if my puppy does not respond to the Come command even with extra encouragement?

If your puppy does not respond to the Come command, it is a sign that he needs more practice with the command. You should practice the Come command with your puppy over shorter distances and with fewer distractions. Once your puppy starts consistently responding to the Come command, you can try to play Puppy Ping Pong again over short distances and with minimal distractions.

How can I make this game more challenging for my puppy?

Once your puppy is familiar with the game, you and your helper can stand in separate rooms. Your puppy will enjoy the extra challenge of seeking you out, but you should avoid allowing your puppy to rush up stairs until he is physically mature. Also, remember to call your puppy with the Come command only once. You can encourage him to come to you by whistling or speaking excitedly as he approaches you.

Variations

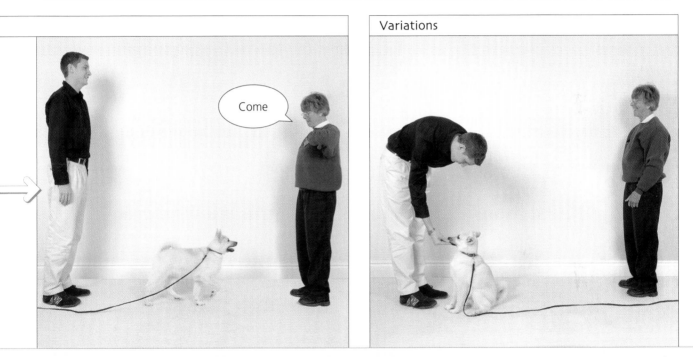

7 After your puppy has finished eating his treat, have your helper call the puppy with the Come command.

8 As the puppy runs back across the room, your helper should verbally praise the puppy.

9 When your puppy gets to your helper, your helper should reward him with a treat.

10 After your puppy has finished eating his treat, repeat steps 4 to 9 two more times.

• You can also use this game to reinforce the Sit command by having your puppy sit before receiving his treat in steps 6 and 9. See page 138 for information on the Sit command.

• Once your puppy is used to playing Puppy Ping Pong indoors, you can try playing outdoors in a large, fenced yard with your puppy wearing a yardline.

Note: For information on yardlines, refer to page 44.

Targeting Tricks

The "Touch It" and "Ring the Bell" tricks teach your puppy to target, or touch, an item with his nose. "Touch It" teaches puppies to touch people's hands instead of nipping at them. This trick is also useful for regaining your puppy's attention in distracting environments since you can use the "Touch It" command to get him to focus on you.

You can start teaching "Touch It" right after you bring your puppy home, but keep the lessons short and fun. As you practice, gradually move your hand further away from your puppy's nose. Eventually he should respond to the command from across the room.

"Ring the Bell," a variation of "Touch It," may be too exciting for some puppies at first. If your puppy can't resist biting the bell, try waiting until he is calm and attempt the trick again.

Touch It

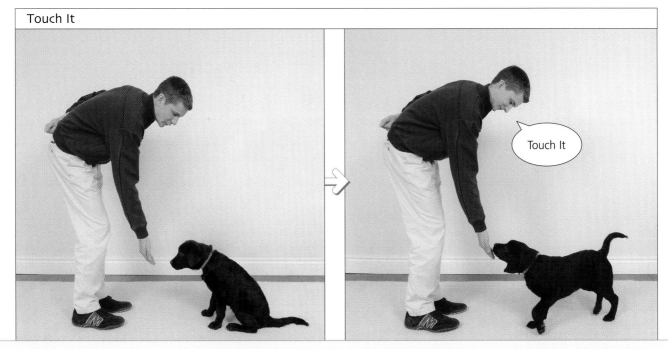

Touch It

- The "Touch It" trick teaches your puppy to focus his attention and bump a target with his nose.

1 Place a treat in your left hand.

2 Stand in front of your puppy with your left hand behind your back.

3 Place your right hand about 4 inches in front of your puppy's nose, with your palm facing the puppy and your fingers pointing down.

4 Say the command "Touch It."

5 Encourage your puppy to investigate the palm of your right hand by looking directly at your hand. Do not make eye contact with your puppy.

6 When your puppy touches the palm of your hand with his nose, praise him and give him the treat from your left hand.

7 Repeat steps 1 to 6 three more times.

Tip

How can I incorporate the "Touch It" trick into the rest of my puppy's training?

You can use the "Touch It" trick to distract your puppy from doing something undesirable. For example, if your puppy is about to chew the legs of a coffee table, have him perform the "Touch It" trick and bump your hand with his nose instead. You can also use "Touch It" to refocus an over-stimulated puppy. For example, if your puppy wants to chase a distant squirrel, having him perform the "Touch It" trick makes him concentrate on you instead.

Tip

How can I advance the "Ring the Bell" trick?

When your puppy consistently rings the bell in response to the "Touch It" command, you can start moving the bell further and further away from your puppy's nose until you are on the other side of the room. You can also hang the bell from a doorknob and direct your puppy to ring the bell when you give him the "Touch It" command.

Ring the Bell

- When your puppy consistently performs the "Touch It" trick, you can try the "Ring the Bell" trick.

- For this trick, you will need a large, jingle-type bell securely attached to a piece of heavy string.

1 Stand in front of your puppy. Holding the string, hang the bell 4 inches in front of your puppy's nose.

2 Say the command "Touch It."

3 When your puppy sniffs and touches the bell with his nose, praise him and give him a treat.

- If your puppy seems disinterested, encourage him to investigate the bell by pointing towards the bell with your other hand.

Note: If your puppy bites the bell, take the bell away for 15 seconds and then repeat steps 1 to 3.

4 Repeat steps 1 to 3 three more times and then put the bell away.

Walk With Me

Although this game teaches your puppy to walk without pulling on his leash, you don't actually hold the leash while playing. As you play "Walk With Me," your puppy will earn treats when you start to walk alone and he decides to follow you. Once your puppy has learned to stay close to you when you're not holding the leash, it will be easier for him to do the same thing during regular walks, when you are holding the leash.

You can start playing this game as soon as your puppy is comfortable wearing a collar. Start in a room that is closed-off and distraction-free. When you finish playing, give your puppy lots of praise and introduce a different activity, like feeding him his meal.

Walk With Me

1 Attach a leash to your puppy's collar.

• Allow the leash to drag behind your puppy. Do not hold the leash.

2 Stand beside your puppy and give him a treat.

3 When your puppy has finished eating the treat, slowly walk away from your puppy. Do not call him or otherwise encourage him to follow you.

4 When your puppy follows you, stop as soon as he catches up to you. Give him a treat and plenty of praise.

• If your puppy does not follow you at first, do not call him. Instead, keep walking around. Your puppy's curiosity should eventually compel him to walk toward you.

My puppy won't follow me. What should I do?

Make sure that you play "Walk With Me" when your puppy is hungry, well-rested and alert. You can even take a couple of handfuls of his food to use as treats and play the game right before your puppy's mealtime. Unless there are distractions while you are playing or your puppy is full or sleepy, there's no reason why your puppy won't love this game.

How can I advance this game?

After your puppy has become used to playing "Walk With Me" inside the house, you can try taking the game outdoors. It's a good idea to start teaching the game in a quiet, fenced area, like a backyard, that will have only minimal distractions. When you play "Walk With Me" outside, make sure you attach a yardline (see page 44) instead of a leash to your puppy's collar. The yardline will allow you to better control your puppy if there are any unexpected distractions outside.

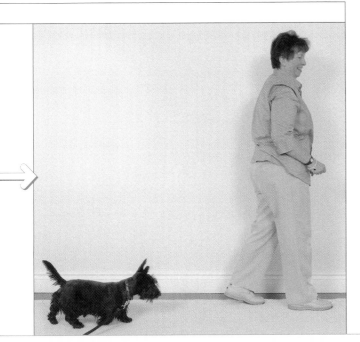

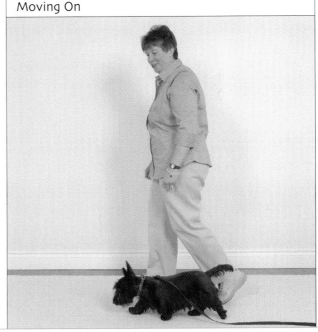

Moving On

5 When your puppy has finished eating the treat, slowly walk away from your puppy in a different direction.

6 When your puppy follows you, stop as soon as he catches up to you. Give him a treat and plenty of praise.

- If your puppy runs ahead of you, immediately turn and walk in a different direction.

7 Repeat steps 5 and 6 four or five more times. Then remove the leash from your puppy's collar and end the game.

- Once your puppy is following you reliably, you can walk at a normal pace and gradually begin to increase the distance you walk before stopping to give him a treat and praise.

- Eventually, your puppy should walk happily at your side with or without a leash.

Gimme Five

As most puppies can learn the "Gimme Five" trick fairly quickly, it's an easy way for your puppy to earn treats and for you to reinforce your leadership.

To help prevent your puppy from pawing you for attention once he has mastered the "Gimme Five" trick, make sure you ignore him if he paws you when you have not given him the "Gimme Five" command.

After your puppy has learned "Gimme Five" with his left paw, you can teach him to perform the trick with his right paw by using your right hand to hold the treat and extending your left hand beneath your puppy's right paw.

Training with a Treat

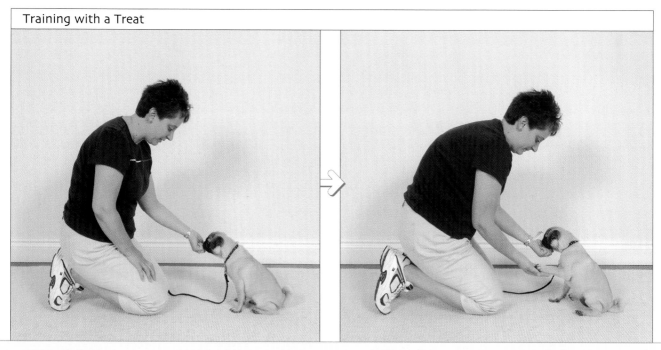

1 Attach a houseline (see page 44) to your puppy's collar.

2 Kneel on the floor facing your puppy, with your puppy in the Sit position (see page 138).

3 Hold a treat in your left hand, with your palm facing upward and your fingers closed around the treat.

4 Place your closed left hand in front of your puppy's nose.

5 Move your left hand to the left.

- As your puppy moves his head to follow the treat, his left paw will lift off the floor.

6 Place your right hand, fingers extended and palm up, underneath your puppy's left paw so his paw touches your palm.

7 Immediately give your puppy the treat and praise him.

How high can I expect my puppy to raise his paw?

Your puppy's shoulder structure and the length of his legs will determine how high he is able to lift his paw when performing this trick. If your puppy can't lift his paw very high, you may have to kneel down low when teaching him the "Gimme Five" trick. As your puppy grows, you can gradually progress from kneeling to crouching or standing, depending on your puppy's size.

Can I use the "Gimme Five" trick to teach my puppy to shake a paw?

Once your puppy has learned the "Gimme Five" trick, you can start teaching him how to shake a paw. Follow the steps on page 173 for "Gimme Five," but instead of only touching your puppy's paw, you should gently hold his paw for a second before releasing it. Gradually increase the length of time that you hold your puppy's paw and start to gently shake his paw. Also, use the command "Shake a Paw" instead of "Gimme Five."

The Command and Hand Signal

- When your puppy is regularly raising his paw as he follows the treat, you can repeat steps 1 to 7 on page 172 and begin saying the command "Gimme Five" at the same time you move the treat in step 5.

- When your puppy is reliably responding when you lure him with a treat and say the "Gimme Five" command, you can stop using the treat to guide your puppy. You can use just the "Gimme Five" command and introduce a hand signal instead.

1 Perform steps 1 and 2 on page 172.

2 Say the command "Gimme Five."

3 Extend your right hand, fingers extended and palm facing up, toward your puppy's left paw. This is the hand signal for "Gimme Five."

4 When your puppy raises his paw to your hand, praise him and give him a treat.

Note: If your puppy does not raise his paw, do not give him a treat and repeat steps 1 to 4. After three unsuccessful attempts, return to training with a treat lure.

Scavenger Hunt

For puppies, mental exercise is just as important as physical exercise. Mentally stimulating games like "Scavenger Hunt" help puppies develop their retrieving skills and strengthen their bond with their owners.

You can start playing "Scavenger Hunt" as soon as your puppy comes home. To make the game easier when your puppy is very young, you should place his toy in a location so that it is still mostly visible.

If your puppy isn't interested in playing this game, he could be tired, distracted or simply not hungry.

Once your puppy has learned to play "Scavenger Hunt" indoors, you can progress to playing outside in a fenced-in area. Playing outdoors is a great way to challenge your puppy because he will have to ignore many distracting sounds and smells and focus on finding his toy.

Scavenger Hunt

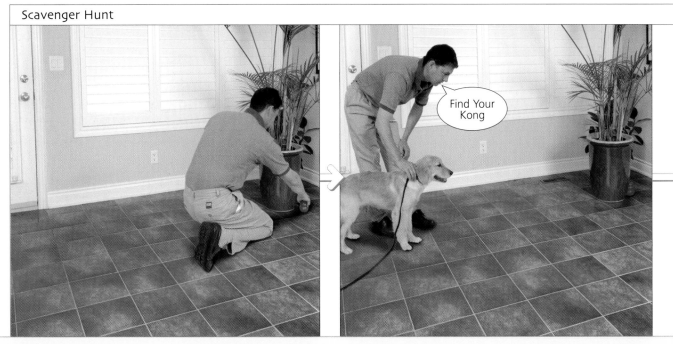

1 Place several treats in a food-stuffable toy, such as a Kong™.

2 Hide the toy in a spot where it will be easy for your puppy to find.

Note: When you first start playing this game, the room where you hide the toy should have very few distractions.

3 Attach a houseline (see page 44) to your puppy's collar.

4 Bring your puppy into the room where you have hidden the toy.

5 Say "Find Your" followed by the name of the toy you have hidden. For example, if you have hidden a Kong™, say "Find Your Kong."

Is there a different way to play the Scavenger Hunt game?

After your puppy has learned how to play "Scavenger Hunt," you can teach him how to find people instead of a toy. To tell your puppy who you want him to find, say "Find," followed by the hider's name. If your puppy is unsure of what you want him to do, you can help your puppy to find the person or have the hider call out to your puppy.

What other searching games can I play with my puppy?

Once your puppy knows how to find a toy, you can teach him to search for his supper. First, take half of your puppy's meal and divide it into several small portions. Next, create a trail of small piles of food in your house or yard that leads to your puppy's food bowl, which contains the other half of his meal. Bring your puppy to the start of the trail, say "Find Your Supper" and encourage him to follow the trail to his dinner.

Advancing the Game

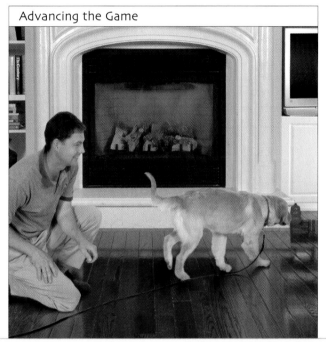

6 Allow your puppy to use his sense of smell to search for the toy.

Note: If your puppy seems unsure of what to do, help him find the toy by walking toward and pointing to the toy. Give your puppy plenty of encouragement.

7 When your puppy finds the toy, praise him enthusiastically and allow him to eat the treats inside the toy.

• Once your puppy can reliably find a food-stuffed toy in an easy-to-find hiding spot, begin hiding the toy in more difficult spots and other rooms around the house.

• When your puppy can easily find a food-stuffed toy, start hiding a toy that is not stuffed with food. This is more challenging for your puppy since a toy that is not stuffed with food will have less scent for him to follow.

Puppy Dress Up

Believe it or not, dressing your puppy has benefits beyond making him look adorable. This game helps your puppy to better accept being handled and wearing things like bandages and Elizabethan collars, which are funnel-shaped veterinary collars.

This game is best played once your puppy has been introduced to basic handling (see page 117). You'll need a loose-fitting T-shirt and pair of socks.

The first few times you play, however, you should only dress your puppy in the T-shirt or the socks, but not both.

While playing, don't get frustrated if your puppy doesn't sit perfectly or moves out of the Sit position. This game is all about having fun. Just remember to praise your puppy calmly throughout the game and be gentle when putting on and removing the clothing.

Putting on a T-shirt

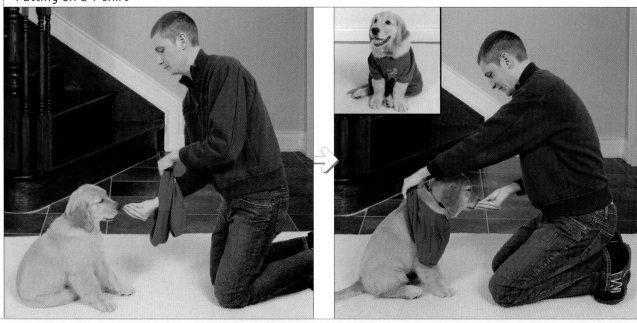

1 Kneel on the floor facing your puppy, with your puppy in the Sit position (see page 138).

2 Roll up the body of a T-shirt and hold it in your left hand.

3 Hold a treat in your right hand with your fingers closed around the treat.

4 Move your right hand through the neck hole of the T-shirt and place your right hand in front of your puppy's nose.

5 While your puppy is sniffing your right hand, gently pull the neck hole of the T-shirt over his head. Then give your puppy the treat and praise him.

6 Unroll the T-shirt down your puppy's body. Then give your puppy another treat and praise him.

7 Gently lift your puppy's left front paw and place it through the left armhole of the T-shirt. Then give your puppy another treat and praise him.

8 Repeat step 7 with his right front paw.

Tip

How long should I keep my puppy dressed up?

Initially, you should only keep your puppy dressed for 10 to 15 seconds at a time. As he becomes used to the game, you can increase the amount of time that your puppy stays dressed. Eventually, he should become completely at ease wearing clothing and you should even be able to practice obedience training while he's dressed. Just remember that your puppy should never be left alone when he is dressed up as he could chew on the clothing and potentially choke.

Tip

What should I do if my puppy doesn't like being dressed up?

If your puppy struggles when you try to play this game, take things more slowly. For example, instead of pulling the shirt over his head, just encourage him to poke his nose a little way through the neck hole to get a treat. If your puppy starts biting the clothing, give him a chewy treat or some peanut butter to keep his mouth busy. Finally, if you find yourself getting frustrated, just take a break and try again when you are both more relaxed.

Putting on Socks

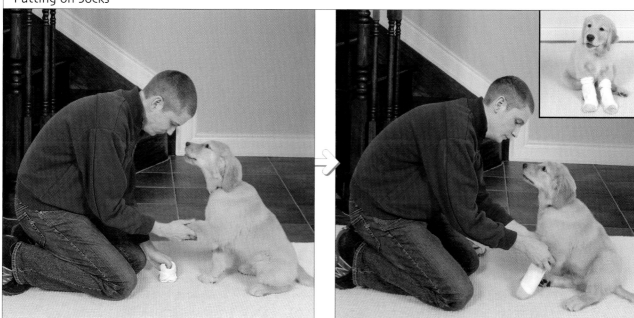

1 Kneel on the floor facing your puppy, with your puppy in the Sit position (see page 138).

2 Roll one sock down to the heel and hold it in your left hand.

3 Using your right hand, gently lift your puppy's left front paw and place his paw inside the rolled-up sock.

4 Let your puppy put his paw back on the ground. Then give him a treat and praise him.

Note: When you place your puppy's paw inside the sock, be careful not to catch his claws.

5 Slowly unroll the sock up your puppy's leg. Then give your puppy a treat and praise him.

6 Repeat steps 2 to 5 with his right front paw.

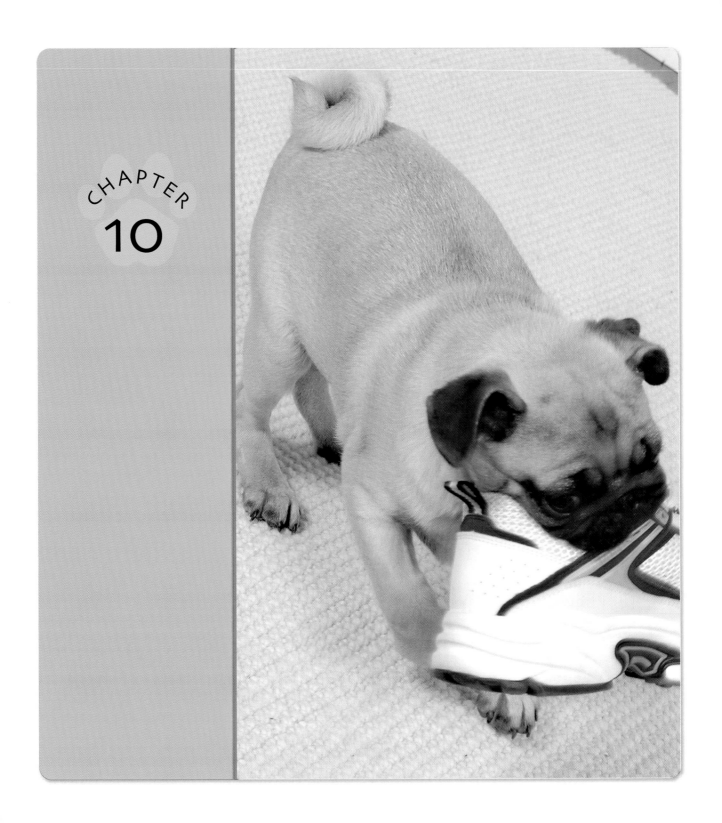

Preventing
Problem Behaviors

Doorway Manners

Prevent Begging

Dealing With Your Puppy's Nipping

Prevent Destructive Chewing

Prevent Jumping Up

Prevent Unnecessary Barking

Teach Your Puppy to Be Alone

Prevent Possessive Food Behavior

Prevent Aggressive Behavior

Doorway Manners

Teaching your puppy good doorway manners can mean the difference between a pet who waits calmly to go outside and one who runs through every open door. A puppy that tries to escape when the door is opened can easily become lost or get hurt if he runs out into the street.

Teaching your puppy to restrain himself is the best way to control his behavior at doorways that lead outside. Restraining a puppy by holding his collar will only make him frustrated and can actually encourage aggressive behavior. Once your puppy has mastered the Sit command (page 138), you can use this command to maintain control of your puppy near doorways. Your puppy will eventually learn that sitting still is rewarded with a trip outside and he will start to sit automatically by any doorway.

Doorway Manners

- When you start teaching your puppy to wait before going through a doorway, practice on a doorway within your house.

1 Attach a leash to your puppy's collar.

2 Give your puppy the Sit command (see page 138).

3 When your puppy is sitting, open the door and step through the doorway.

   Note: If your puppy gets up, immediately close the door. Help him back into the Sit position and then perform step 3.

4 Say your release word (see page 137) and encourage your puppy to come through the doorway.

5 When your puppy is through the doorway, give the Sit command again.

6 When your puppy is sitting, give him praise and a treat. Then say the release word.

- When your puppy is reliably sitting before and after going through doorways inside the house, practice these steps using doors that lead outside.

Prevent Begging

Believe it or not, puppies learn to beg thanks to their owners. When you feed your puppy at your mealtime, or any time you eat, you reinforce the idea that he can have some of whatever you are eating. You can stop begging before it becomes a bad habit by ignoring your puppy when he begs for your food. Resisting these demands will also strengthen your leadership position.

By refusing to feed your puppy during or after your meals, he will learn that your food is off-limits and he will eventually ignore people who are eating. When you are entertaining guests who don't know the rules, keep your puppy away from the table. This will prevent him from eating dropped food or sneaking a treat from a well-meaning guest.

Prevent Begging

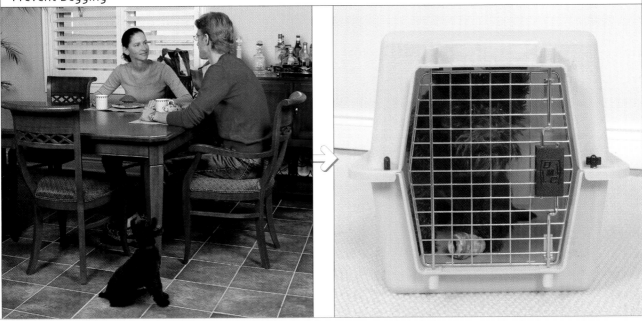

- Puppies beg to try to obtain the food you are eating.

- A begging puppy may sit beside you, drooling, whining and staring intensely at you while you eat.

- You should never give your puppy food when he is begging. This will only reinforce his begging behavior.

- You should ignore any begging behavior displayed by your puppy.

- To prevent your puppy from developing a habit of begging, keep him away from the table while you are eating.

- Before you sit down for a meal, place your puppy in his crate with a Kong™ or other suitable chew toy.

Note: If your puppy has learned to remain in the Down position with distractions, you can have him lie in the Down position while you eat instead of placing him in his crate. For information on the Down command, see page 140.

Dealing With Your Puppy's Nipping

For puppies, the best way to explore the world around them is to examine every new object by putting it in their mouths. Although nipping and mouthing is normal, young puppies may have difficulty controlling the strength of their bites, especially when they are overexcited.

To help inhibit your puppy's biting, you should teach him to use his mouth only on appropriate objects, such as chew toys. Also, remember to reward your puppy when he uses his mouth appropriately. For example, praise your puppy when he uses his mouth gently to take a toy from you.

Owners can help their puppies learn how to use their mouths gently through bite inhibition training. When they mature, dogs that have learned bite inhibition as puppies are less likely to cause harm if they ever do bite as adults.

Why Puppies Nip

- Nipping, play biting and mouthing are normal behavior for puppies.

- This puppy behavior allows your puppy to learn about the world around him and learn about the strength of his bite.

- Your puppy is not misbehaving when he nips or mouths you or your possessions.

- Remember that nipping and mouthing is just part of a stage in your puppy's development.

- Try to remain calm and patient until your puppy grows out of the nipping stage.

Tip

Should I punish my puppy in response to nipping or mouthing?

You should never physically punish your puppy if he nips or mouths you. For example, if you respond to nipping by shaking your puppy or holding his muzzle, you will only frighten your puppy or make him more excited, which can make the nipping worse. Instead, you should remove yourself from his reach and calmly redirect his attention to a chew toy.

Tip

When will my puppy's nipping and mouthing end?

Your puppy's nipping and mouthing should taper off sharply once he has finished teething. When your puppy is about three to four months old, his adult teeth will start to replace his puppy teeth. When he is about six or seven months old, your puppy should have all his adult teeth. Try to be patient and sensible during this stage and remember that your puppy will eventually grow out of this behavior.

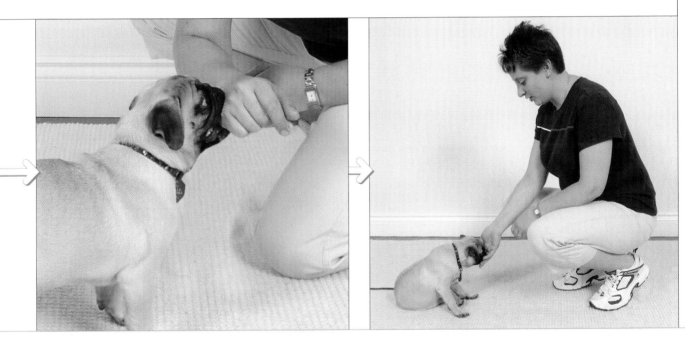

- Puppies have sharp teeth, so their nipping and mouthing can hurt, but it usually will not cause serious pain or injury.
- A puppy may nip more when he is excited.
- To avoid getting your puppy overly excited, remember to avoid inappropriate play with him. Do not play wrestling, chasing, teasing or tugging games with your puppy.
- You can teach your puppy to use his mouth softly, or "inhibit" his bite.
- Puppies begin learning bite inhibition when they are still with their littermates and their mother.
- When you bring your puppy home, you can continue his bite inhibition training and teach him that nipping is not acceptable.
- See page 184 for ways to deal with your puppy's nipping and mouthing.

CONTINUED

Dealing With Your Puppy's Nipping continued

There are a few simple ways to teach your puppy bite inhibition and appropriate chewing behaviors. First, don't allow your puppy to tug on clothing or toys when you are playing with him. You can help to discourage tugging by praising your puppy when he releases an object he has tried to tug.

Second, you should attach a houseline or a leash to your puppy's collar so that if your puppy nips,

you can use the houseline or leash to gently guide your puppy away from you. See page 44 for information on houselines and page 43 for information on leashes.

Lastly, make sure to give your puppy plenty of chew toys—it's important that your puppy has an appropriate way to satisfy his desire to chew.

No Tug-of-War

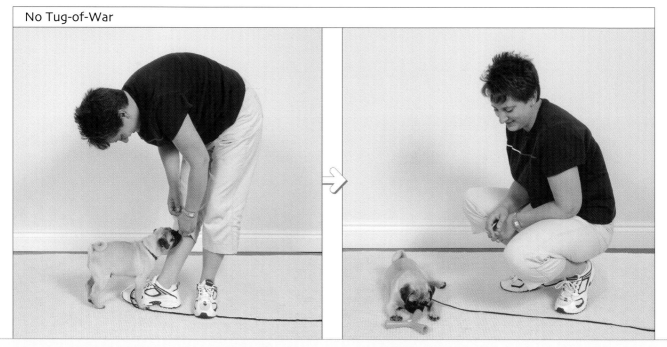

- When your puppy grabs your clothes with his teeth and tries to play tug-of-war, you must show him that this is not acceptable behavior.

1 Gently remove the item that he is tugging from his mouth.

Note: If your puppy has a houseline attached to his collar, you can use the houseline to gently restrain the puppy. See page 44 for information on houselines.

2 Immediately give the puppy an appropriate chew toy to redirect his behavior.

Note: You should have a chew toy handy whenever you are with your puppy. You can use the chew toy to redirect his behavior any time he starts nipping or chewing inappropriately.

- If your puppy tugs or chews on his houseline or leash, spray the houseline or leash, when it is not attached to your puppy's collar, with a bitter-tasting spray.

Note: You can purchase bitter-tasting spray from your local pet supply store.

Are there any tricks or games that can help teach my puppy bite inhibition?

Tip

The "Touch It" trick helps teach puppies bite inhibition. In this trick, puppies are rewarded for touching your hand and other objects, rather than mouthing them. See page 168 for information on the "Touch It" trick. The "Get It" game helps teach puppies to use their mouths gently. If a puppy tries to snatch a treat from you, he won't be rewarded. See page 160 for information on the "Get It" game.

 What else can I do to manage my puppy's nipping behavior?

Tip

The best way to manage your puppy's nipping is to think ahead. Try to anticipate what situations will make your puppy overexcited and more likely to nip and remove him from those situations. For example, if your puppy nips at your children when they return from school, put him in his crate before they are scheduled to arrive home.

Ouch!

- You can teach your puppy not to nip you.

1 When your puppy nips you, immediately say "Ouch!" in a firm voice.

2 Stand and turn your back to your puppy.

3 After standing still for 20 seconds, return your attention to your puppy.

4 You can give your puppy a chew toy to redirect him from nipping you again.

- Repeat steps 1 to 3 each time your puppy nips you.

Note: If your puppy does not pay attention when you say "Ouch" in step 1, try using a louder voice or lower tone the next time you perform the steps.

- If your puppy nips you three times in a row, give your puppy a command that he has mastered, such as Sit (see page 138). Then reward your puppy with a safe chew toy and place him into his crate for some quiet time to chew on the toy.

Prevent Destructive Chewing

If there's one thing puppies are known for, it's their ability to destroy expensive shoes in a matter of minutes. Puppies chew for many reasons—teething, instinct and to explore their surroundings. You can better control your puppy's chewing through supervision, puppy proofing your house and giving your puppy appropriate chew toys. Be clear about what things your puppy is allowed to chew. Don't let him chew an old slipper if you don't want him eating your new shoes because he can't tell the difference.

Make sure your puppy always has access to safe chew toys. His desire to chew may fade over time, but chew toys will keep his teeth clean and exercise his jaws. Consult your veterinarian before giving your puppy edible toys like rawhide bones.

Prevent Destructive Chewing

- Puppies chew for many different reasons. They chew on items in their environment to learn about the objects, just the way a baby automatically puts objects in his mouth to learn about them.

- Puppies also chew when they are bored and when they have too much energy from not getting enough exercise.

- As your puppy's owner, it is your job to teach your puppy about the items he is allowed to chew and keep inappropriate items out of his reach.

- Puppies also go through teething periods between 3 and 7 months of age.

- When your puppy is teething and trying to chew everything in sight, remember that this is just a phase and it will not last forever.

- During teething, make sure your puppy has appropriate things to chew, such as a Kong™ or other puppy-safe teething toys.

- Teething puppies may also enjoy chewing a rope bone that has been soaked in water and then frozen.

How can I safely help my puppy into the Sit position when he is too excited to comply on his own?

Tip

To help your puppy into the Sit position, pull up gently on his collar or leash with one hand while lightly guiding his rear towards the ground with your other hand. The teeter-totter motion of your puppy's head coming up while his rear comes down will take the pressure off your puppy's hips. Once your puppy is seated, release all tension on the collar or leash. Avoid pushing straight down on your puppy's rear as this can injure and frighten him.

My puppy has not yet mastered the Sit command. What can I do to prevent him from jumping up on visitors?

Tip

You should place your puppy in his crate before your visitors arrive. Once they have settled in, you can attach a leash to your puppy's collar and practice the Sit command away from the guests. Gradually bring your puppy closer to the guests, give him the Sit command and ask one of your guests to calmly pat your puppy. This will help your puppy learn that when he sits nicely he will be rewarded with attention.

Jumping Up on Visitors

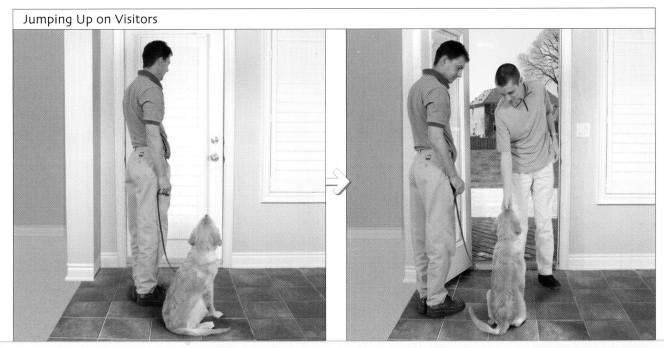

- Even if you have a tiny dog, you should teach your puppy not to jump up on people at the door. Even a small dog jumping up could cause injury by tripping someone or knocking them off balance.

1 When a visitor comes to your door, before opening the door, attach your puppy's leash to his collar.

2 Give the Sit command (see page 138).

3 When your puppy is sitting, open the door and ask the visitor to enter.

4 Ask the visitor to give your puppy a treat while he is sitting.

- If your puppy jumps up, ask your visitor to turn away from your puppy and ignore him until he stops jumping up. Then perform steps 2 and 3 on page 188.

CONTINUED

Prevent Jumping Up continued

Your puppy may look cute snuggled up with the couch cushions, but after a few months of vacuuming puppy fur, you may regret letting him up there in the first place. The best way to keep your puppy off the furniture is to make it off limits from day one. Supervision is also important—you should always know where your puppy is so he doesn't try to climb onto the sofa when you're not looking.

Some puppies, especially larger breeds, love to put their paws and noses up on the kitchen counter in search of food. You can discourage this behavior by making sure your puppy never gets the chance to steal a treat from the countertop. This will prevent him from thinking of the counter as a place to look for food.

Jumping Up on Furniture

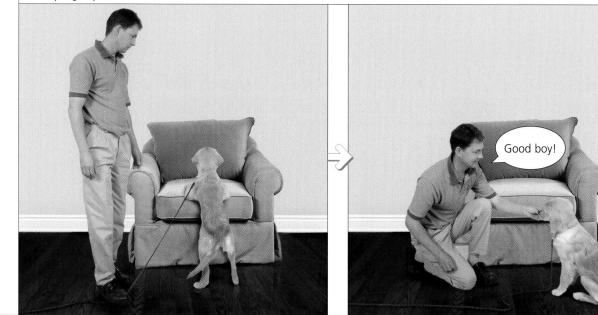

Good boy!

- Before you bring your new puppy home, you should determine whether the puppy will be allowed up on the furniture.

- If you do not want your puppy to jump up on your furniture, you must never invite him up onto the furniture.

1 To prevent your puppy from jumping up on your furniture when you are able to supervise the puppy, attach a houseline (see page 44) to his collar.

2 If your puppy attempts to jump up on the furniture, step on the houseline to prevent him from jumping.

3 When your puppy moves away from the furniture, praise him and give him a treat.

- When you are unable to supervise your puppy, you should place him in his crate.

Note: If your puppy is housetrained, you can create a cozy place for him to relax, such as a dog bed, so he does not feel the need to get up on your furniture.

My small puppy puts his front paws up on the coffee table. What should I do?

Tip

Make sure there isn't anything edible or interesting on your coffee table and supervise your puppy so he doesn't have the chance to steal things from the top of the table. When puppies are able to find delicious treats on a table, they will usually go back for more. You can also attach a houseline (see page 44) to your puppy's collar so if he puts his front paws up on the table, you can use the houseline to gently guide him off.

Is there anything else I can do to deter my puppy from jumping up on the counter?

Tip

Once your puppy has mastered the Down command (page 140), you can use this command to keep him off the counter. To practice, give your puppy the Down command and pretend to prepare food on the countertop. Your puppy should gradually learn to remain in the Down position while you cook. You can also place a wide strip of double-sided tape along your counter's edge. The tape helps deter your puppy from jumping up because it feels sticky and strange when he touches it with his paws.

Jumping Up on the Counter

- People spend time standing at the kitchen counter preparing food, so puppies cannot help being interested in what is on the counter.

- Large breeds of puppies may be tempted to jump up and put their paws on the counter so they can get a better view. This is often called counter-surfing.

- To prevent your puppy from being able to get food off the counter, keep items such as the fruit bowl or cookie jar pushed well back from the edge of the counter so the puppy cannot reach them.

1 To prevent your puppy from jumping up on the counter when he is in the kitchen with you, attach a houseline (see page 44) to his collar.

2 If your puppy attempts to jump up on the counter, use the houseline to gently guide him back to the floor. Do not speak to or touch your puppy as you guide him down.

3 When your puppy moves away from the counter, praise him.

- When you are unable to supervise your puppy, you should place him in his crate.

Prevent Unnecessary Barking

Whoever said that a dog's bark is worse than his bite knew what he was talking about. Not only can excessive barking upset your neighbors, it is also a hard habit to break.

Barking is a natural puppy behavior, although some breeds bark more than others. Excessive barking is often caused by loneliness. When puppies are frequently left alone they can become bored, stressed and are more likely to bark around the house and even in their crates.

For information on dealing with puppies who bark in their crates, see the top of page 71.

You can help prevent unnecessary barking by providing your puppy with many opportunities to experience new people, sights and sounds. Another way to discourage barking is to ignore the behavior. Giving a puppy attention when he barks, even undesirable attention like raising your voice, only helps to reinforce the behavior.

Prevent Unnecessary Barking

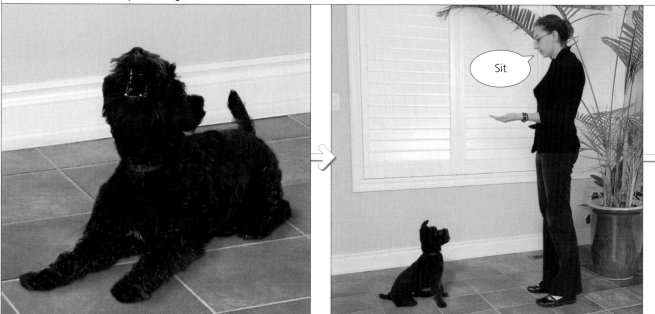

- Puppies bark for a number of reasons. Barking is a natural form of communication for puppies and it is usually acceptable if it is not excessive.

- Your puppy may bark when he is lonely or wants your attention.

- If your puppy barks, do not give him your attention. Do not talk to, shout at or touch your puppy. This form of extra attention rewards your puppy for barking.

  Note: Remember that even scolding your puppy for barking is giving him attention.

- When your puppy begins to bark, ignore him until he has been quiet for a few seconds. Then work with him on a training command, such as Sit (see page 138).

  Note: Training commands disrupt your puppy's barking and gives him attention on your terms, instead of you responding to his demands.

- Make sure your puppy gets plenty of exercise and play time. A tired puppy is a happy puppy.

- To prevent your puppy from barking due to loneliness outside, do not leave him alone outside.

Is there anything else I can do to help prevent my puppy from barking?

Tip

You may be able to discourage your puppy from excessive barking by having him wear a correctly-fitted Gentle Leader® head collar while he accompanies you around the house. Although the Gentle Leader® is not a muzzle and does not prevent barking, having your puppy wear one may help to calm his desire to bark. Your trainer or veterinarian can provide you with more information about head collars and advise you as to whether or not the Gentle Leader® would benefit your puppy.

How can I prevent my puppy from barking at the window?

Tip

You can prevent your puppy from barking at the window by blocking his access to the area. When a puppy can't see or hear the distractions outside, he won't be as tempted to bark at them. If you are not able to keep your puppy away from the window, you should try to distract him from what is making him bark. Use a houseline (see page 44) to gently move him away from the window or practice the Come command (page 142) to distract him, which should help to stop his barking.

- Your puppy may bark when he is worried or startled, such as when he hears a sudden loud noise.

- Be calm if your puppy seems worried to help him remain calm too.

- Praise your puppy calmly when he is quiet. You can then give your puppy a treat.

- Your puppy may bark when he sees or hears things that are exciting to him, such as when he is out in the yard.

- When socializing your puppy, give him lots of experience with different sights and sounds so he will be used to them.

- If your puppy barks excessively because he is excited by sights and sounds, put him into his crate for 10 minutes to remove him from the distractions.

Teach Your Puppy to Be Alone

When puppies are left alone for long periods of time, they can feel anxious and may engage in destructive behavior. Teaching your puppy to feel safe and comfortable when he is at home alone will help eliminate these problems and is an important part of training. In addition, a structured daily routine for your puppy can help him to feel generally calm.

When you are just about to leave, try not to act overly emotional or guilt-ridden. Your puppy is attuned to your feelings and changes in your behavior can make him nervous and upset.

Never leave a puppy outside when you are not home. He could easily get hurt or stolen while you are away and if the puppy barks excessively it might upset your neighbors.

Teach Your Puppy to Be Alone

- You can teach your puppy to be calm when he is at home alone.

- Separation anxiety starts with a puppy being uncomfortable when he is home alone and may develop into behaviors such as barking, howling, chewing or soiling inside the house.

- Most anxiety behaviors occur within 5 to 10 minutes after you leave the house.

- You should begin teaching your puppy to be comfortable being alone as soon as you bring him home.

- You should get your puppy used to being alone in his crate or long-term confinement area when you are home.

  Note: For information on crate training your puppy, see page 70. For information on long-term confinement areas, see page 80.

- When in his crate or confinement area, give your puppy a stuffed Kong™ or other safe chew toy to keep him occupied and happy.

  Note: If the puppy whines or barks in his crate or confinement area, ignore him as long as you are sure he does not need to relieve himself.

Tip

What else should I do to make it easier for my puppy to be alone?

You can help your puppy to be alone by letting him entertain himself when you are home rather than always giving him your attention. For example, let him chew on a chew toy while you read a book or put him in his crate for short periods of time. If your puppy is used to doing quiet things by himself while you are home, he won't mind as much doing the same when you are out.

Tip

Should I punish my puppy if he has misbehaved in my absence?

If your puppy does misbehave in your absence, he should not be punished when you get home. The puppy may associate your return with punishment, which could make him more anxious the next time he is left alone. A puppy should be left in his crate or long-term confinement area (see page 80) when he is at home alone so that he stays safe and doesn't have a chance to misbehave.

- When you leave your house, keep your departure low-key so your puppy hardly notices that you are gone.

- You should start with short absences when your puppy is very young, since young puppies cannot hold their bladders very long.

- You may want to leave the television or radio on for background noise for your puppy.

- When you arrive home after being away, enter the house quietly. Do not make a big deal of your arrival.

  Note: If you can hear your puppy barking before you enter your house, wait until he is quiet for a few seconds before you enter.

- Ignore the puppy for a few minutes after you enter the house. Then let him out of his crate or confinement area and take him out to his potty area.

Prevent Possessive Food Behavior

Have you ever seen a dog growl, freeze or snap to protect their food? Puppies learn this possessive behavior, also called resource guarding, when they are very young. Some puppies become assertive to protect their food and toys from their littermates.

Most puppies, however, don't behave this way towards people. You can help to avoid potential possessive food behavior if you teach your puppy early on to become comfortable with people around his food bowl. Make sure that you don't respond aggressively to any possessive behavior that your puppy may exhibit. Yelling at your puppy can actually make him more possessive.

If your puppy shows signs of possessiveness, such as freezing or growling, when you are working through these exercises, stop immediately and contact a professional trainer to help you.

Prevent Possessive Food Behavior

- Start working with your puppy as soon as you bring him home to prevent food possession issues.

- Placing treats in your puppy's dish while he is eating teaches him that hands near his food bowl are a good thing.

1 Sitting on the floor, occasionally drop treats, such as small pieces of liver, chicken or cheese, into his food bowl while he is eating.

2 Repeat step 1 three times. Then leave the puppy alone to finish the rest of his meal.

3 Repeat steps 1 and 2 for a few meals.

4 When your puppy shows no sign of being bothered by your hand near his food bowl, repeat steps 1 to 3, except place your hand in the puppy's food bowl and hand-feed him the treats in step 1.

Tip

What are the early signs of possessive food behavior?

Common signs of possessive food behavior include:

✓ rapid eating which gets faster when someone approaches

✓ hunching up or freezing over food or toys when someone approaches

✓ growling

✓ snapping

If your puppy is showing any of these behaviors, you will need the help of a professional. A trainer can work with your puppy and help to modify his behavior.

Tip

Can puppies be possessive of other items besides food?

Puppies can be possessive of anything, such as toys, laundry baskets or even a piece of facial tissue. To prevent this behavior, you need to teach your puppy that everything belongs to you. Control your puppy's access to toys by leaving only a few out at a time. Play the "Give and Take" game (see page 156) to prevent your puppy from being possessive of his toys. Consult a professional trainer if your puppy becomes possessive of furniture, as this could indicate more serious leadership issues.

5 When your puppy shows no sign of being bothered by your hand in his food bowl, gently stroke the puppy's back and sides while he eats out of your hand. Gradually work toward stroking his head as he eats.

6 Repeat step 5 every day until your puppy begins to wag his tail and look up from his bowl when you approach. Continue performing step 5 a few times per week until your puppy is mature and then occasionally throughout your dog's lifetime.

7 In addition to stroking and hand-feeding your puppy, you should occasionally lift up his bowl while he is eating, place a special treat in the bowl and then return the bowl to your puppy.

● When your puppy is completely happy having you touch him and his food bowl, have other adults perform steps 1 to 5.

Note: Children should not perform these steps until the puppy is completely happy with several adults touching his food and never without close adult supervision.

Prevent Aggressive Behavior

Aggressive behavior is much easier to prevent than correct. There are many different reasons why puppies display aggressive behavior, but all aggression should be handled with the help of a professional.

Puppies may use aggressive behavior to escape from a frightening situation. When puppies are not socialized properly they are more likely to be fearful. You can help a fearful puppy to become more confident by gradually introducing him to new people and situations and by rewarding any signs of confidence. You can work to avoid aggressive behavior by using preventative measures as soon as you bring your new puppy home. For information on preventing aggression when your puppy is eating or playing with toys, see page 196.

Prevent Aggressive Behavior

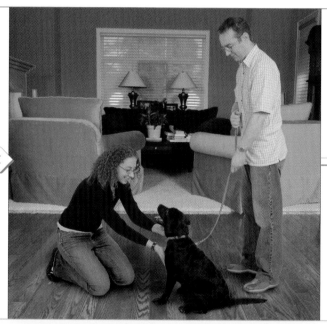

- Dogs show aggression by giving hard stares, growling and biting. Aggression is often the result of a dog feeling stressed or fearful.

- If your puppy shows any signs of real aggression, you have a serious problem that requires the help of a professional trainer.

  Note: You can ask your veterinarian for trainer recommendations.

- The best way to help your puppy be relaxed with all kinds of situations is to be sure he is well socialized when he is a puppy and throughout his life.

  Note: See pages 120 to 125 for information on socialization.

- When socializing your puppy, make sure he has many good experiences with different people and different places.

Should I worry about my puppy being aggressive with other dogs?

Tip

You shouldn't worry when your puppy wrestles with other puppies. This behavior is not truly aggressive, just playful. Although most puppies are not naturally aggressive, you can ensure that your puppy gets along with other dogs by socializing him with other dogs from a young age. Provide safe opportunities for him to meet other dogs, such as puppy classes. If a situation does arise where your puppy encounters an aggressive dog, you should stay calm, use the "Let's Go" command (page 146) and leave.

What else could cause my puppy to show aggression?

Tip

If your normally happy puppy displays signs of aggression, such as growling or snapping, when you touch him, it would be a good idea to have him examined by a veterinarian. You may find that his aggression is not due to a behavior or socialization problem, but is instead caused by a painful health problem.

- A puppy may develop aggression issues when he is unsure of your role as his "pack leader" and feels insecure. There are many ways you can establish your leadership position.

- Begin working on training commands, such as Sit, as soon as you bring your puppy home. Learning to obey your commands will help the puppy see you as his leader.

- Feed your puppy at specified times throughout the day and then take the food bowl away between meals. Your puppy needs to know that his food comes from you.

- Do not leave the puppy's toys out all the time. Instead, provide a few toys at a time and practice taking them away from him with the Give and Take game (see page 156). Your puppy needs to know that the toys he enjoys come from you and he should learn to give them up easily.

- Have your puppy do some work for the things he likes. For example, before you pet him, have him practice a training command first, such as Come (see page 142). Then pet him as praise.

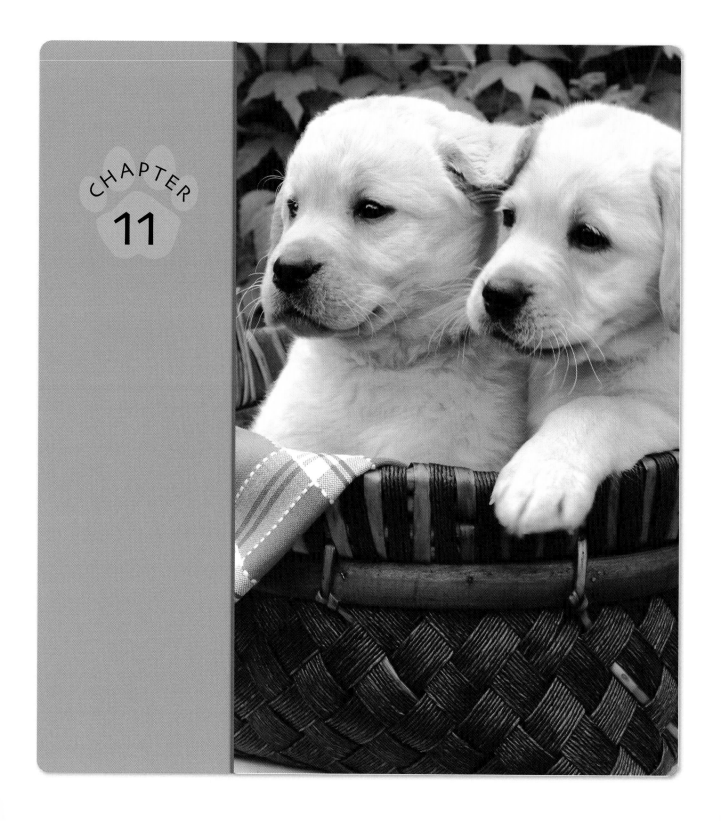

Keeping Your Puppy Healthy

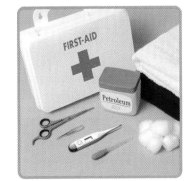

Standard Vaccinations

Fleas and Ticks

Your Puppy's Respiratory Health

Eye and Ear Concerns

Your Puppy's Digestive Health

Heartworms and Intestinal Parasites

Skin Concerns

Spay or Neuter

First-Aid Kit Essentials

Standard Vaccinations

Sometimes the best defense is a good offense. This is especially true when you are trying to protect your puppy's health. Vaccinating your puppy can help prevent serious and potentially fatal diseases like distemper, hepatitis and leptospirosis.

When a puppy is vaccinated, a small amount of the disease organism is injected into the puppy's body.

The puppy's immune system is then prepared to fight off that organism in the future.

Some diseases can be transmitted from puppies to people, so by vaccinating your puppy, you are also protecting the health of your family.

COMMON VACCINES

Talk to your veterinarian to determine which vaccinations your puppy should have. This can vary depending on which diseases are prevalent in your area, your puppy's breed and his risk factors for specific diseases.

Rabies Vaccine

The rabies vaccine is the most commonly administered vaccine. The rabies virus can be transmitted to animals and also to humans.

DHLPP Vaccine

The DHLPP vaccine is commonly administered to puppies. The DHLPP vaccine protects against several different diseases, including distemper, hepatitis, leptospirosis, parvovirus and parainfluenza.

Kennel Cough Vaccine

Your veterinarian may recommend a kennel cough vaccine if your puppy will be around a lot of other dogs. Kennel cough is not fatal, but it can make your puppy feel uncomfortable—much like how a human with a cold feels.

Lyme Disease Vaccine

Lyme disease infections can be quite serious, leading to joint, heart or neurological disease. Your veterinarian may recommend a Lyme disease vaccination if the ticks that carry the disease are found in your area.

SETTING UP A VACCINATION SCHEDULE

Your puppy will need regular vaccinations throughout his life to protect him from infectious diseases. Your veterinarian will set up a vaccination schedule for your puppy and help you determine the best vaccines for him.

Your puppy's vaccination schedule will depend on several factors, including your geographical location and your veterinarian. Some veterinarians may decide to spread vaccinations for different diseases over a few visits, rather than give them together in a single injection.

Most puppies will have their first shots before they leave the breeder. When you pick up your puppy, the breeder should provide you with proof of the vaccinations that you can take to your own veterinarian.

Sample Vaccination Schedule

Age	Vaccination
6 to 8 weeks	DHLPP
10 to 12 weeks	DHLPP
15 to 16 weeks	DHLPP and possibly rabies
Annually	DHLPP
Every 1 to 3 years	Rabies

VACCINES AND LOCAL LAWS

Puppy owners can be required by law to vaccinate their pets against certain diseases. For example, in some areas puppies must be vaccinated against rabies. The laws regarding vaccinations vary from place to place, so make sure you are familiar with local regulations.

YOUR YOUNG PUPPY'S SAFETY

Puppies are not fully vaccinated until they receive their shots around 16 weeks old. When introducing your puppy to other dogs and animals, first make sure the animals are healthy and up to date on their vaccines. You should avoid taking your puppy to public parks and areas visited by other dogs until your veterinarian tells you it is safe to do so.

Fleas and Ticks

Fleas and ticks are rarely more than a nuisance for puppies, but they can spread serious diseases if left unchecked.

Flea bites can irritate your puppy's skin and even transmit tapeworms. Since puppies can pick up fleas anytime they go outside in warm weather, it's a good idea to comb your puppy with a fine-toothed comb after outdoor walks. You can also talk to your veterinarian about using flea-preventative shampoos.

Ticks use dogs as a source of food and dogs can pick up ticks after an outing in the woods or an area known for having ticks. If you see a tick on your puppy, put on latex gloves and remove the tick immediately. The sooner you remove a tick, the less likely it is to give your puppy a serious illness such as Rocky Mountain spotted fever or Lyme disease. Consult your veterinarian if you notice any redness or swelling around a tick bite.

Fleas

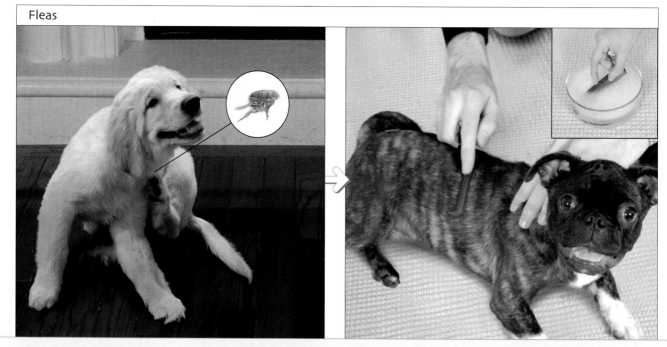

- Fleas are tiny insects that get into a puppy's coat and feed on the puppy's blood, causing intense itching.

- Puppies can pick up fleas almost anywhere. Fleas can jump onto your puppy from grass, carpets or even other dogs.

- If your puppy begins to scratch or lick himself excessively, you should check him for fleas.

- To examine your puppy for fleas, use your hands to part his fur and check his skin for fleas or flea dirt. Flea dirt looks like specks of black pepper.

1 To remove fleas from your puppy, thoroughly comb his coat with a fine-toothed comb.

2 As you comb the fleas off of your puppy, dip the comb in soapy water to drown the fleas.

3 To kill any fleas that you missed while combing your puppy, bathe him using a flea-killing shampoo. See page 108 for information on bathing your puppy.

Note: Ask your veterinarian to recommend a flea-killing shampoo that is appropriate for your puppy's age and weight.

How do I clean up my house after a flea infestation?

Tip

If you have found fleas on your puppy, it's likely that your home could be infested. Fleas can jump several feet at once, so you should treat every room in your house. Vacuum all carpets and pay extra attention to areas that your puppy sleeps in or walks through. When you've finished vacuuming, place the vacuum bag inside a plastic garbage bag and throw it out immediately. You should also wash your puppy's bedding using hot water and anti-flea detergent.

How can I eliminate and prevent fleas and ticks?

Tip

There are effective medications that can help to protect your pet from fleas and ticks and even prevent other parasites. Some medications are applied to the skin and others are given orally, but both types are usually administered once a month. Consult your veterinarian to determine the best way to prevent your puppy from getting fleas and ticks. Your veterinarian may also be able to advise you about natural preventative methods for fleas and ticks.

Ticks

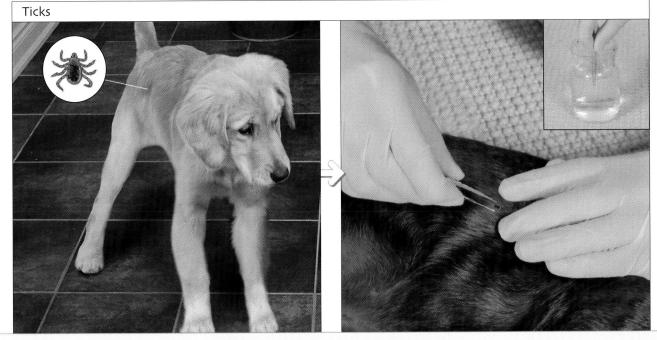

- Ticks are small bugs that attach to a puppy's skin and feed on the puppy's blood. Ticks can range in size from a small speck to the size of a kernel of corn.

- Unlike fleas, ticks do not generally cause much discomfort for a puppy, but they do carry diseases that can be passed on to your puppy and people. Ticks should be removed immediately.

1 To remove ticks from your puppy, put on a pair of latex gloves and use your hands to part his fur until you locate a tick.

2 Using a pair of fine-pointed tweezers, firmly grasp the head of the tick as close to the puppy's skin as possible, being careful not to crush the tick.

3 Gently pull the tick away from your puppy's skin without twisting the tweezers.

4 Place the tick in a sealed jar of bleach or rubbing alcohol to kill the tick.

5 Repeat steps 1 to 4 until all of the ticks have been removed.

Your Puppy's Respiratory Health

While sneezing and a runny nose are not usually major concerns for humans, these symptoms can indicate a potentially serious problem in puppies.

If you notice that your puppy has typical cold symptoms like coughing, sneezing, a runny nose or a change in his breathing pattern, you should contact your veterinarian.

Sneezing and Runny Nose

The old story that a warm, dry nose is an indication of a sick puppy is a myth. Puppies that are ill can just as easily have cool, wet noses.

You should see your veterinarian if you notice secretions from your puppy's nose that continue for more than a few hours or are opaque. You should also have your veterinarian examine your puppy if he continually sneezes or has sneezes that are accompanied by secretions from his nose or eyes.

Coughing

Coughing is a common ailment that affects puppies. It isn't always a cause for concern, but coughing can be an effort to expel a foreign object that is stuck in the puppy's airway. Coughing can also be a sign of a collapsed windpipe or fluid build-up in the lungs resulting from a respiratory disease.

If your puppy develops a cough, but the condition doesn't seem to be bothering him, you should call your veterinarian for advice. However, if your puppy seems to be in distress or has a persistent cough, you should see your veterinarian immediately.

Rapid Breathing

Puppies will often breathe quickly in extreme heat, after vigorous exercise or if they are stressed or excited. If you notice your puppy breathing rapidly under any other circumstances, you should take him to the veterinarian right away.

Noisy Breathing

Noisy breathing is relatively common in some breeds that have short faces, such as Pugs. Short-faced breeds have uniquely formed throats and nasal passages which can cause snoring, snorting or heavy breathing. Noisy breathing in other types of dogs can often be attributed to some sort of obstruction in their airway, but it can also be a sign of heart failure or lung disease. It's wise to have noisy breathing investigated by a veterinarian who can accurately diagnose the cause.

Eye and Ear Concerns

You should always be on the lookout for eye and ear problems in your puppy. An excellent time to check your puppy is when you are grooming him or practicing handling (see page 117).

Persistent eye and ear problems may be an indication of serious health concerns and should be investigated by your veterinarian.

Eyes

Excessive tearing and redness of the eyes, as well as swelling in or around the eyes, can be evidence of an infected or injured eye. These symptoms can be caused by allergies, scratches, in-grown eyelashes or a small object in the eye. You should carefully examine both eyes and if the tearing or redness persists, consult your veterinarian.

Conjunctivitis

Conjunctivitis is an infection, often bacterial, of the membrane that lines the inner sides of the eyeball. With conjunctivitis, you may begin to see discharge at the corner of your puppy's eye and his eye may appear reddened. Conjunctivitis can be passed along to humans, so be sure to thoroughly wash your hands after touching the area around your puppy's eyes.

Ears

If your puppy is having problems with his ears, he may rub the side of his head against the floor, vigorously scratch his ears and whine or pull away when you touch the area around them. You may also notice a foul odor coming from his ears, the ear flap may be reddened and a crusty brown substance may appear inside the ear.

Ear infections are a likely cause of irritated ears. These infections are more common in dogs that have floppy, hairy ears. If a puppy swims often, lives in a humid climate or does not have his ears cleaned regularly, he will be more prone to ear infections. Another common source of ear irritation can be ear mites. These tiny bugs can cause inflamed and itchy ears.

Your Puppy's Digestive Health

Every puppy will occasionally experience digestive problems, which may produce symptoms such as vomiting, constipation or diarrhea. If your puppy shows signs of a digestive problem, you should consult your veterinarian. Fortunately, your veterinarian can often treat digestive problems easily.

Vomiting

Eating too quickly or overeating can cause puppies to vomit, but vomiting can also be a sign of a serious disease. You should consult your veterinarian if the vomit contains blood, if the vomiting doesn't stop, if your puppy is sluggish or seems to be in pain.

Diarrhea

Diarrhea is a condition in which a puppy has loose stools resulting from an irritation of the digestive tract. This irritation can be caused by overexcitement, food allergies or changes in diet, as well as several other conditions. If the diarrhea persists or if your puppy also seems lethargic and unwell, consult your veterinarian.

Constipation

Puppies who are constipated are unable to defecate, although they may strain and whimper while attempting to do so. Inappropriate diet is the most common cause of constipation, but it could also occur if a puppy has swallowed something that is blocking his digestive tract. Consult your veterinarian if your puppy is constipated.

Frequent Urination

Frequent urination can be a symptom of kidney problems or a bladder infection. If your puppy takes frequent trips to the potty area without producing much urine, urinates indoors after he's been housetrained or urinates without warning, consult your veterinarian.

Bloat

A build-up of fluid or gas can cause a puppy's stomach to swell and become bloated. This can be the result of having too much dry kibble at a meal, exercising vigorously after meals or eating too quickly. Signs of bloat include restlessness, drooling, pain, unsuccessful attempts to vomit or defecate and a stomach that feels tense to the touch. You should consult your veterinarian immediately if you think your puppy is suffering from bloat.

Heartworms and Intestinal Parasites

Heartworms and intestinal parasites can be very dangerous and even fatal for your puppy if left unchecked. Your veterinarian will complete a routine annual blood test to check for heartworms. If intestinal parasites are suspected, your veterinarian can check for these by analyzing a sample of your puppy's stool. As a good defense against heartworms and intestinal parasites, your veterinarian may recommend a monthly preventative medication.

Heartworms

Heartworms are small worms that are transmitted through mosquito bites. If left untreated, the worms will grow to be up to several inches in length. These adult worms will begin to restrict blood flow in the heart and lungs, possibly leading to heart failure.

Puppies do not often show symptoms of heartworm infestation because these organisms take more than a year to grow to the point where they cause noticeable symptoms. For this reason, your vet will recommend a yearly heartworm test for your puppy. While it can be deadly, heartworm is a condition that is easily avoided through regular preventative medication that is available from your veterinarian.

Intestinal Parasites

Intestinal parasites are harmful organisms that can live in a puppy's intestinal tract. These parasites cause symptoms such as diarrhea, excessive gas, bloating, vomiting, bloody or watery stools, increased appetite, abdominal pain and rectal itching. Dogs can become infected with intestinal parasites by eating stools of other infected animals (which puppies sometimes do) or by drinking water that contains the parasites. Common intestinal parasites include coccidia, giardia, hookworms, roundworms, tapeworms and whipworms.

If your puppy shows signs that he may have intestinal parasites, you should examine the area around his anal opening and his stools for signs of worms. If you do notice any worms, try to capture one using rubber gloves and tweezers. Place the worm in a sealed jar and then take the worm, along with a stool sample, to your veterinarian.

Be aware that some intestinal parasites can be passed on to humans. If your puppy is infected, you must clean up his stools immediately and then wash your hands thoroughly.

Skin Concerns

There are a number of skin conditions that can affect your puppy and lead to problems such as hair loss, inflammation, swelling and itching. The best way to monitor these problems is to groom your puppy on a regular basis.

If you notice a problem, take your puppy to the veterinarian to be examined for evidence of skin parasites, allergic reactions or bacterial infections. By identifying skin conditions and receiving treatment early, you can often prevent these problems from becoming serious.

Skin Parasites

Skin parasites are tiny bugs that live on your puppy's skin and cause intense itching and sometimes hair loss. Common parasites that affect puppies include demodex, sarcoptic mange and fleas. See page 204 for more information on fleas. Your veterinarian will be able to identify and suggest an appropriate treatment for skin parasites.

Allergic Reaction

Just like humans, puppies can have allergic reactions to foods, fabrics, detergents, molds and fungi. An allergic reaction may cause your puppy to scratch constantly or excessively lick and chew his fur. If you suspect that your puppy is experiencing an allergic reaction, try to slowly eliminate new substances he has been exposed to. Consult your veterinarian, who can suggest a shampoo or ointment to help with the itching and advise you about whether you should change your puppy's diet due to a food allergy.

Bacterial Infection

Bacterial infections of your puppy's skin are extremely itchy. They can cause intense and continuous scratching, licking and chewing that leads to hair loss or moist, quarter-sized red patches called "hot spots." Open sores and crusted areas can also develop as a result of a bacterial infection. If you notice any of these symptoms, you should take your puppy to the vet immediately.

Skin Fold Infection
Dogs with thick, baggy skin, such as Bulldogs and Bloodhounds, can develop infections between the folds of their skin. Inflamed skin and a foul odor coming from areas of folded skin are often evidence of an infection. Consult your veterinarian for antibiotic treatment options if you notice an infection.

Spay or Neuter

Many veterinarians recommend that spaying and neutering be performed on puppies at about 6 months of age. This medical procedure is performed to prevent dogs from reproducing and contributing to the problem of dog overpopulation.

Contrary to some people's beliefs, spaying and neutering will not alter a puppy's personality or decrease natural hunting and watch-dog abilities. Unless you are planning to breed your dog, spaying or neutering will make your puppy's life much less complicated.

Spaying

Spaying is a medical operation that removes the ovaries of a female dog to prevent her from having puppies. With this procedure, the possibility of ovarian cancer is eliminated and your puppy is less likely to develop breast, uterine and cervical cancers. As well, estral bleeding, which normally occurs twice a year, is eliminated.

An unspayed female dog will have to be kept indoors while she is in heat to prevent her from mating with a male dog.

Spaying is best performed before a female puppy goes into heat for the first time. A puppy must be anesthetized for this procedure and it normally takes between 5 and 14 days to fully recover.

Neutering

Neutering is a medical operation that removes the testicles of a male dog to prevent him from breeding with female dogs. This operation ensures that your dog will not develop testicular cancer and may make prostate cancer less likely. A neutered male puppy will be less likely to fight with other dogs. He is also not as likely to wander away from home or mark his territory.

A male dog that is not neutered may resort to extreme measures to follow his instinct to mate with a female dog. He could try to escape confinement, break leashes or cross heavily traveled roads to get to a female in heat.

A puppy must be anesthetized for a neutering operation. It normally takes between 5 and 10 days to recover from this surgery.

First-Aid Kit Essentials

Puppies love to explore the world around them, but sometimes a puppy's curiosity and adventurous nature can cause him to get hurt. Having a first-aid kit on-hand can help you be prepared for minor injuries your puppy may sustain.

While you should not think of a first-aid kit as a substitute for medical attention when your puppy is seriously ill, having the proper first-aid supplies on hand will allow you to treat your puppy for minor injuries. You can purchase supplies for a puppy first-aid kit at a drugstore or you can buy a ready-made kit at a pet supply store. Keep your first-aid kit in a convenient location and check it from time to time to make sure the supplies are up to date.

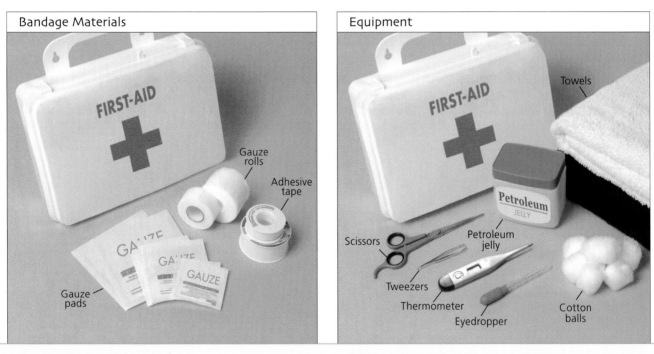

Bandage Materials

- Gauze pads of various sizes.
- Gauze rolls or strips of cloth to wrap around a wounded area.
- Adhesive tape.

Equipment

- Scissors and tweezers.
- A thermometer.

  Note: A dog's normal temperature ranges between 100.5 and 102.5 degrees Fahrenheit.

- An eyedropper for giving your puppy medicine orally.
- Petroleum jelly.
- Cotton balls, clean towels and a large sheet or towel you can use to carry the puppy if he cannot walk.

Tip

What type of container should I use for my puppy's first-aid kit?

The best way to organize your first-aid supplies is to put them in a small, plastic container. Tool boxes, tackle boxes, cosmetic containers and sewing boxes are all suitable to hold your first-aid supplies. To determine the size of container that you will need, purchase all of your first-aid supplies first to see how large of a container you will need to fit in all of the items.

Tip

Is there anything else a first-aid kit should include?

Your first-aid kit can include hot and cold packs and a drink, like Gatorade, to treat dehydration. Puppies may act aggressively if they are frightened or in pain, so first-aid kits should have a muzzle to help keep scared or hurt puppies under control. The muzzle should fit properly and never be used if the puppy is vomiting.

Medicine

Paperwork

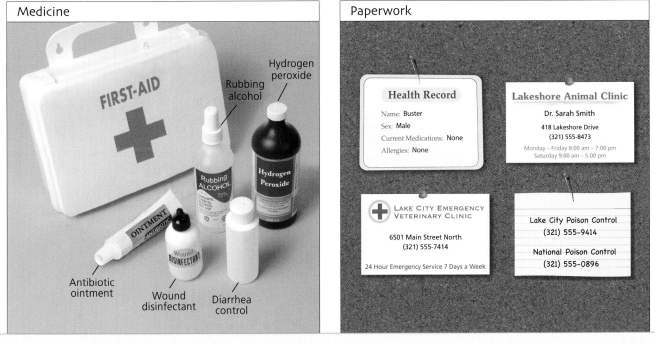

- Antibiotic ointment, wound disinfectant and rubbing alcohol.

- Diarrhea control medicine and hydrogen peroxide for inducing vomiting.

Note: Contact your veterinarian to discuss appropriate doses and treatment before giving your puppy any medicine.

- Your puppy's health record and list of current medications.

- Your veterinarian's regular clinic hours and telephone number.

- The hours and telephone number of the local emergency veterinary clinic.

- The telephone numbers of the local and national poison control centers.

Reference

Puppy and Dog Resources

Glossary of Terms

Puppy and Dog Resources

The Internet can be a fantastic resource for dog enthusiasts. Many Web sites have information about dog breeds that can help you decide which breed will be best for you and your family.

You can read online articles about how to keep your puppy happy and healthy throughout his life. You can also find useful information on dog breeders and trainers.

Kennel Clubs

The Web sites for various kennel clubs from around the world provide authoritative and detailed information about breeds, breed clubs and events such as obedience, conformation and agility trials. They also present information on how to care for your puppy.

American Kennel Club
www.akc.org

Canadian Kennel Club
www.ckc.ca

The Kennel Club (United Kingdom)
www.the-kennel-club.org.uk

Australian National Kennel Council
www.ankc.aust.com

Pet Dog Trainers

If you need a professional to assist you with puppy training, the Web sites of various dog training associations can help you locate a trainer in your area. Trainers who are members of one of these associations have agreed to uphold the principles of fair and kind training. They have also agreed to follow the association's strict code of ethics.

Association of Pet Dog Trainers (United States)
www.apdt.com

Canadian Association of Professional Pet Dog Trainers
www.cappdt.ca

Association of Pet Dog Trainers (United Kingdom)
www.apdt.co.uk

Association of Pet Dog Trainers (Australia)
www.apdt.com.au

Certification Council for Pet Dog Trainers
(United States, Canada)
www.ccpdt.org

Pet Health & Safety

American Animal Hospital Association

The American Animal Hospital Association Web site will help you find an AAHA-accredited veterinarian for your puppy's care.

www.healthypet.com

ASPCA Animal Poison Control Center

The ASPCA Animal Poison Control Center operates a 24-hour emergency call center to help when you think your puppy may have eaten something toxic. The phone number is 1-888-426-4435. There is a fee for using this emergency service.

Animal Welfare

Several prominent animal-welfare organizations operate Web sites that provide general canine health information and tips on how to help animals in need.

American Society for the Prevention of Cruelty to Animals
www.aspca.org

Humane Society of Canada
www.humanesociety.com

Royal Society for the Prevention of Cruelty to Animals (United Kingdom)
www.rspca.org.uk

Royal Society for the Prevention of Cruelty to Animals (Australia)
www.rspca.org.au

Shopping, Entertainment & Education

Dog Owner's Guide

This is an online magazine for dog owners. It offers hundreds of informative articles organized into categories such as choosing the right dog, manners and training and kids and dogs.

www.canismajor.com/dog

Kong™ Company

Kong™ toys are some of the most popular toys in the canine world. The company Web site offers information on the various Kong products along with recipes for food to stuff inside Kong toys.

www.kongcompany.com

DogFriendly

This site offers guides to dog-friendly places and services in more than 70 cities. You can find listings for dog-friendly beaches, events, hotels and parks.

www.dogfriendly.com

Pets on the Go

This Web site provides travel tips for people traveling with pets and it allows you to search for accommodations where dogs are welcome.

www.petsonthego.com

Gentle Leader Headcollar

Many trainers recommend the Gentle Leader headcollar for puppies who need some extra control. The company Web site provides information about the Gentle Leader.

www.gentleleader.com

Dogster

This site is a fun virtual community for dog lovers and their pets. On Dogster, you can create a Web page for your puppy, post photos, tell dog stories and make friends with other dog owners.

www.dogster.com

Glossary of Terms

A

American Kennel Club
The American Kennel Club (AKC) is a not-for-profit organization that maintains the world's largest registry, or list, of purebred dogs. The AKC also administers tests, competitions and other activities for purebred dogs and their owners.

Animal Shelter
An organization that cares for puppies and dogs of all types until permanent homes can be found.

Association for Pet Dog Trainers
An association for dog trainers. When looking for a trainer for your puppy, you should find a trainer who is a member of the Association for Pet Dog Trainers (APDT).

B

Begging
Any unwanted behavior a puppy uses to try to obtain food or attention, such as staring, whining or pawing at you.

Bite Inhibition
A puppy's ability to control his bite and use his mouth softly. You should begin teaching your puppy to control his bite as soon as you bring him home.

Bloat
A potentially fatal condition in which a dog's stomach swells due to an accumulation of fluid or gas. Puppies may develop bloat if they gulp their food or water too quickly or exercise too much after eating.

Breed
A type of dog. For example, German Shepherd is one breed of dog and Pug is another.

Breed Rescue Group
An organization that cares for abandoned puppies and dogs of a specific breed, or type, until permanent homes can be found.

Breeder
A person who raises puppies of a specific breed, or type. Reputable breeders are very concerned about the welfare of their puppies and breed carefully to comply with established breed standards.

C

Collar
A strap that goes around a puppy's neck. You can attach a leash to the collar. The first collar you buy for most young puppies should be a flat collar made out of nylon, with either a traditional metal buckle or a plastic quick-release snap.

Collar Hold Game
A game you can play with a puppy to teach him to become accustomed to having his collar held and prevent him from dodging when you reach for him.

Come
The command you use to have a puppy stop what he is doing and return to you. A basic obedience command.

Confinement Area
An area in your home with floors that are easy to clean, such as a laundry room, where you can keep your unhousetrained puppy when you are away from home for an extended period of time.

Counter-Surfing
Refers to the act of a puppy or dog jumping up and putting his paws on the counter so he can have a better view and possibly steal food.

Crate

A metal or plastic box with a wire-mesh door that can be latched shut to keep a puppy inside. A crate is useful for housetraining and for preventing inappropriate behavior when you cannot supervise the puppy.

Crate Training

Teaching a puppy to be comfortable in his crate so he will eventually automatically go to his crate to relax or sleep.

D

Distractions

Objects, people or sounds which divert a puppy's attention. When you begin training commands and tricks or playing games, you should start in a location free of distractions so you can have the puppy's full attention. You can gradually introduce visual distractions, such as a toy lying on the floor in the room, and sound distractions, such as clapping. Introducing distractions helps ensure the puppy will respond to your commands even when faced with real-life distractions.

Do Your Business

The command you use to have a puppy eliminate on cue. A housetraining command.

Down

The command you use to have a puppy lie down on the ground. A basic obedience command.

E

Ear Mites

Tiny insects that live in a dog's ear and feed on the outer layer of skin. Mites should be diagnosed and treated by a veterinarian.

Exercise Pen

A foldable fence you can set up indoors or outdoors to give a puppy a confined area that he can move around in.

F

Fear Imprint Period

A period that occurs between 8 and 12 weeks of age and again between 5 and 14 months of age in which a puppy may be especially fearful or cautious. Owners must ensure that a puppy has happy, positive experiences during fear imprint periods, since any frightening experience during this time can have lasting negative effects.

Fleas

Tiny insects that get into a puppy's coat and feed on his blood, causing intense itching. Puppies can pick up fleas almost anywhere. Fleas can jump onto a puppy from grass, carpets or even other dogs.

G

Get It

A game you can play with a puppy. The in-hand version of Get It teaches a puppy to take treats calmly and gently. The floor version of Get It teaches a puppy to wait until he is permitted to eat food that is on the floor.

Gimme Five

The command you use to have a puppy raise his front paw to connect with your hand. This is a trick you can teach your puppy.

Give

The command you use to have a puppy release an item from his mouth into your hand. A basic obedience command.

Glossary of Terms

Give and Take
A game you can play with a puppy to teach him to give up valued objects, such as toys, without protest.

Grooming
Keeping a puppy clean by performing tasks such as brushing his coat, trimming his nails, caring for his teeth and bathing him.

H

Handling
Teaching a puppy to be comfortable with being touched by you or by someone else.

Head Halter
A type of collar that is used to handle puppies who need some extra control. Head halters fit around a puppy's nose and neck and make it easier to guide a puppy who pulls on his leash. Head halters should not be used on puppies under 4 months of age and must be fitted with the guidance of a trainer or veterinarian.

Heartworm
A parasite that lives in the blood vessels of the heart and lungs of an infected dog. Heartworm can be fatal, but is usually avoided using preventative medication.

Houseline
A six- to ten-foot long training leash that is designed to loosely drag behind a puppy that is being trained when he is inside the home. You can step on or pick up the houseline when you need to stop a puppy from running off or guide him away from something inappropriate, such as trying to jump up on the furniture.

Housetraining
Teaching a puppy to eliminate in his outdoor potty area or litter box.

K

Kibble
Dry dog food.

Kong™
A hollow, rubber chew toy you can fill with treats or kibble.

L

Leash
A length of nylon, cotton or leather with a clip that attaches to a puppy's collar. Short, four- to six-foot leashes are used for walking and training a puppy. Long, 25- to 30-foot leashes are essential for working with a puppy in large spaces, such as parks and fields.

Let's Go
The command you use to have a puppy walk politely with you, without pulling on the leash. A basic obedience command.

Life Reward
An activity a puppy enjoys, such as chewing a toy, going for a walk or playing a game. You can give your puppy a life reward, instead of a food treat, when he responds to a command or displays appropriate behavior. See also Reward.

Lure
When you first start training a puppy to perform a command, you will usually use a lure to guide him into position. Using a lure allows you to show the puppy what to do without using your hands or a leash to push or pull him into position. You will often use a food treat as a lure.

M

Martingale Collar

A loose-fitting, nylon collar that does not have buckles but features a loop that tightens to make the collar fit more snugly if a puppy pulls at his leash. A martingale collar is useful for a puppy who is prone to pulling out of his collar.

Meet the Puppy Game

A game you can play when a puppy first comes home and is meeting younger family members for the first time. This game keeps children sitting quietly and allows the puppy to explore each person on his own.

Mixed Breed

A puppy whose parents are different breeds, or types, of dog. For example, a Labradoodle has one Labrador parent and one Poodle parent.

Mouthing

Play biting and nipping by puppies. Mouthing is a natural, normal puppy behavior.

N

Neuter

A surgical procedure to prevent male dogs from reproducing. If you do not plan to breed your male dog, you should have him neutered.

O

Off-Leash Park

A controlled space in which dogs can socialize with you, other dogs and other dog owners without a leash. You should not take a puppy younger than 6 months and who does not come when called to an off-leash park.

Outside

The command you use to stop a puppy when he is eliminating in an inappropriate area, such as in the house, so you can take him outdoors. A housetraining command.

P

Pass the Puppy

A game you can play with a young or small puppy that teaches him to accept and welcome handling from different people.

Positive Training

Rewarding a puppy with food, toys or an enjoyable activity when he responds to a command or acts in an appropriate manner to reinforce his good behavior.

Possessiveness

A dog's unwanted behavior of acting in a possessive and possibly threatening manner when he has an item, such as his food bowl, and someone approaches. Possessiveness can be a serious behavior problem that requires professional help to overcome. Also called resource guarding.

Puppy Dress-Up

A game you can play with a puppy to help him become accustomed to handling. In this game, you dress a puppy in a T-shirt or socks.

Puppy Fetch

A game you can play with a puppy that allows him to practice retrieving an object that you throw, returning to you and giving you the object.

Puppy Party

A fun way to introduce your child's friends to a new puppy. The puppy has a chance to become accustomed to handling by children and you have a chance to educate the children about the importance of being calm around the puppy and not rewarding him for unwanted behaviors, such as jumping up.

Puppy Ping Pong

A game you can play with a puppy to help him practice the Come command. This game also reinforces the skill of the puppy being able to find his owners and helps to expend some of the puppy's energy.

Purebred

A puppy whose mother, father and ancestors are all of the same breed, or type, of dog.

R

Registered Name

The name that will appear on a purebred puppy's official papers. The breeder's kennel name usually makes up the first part of the registered name, followed by the name you want to use for the puppy. A puppy may be called by his registered name or by a nickname.

Relax Command

The command you use to have a puppy relax and be calm in a sitting or lying position. A basic obedience command.

Release Word

A word you can use at the end of a stationary command, such as Sit, to tell a puppy he is now free to move.

Reward

A reward can be praise or an item a puppy likes, such as food or a toy. When training, you give a puppy a reward when he responds to a command so he will be more likely to respond to the command in the future. See also Life Reward.

S

Scavenger Hunt

A game you can play with a puppy that is mentally stimulating for the puppy, helps with retrieving skills and increases bonding with you.

Separation Anxiety

A puppy's feelings of stress and panic when he is left alone. Excessive panting, pacing, barking and destructive behavior can be signs of separation anxiety. Separation anxiety can be a serious behavior problem that requires professional help to overcome.

Sit

The command you use to have a puppy sit with his hind quarters on the ground. The most basic obedience command.

Socialization

Teaching a puppy to be comfortable with a variety of places, situations, people and sounds. Socialization is the key to having a stable, reliable dog and should be the top priority in your early training process. The main periods for socialization are from 2 to 4 months and from 7 to 9 months of age.

Spay

A surgical procedure to prevent a female dog from reproducing. If you do not plan to breed your female dog, you should have her spayed.

T

Teething

Puppies go through teething periods between 3 and 7 months of age. During teething, make sure your puppy has appropriate things to chew, such as a Kong™ or other puppy-safe teething toys.

Ticks

Small insects that attach to a puppy's skin and feed on his blood. Ticks can range in size from a small speck to the size of a kernel of corn. Ticks do not generally cause much discomfort for a puppy, but they do carry diseases that can be passed onto the puppy and people.

Touch It

The command you use to have a puppy focus his attention and bump a target with his nose. This is a trick you can teach your puppy.

Training Pouch

A pouch or large pocket you can strap around your waist or clip to your belt to hold food treats and toys when training a puppy.

V Vaccination

A disease organism that is injected into a puppy's body to help prepare the puppy's immune system to fight off that organism in the future. Puppies are not fully vaccinated and safe from disease until they receive their shots around 16 weeks of age.

W Walk With Me

A game you can play with a puppy to help him with loose-leash walking. This game teaches a puppy that staying near you while you walk is fun, whether you hold his leash or not.

Where's Your Tummy?

The command you use to have a puppy roll onto his back and lie with his tummy exposed. This is a trick you can teach your puppy.

Y Yardline

A 16-foot long training leash that is designed to loosely drag behind a puppy that is being trained when he is outside in a fenced area. You can step on or pick up the yardline when you need to stop the puppy from running off or guide him away from something inappropriate, such as digging in the garden.

Puppy Bloopers

It's not every day that we get to work with some of the most adorable creatures in the world, but for this book, we did have the immense pleasure of taking pictures of some very cute puppies. If there's one thing we learned, however, it's that no matter how much praise or freeze-dried liver is involved, sometimes a puppy just has to be a puppy.

It's about time for my nap!

May I have this dance?

Just a little to the right...

All dressed up and nowhere to go.

I'm outta here!

Look, Ma...I can fly!

"Sit"...that means go play with my toys, right?

Did you hear what she just said?

Are you talking to me?

Modeling is hard work!

Index

Index

Index

Index

lures, 132, 220
 stopping using, 134
positive methods, 130
pouch, 223
praise, 133
release words, 137
rewards, 132-133, 222
sessions, 130
teaching puppy his name, 136
using crates, 219
transporting, puppies, 62-63
treats
 food, 95, 132-133, 222
  stopping using, 135
 lures, 132, 220
  stopping using, 134
tricks
 benefits, 152
 Gimme Five, 172-173, 219
 Ring the Bell, 168-169
 Roll Over, 165
 Shake a Paw, 173
 targeting, 168-169
 Touch It, 168-169, 223
 Where's Your Tummy?, 164-165, 223
trimming, nails, 107
T-shirts, putting on puppy, 176-177
tug-of-war games, avoiding, 87, 153, 184

U

United Kingdom, Kennel Club, contact information, 216
urination
 due to excitement, 77
 frequent, 208

V

vaccinations, 223
 sample schedule, 203
vaccines, overview, 202-203
veterinarians
 choosing, 53
 first visit, 73
 preparing puppy for visits, 119
vomiting, 208

W

Walk With Me, game, 170-171, 223
warnings, body language signals, 127
water
 bowls, 42
 drinking, 95
West Highland White Terrier, 21
Where's Your Tummy?, trick, 164-165, 223
whipworms, 209
Working group, dogs, 23

Y

yardlines, 44-45, 223
yards, puppies and children in, 87
Yorkshire Terrier, 20

Did you like this book? MARAN ILLUSTRATED™ offers books on the most popular computer topics, using the same easy-to-use format of this book. We always say that if you like one of our books, you'll love the rest of our books too!

Here's a list of some of our best-selling computer titles:

Guided Tour Series - 240 pages, Full Color

MARAN ILLUSTRATED's Guided Tour series features a friendly disk character that walks you through each task step by step. The full-color screen shots are larger than in any of our other series and are accompanied by clear, concise instructions.

	ISBN-10	ISBN-13	Price
MARAN ILLUSTRATED™ Computers Guided Tour	1-59200-880-1	978-1-59200-880-3	$24.99 US/$33.95 CDN
MARAN ILLUSTRATED™ Windows XP Guided Tour	1-59200-886-0	978-1-59200-886-5	$24.99 US/$33.95 CDN

MARAN ILLUSTRATED™ Series - 320 pages, Full Color

This series covers 30% more content than our Guided Tour series. Learn new software fast using our step-by-step approach and easy-to-understand text. Learning programs has never been this easy!

	ISBN-10	ISBN-13	Price
MARAN ILLUSTRATED™ Access 2003	1-59200-872-0	978-1-59200-872-8	$24.99 US/$33.95 CDN
MARAN ILLUSTRATED™ Computers	1-59200-874-7	978-1-59200-874-2	$24.99 US/$33.95 CDN
MARAN ILLUSTRATED™ Excel 2003	1-59200-876-3	978-1-59200-876-6	$24.99 US/$33.95 CDN
MARAN ILLUSTRATED™ Mac OS® X v.10.4 Tiger™	1-59200-878-X	978-1-59200-878-0	$24.99 US/$33.95 CDN
MARAN ILLUSTRATED™ Office 2003	1-59200-890-9	978-1-59200-890-2	$29.99 US/$39.95 CDN
MARAN ILLUSTRATED™ Windows XP	1-59200-870-4	978-1-59200-870-4	$24.99 US/$33.95 CDN

101 Hot Tips Series - 240 pages, Full Color

Progress beyond the basics with MARAN ILLUSTRATED's 101 Hot Tips series. This series features 101 of the coolest shortcuts, tricks and tips that will help you work faster and easier.

	ISBN-10	ISBN-13	Price
MARAN ILLUSTRATED™ Windows XP 101 Hot Tips	1-59200-882-8	978-1-59200-882-7	$19.99 US/$26.95 CDN

MARAN ILLUSTRATED™ Piano
is an information-packed resource
for people who want to learn to
play the piano, as well as current
musicians looking to hone their skills.
Combining full-color photographs and
easy-to-follow instructions, this guide
covers everything from the basics
of piano playing to more advanced
techniques. Not only does MARAN
ILLUSTRATED™ Piano show you how
to read music, play scales and chords
and improvise while playing with
other musicians, it also provides
you with helpful information for
purchasing and caring for your piano.

ISBN-10: 1-59200-864-X
ISBN-13: 978-1-59200-864-3
Price: $24.99 US; $33.95 CDN
Page count: 304

MARAN ILLUSTRATED™ Dog Training
is an excellent guide for both current
dog owners and people considering
making a dog part of their family.
Using clear, step-by-step instructions
accompanied by over 400 full-color
photographs, MARAN ILLUSTRATED™
Dog Training is perfect for any visual
learner who prefers seeing what to do
rather than reading lengthy explanations.

Beginning with insights into popular
dog breeds and puppy development,
this book emphasizes positive training
methods to guide you through
socializing, housetraining and teaching
your dog many commands. You will
also learn how to work with problem
behaviors, such as destructive chewing.

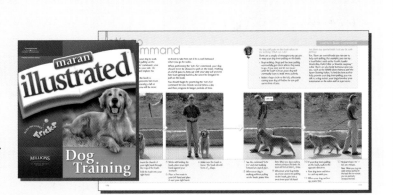

ISBN-10: 1-59200-858-5
ISBN-13: 978-1-59200-858-2
Price: $19.99 US; $26.95 CDN
Page count: 256

MARAN ILLUSTRATED™ Knitting & Crocheting contains a wealth of information about these two increasingly popular crafts. Whether you are just starting out or you are an experienced knitter or crocheter interested in picking up new tips and techniques, this information-packed resource will take you from the basics, such as how to hold the knitting needles or crochet hook, to more advanced skills, such as how to add decorative touches to your projects. The easy-to-follow information is communicated through clear, step-by-step instructions and accompanied by over 600 full-color photographs—perfect for any visual learner.

ISBN-10: 1-59200-862-3
ISBN-13: 978-1-59200-862-9
Price: $24.99 US; $33.95 CDN
Page count: 304

MARAN ILLUSTRATED™ Yoga provides a wealth of simplified, easy-to-follow information about the increasingly popular practice of Yoga. This easy-to-use guide is a must for visual learners who prefer to see and do without having to read lengthy explanations.

Using clear, step-by-step instructions accompanied by over 500 full-color photographs, this book includes all the information you need to get started with yoga or to enhance your technique if you have already made yoga a part of your life. MARAN ILLUSTRATED™ Yoga shows you how to safely and effectively perform a variety of yoga poses at various skill levels, how to breathe more efficiently and much more.

ISBN-10: 1-59200-868-2
ISBN-13: 978-1-59200-868-1
Price: $24.99 US; $33.95 CDN
Page count: 320

MARAN ILLUSTRATED™ Weight Training is an information-packed guide that covers all the basics of weight training, as well as more advanced techniques and exercises.

MARAN ILLUSTRATED™ Weight Training contains more than 500 full-color photographs of exercises for every major muscle group, along with clear, step-by-step instructions for performing the exercises. Useful tips provide additional information and advice to help enhance your weight training experience.

MARAN ILLUSTRATED™ Weight Training provides all the information you need to start weight training or to refresh your technique if you have been weight training for some time.

ISBN-10: 1-59200-866-6
ISBN-13: 978-1-59200-866-7
Price: $24.99 US; $33.95 CDN
Page count: 320

MARAN ILLUSTRATED™ Poker is an essential resource that covers all aspects of the most popular poker games, including Texas Hold'em, Omaha and Seven-Card Stud. You will also find valuable information on playing in tournaments, bluffing, feeling at home in a casino and even playing poker online.

This information-packed guide includes hundreds of detailed, full-color illustrations accompanying the step-by-step instructions that walk you through each topic. MARAN ILLUSTRATED™ Poker is a must-have for anyone who prefers a visual approach to learning rather than simply reading explanations.

Whether you are a novice getting ready to join in a friend's home game or you are an experienced poker player looking to hone your tournament skills, MARAN ILLUSTRATED™ Poker provides all the poker information you need.

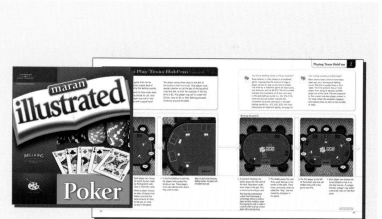

ISBN-10: 1-59200-946-8
ISBN-13: 978-1-59200-946-6
Price: $19.99 US; $26.95 CD
Page count: 240

MARAN ILLUSTRATED™ Guitar is an excellent resource for people who want to learn to play the guitar, as well as for current musicians who want to fine tune their technique. This full-color guide includes over 500 photographs, accompanied by step-by-step instructions that teach you the basics of playing the guitar and reading music, as well as advanced guitar techniques. You will also learn what to look for when purchasing a guitar or accessories, how to maintain and repair your guitar, and much more.

Whether you want to learn to strum your favorite tunes or play professionally, MARAN ILLUSTRATED™ Guitar provides all the information you need to become a proficient guitarist.

ISBN-10: 1-59200-860-7
ISBN-13: 978-1-59200-860-5
Price: $24.99 US; $33.95 CDN
Page count: 320

MARAN ILLUSTRATED™ Cooking Basics is an information-packed resource that covers all the basics of cooking. Novices and experienced cooks alike will find useful information about setting up and stocking your kitchen as well as food preparation and cooking techniques. With over 500 full-color photographs illustrating the easy-to-follow, step-by-step instructions, this book is a must-have for anyone who prefers seeing what to do rather than reading long explanations.

MARAN ILLUSTRATED™ Cooking Basics also provides over 40 recipes from starters, salads and side-dishes to main course dishes and baked goods. Each recipe uses only 10 ingredients or less, and is complete with nutritional information and tips covering tasty variations and commonly asked questions.

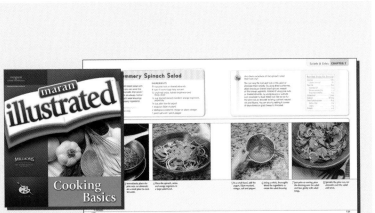

ISBN-10: 1-59863-234-5
ISBN-13: 978-1-59863-234-7
Price: $19.99 US; $26.95 CDN
Page count: 240

illustrated EFFORTLESS ALGEBRA

MARAN ILLUSTRATED™ Effortless Algebra is an indispensable resource packed with crucial concepts and step-by-step instructions that make learning algebra simple. This easy-to-use guide is perfect for those who wish to gain a thorough understanding of algebra's concepts, from the most basic calculations to more complex operations.

Clear instructions thoroughly explain every topic and each concept is accompanied by helpful illustrations. This book provides all of the information you will need to fully grasp algebra, whether you are new to the subject or have been solving quadratic equations for years. MARAN ILLUSTRATED™ Effortless Algebra also provides an abundance of practice examples and tests so that you can put your knowledge into practice. This book is a must-have resource for any student of algebra.

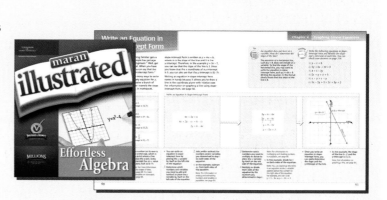

ISBN-10: 1-59200-942-5
ISBN-13: 978-1-59200-942-8
Price: $24.99 US; $33.95 CDN
Page count: 304

illustrated SUDOKU

MARAN ILLUSTRATED™ Sudoku is an excellent resource for anyone who wants to learn how to solve Sudoku puzzles or improve their skills.

This book contains easy-to-follow instructions explaining how to play Sudoku as well as advanced puzzle-solving strategies. The colorful illustrations and step-by-step instructions are perfect for any visual learner. MARAN ILLUSTRATED™ Sudoku also contains over 100 puzzles and answers so you can put your new Sudoku skills to the test!

Whether you have never tried a Sudoku puzzle before or you are an experienced player, MARAN ILLUSTRATED™ Sudoku is the book for you.

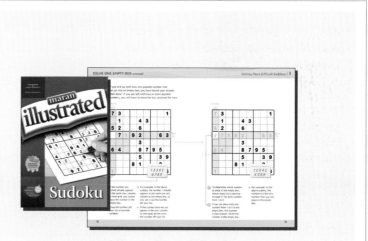

ISBN-10: 1-59863-316-3
ISBN-13: 978-1-59863-316-0
Price: $9.99 US; $13.95 CDN
Page count: 192

MARAN ILLUSTRATED™ Bartending
is the perfect book for those who want to
impress their guests with cocktails that are
both eye-catching and delicious. This
indispensable guide explains everything
you need to know about bartending in
the most simple and easy-to-follow terms.
MARAN ILLUSTRATED™ Bartending has
recipes, step-by-step instructions and over
400 full-color photographs of all the hottest
martinis, shooters, blended drinks and
warmers. This guide also includes a
section on wine, beer and alcohol-free
cocktails as well as information on all
of the tools, liquor and other supplies
you will need to start creating drinks
right away!

ISBN-10: 1-59200-944-1
ISBN-13: 978-1-59200-944-2
Price: $19.99 US; $26.95 CDN
Page count: 256